Will
NATO
Go East?

970066

Canadian Cataloguing in Publication Data

Main entry under title:

Will NATO go east? : the debate over enlarging the Atlantic alliance

Includes index.
ISBN 0-88911-725-X

1. North Atlantic Treaty Organization – Europe, Eastern.
2. National security – Europe. I. Haglund, David G.
II. Queen's University (Kingston, Ont.). Centre for
International Relations.

UA646.5.E852W55 1996   355'.031'091821   C96-931192-3

Will NATO Go East?

The Debate Over Enlarging the Atlantic Alliance

Edited by David G. Haglund

*With a Foreword
by Jeffrey D. McCausland and Robert H. Dorff*

Contents

PART I: THE THEORETICAL AND POLICY SETTING

PART II: SELECTED CASE STUDIES

Foreword

Jeffrey D. McCausland and Robert H. Dorff

"All politics are local."

Thomas "Tip" O'Neill, Former Speaker of the US House of Representatives

Much has been said and written on the topic of NATO enlargement in the few years since the debate began in earnest. Arguments in favour stress the need for stability and security guarantees in the heart of Europe. There is also a moral argument, stressing among other things that this is the right thing to do. Arguments against have focused primarily, though not exclusively, on the potential negative effects of enlargement on Russia and its own security needs, as well as on the possibility that enlargement will make the alliance too cumbersome and too diverse to function effectively. And of course, some critics stress that enlargement will only serve to import the instabilities extant in some of these countries into an otherwise stable and healthy organization.

This book provides some additional and necessary structure to this debate by examining how NATO enlargement is considered within the framework of evolving alliance strategy as well as the context of the policies of respective NATO members and the Russian Federation. At the strategic level, it is clear that the decision to enlarge should be reached through a careful process of analysis and decisionmaking. Unfortunately, the arguments for and against enlargement have heretofore been made largely in the absence of a revised, overarching strategic framework. Small wonder, then, that the debate at times seems so unfocussed and the issues so slippery. Absent this essential strategic framework, the arguments lack clear, consistent logic. In the end, they may rest almost exclusively on underlying, unarticulated assumptions rather than on clearly defined objectives and a sense of how those objectives can be achieved. But the dramatic developments in European security since 1989 also mean that alliance members must not only reexamine the underlying strategic direction of the alliance, but also how this direction relates to the respective national interests of its members. In this regard, the question of NATO enlargement will bring both of these issues to the forefront — domestic input into foreign and security policy as well as the evolution of alliance strategy.

Historians have suggested that during the period 492 to 432 BC the Greek city-states established the League of Delphi to enhance their defence in light of the threats from the Persian Empire. From a historical perspective this may be important for current western security for two reasons. First, once the threat of the Persian "superpower" disappeared, the alliance dissolved and shortly thereafter the Greeks went to war among themselves in the Peloponnesian War. Second, the League of Delphi is the longest continuous alliance of several states in history, lasting about sixty years. It is interesting to consider that the North Atlantic Treaty Organization is now in its 47th year.

Such casual observations are not intended as a thorough review of the historical record or to suggest that, with the disappearance of the Soviet Union, NATO is doomed. However, any survey of the history of alliances does reveal several fundamental points. First, alliances are based on the state as the central actor in the international system. This was true even for the Greek city-states previously mentioned, though they certainly predate the Peace of Westphalia and the beginning of the "modern" nation-state system. From our vantage point on the eve of the 21st century it is clear that, despite arguments to the contrary, the nation-state remains at the centre of the modern international system. Therefore, the behaviour of nation-states will continue to be at the heart of issues facing the alliance. When NATO was originally formed, European and American policymakers formulated three purposes for the alliance: keep the United States involved in European security affairs, keep Germany from once again threatening stability on the continent, and keep the Soviet Union out of Western Europe. Today, the future of the alliance and European security suggest that these strategic purposes may require modification. Furthermore, the principal NATO members (the United States, Britain, France, and Germany) will play critical roles in the refinement of alliance strategy. If NATO is to enlarge, all members must also solicit the endorsement from their respective publics if the unanimous support of the existing membership required by Article 10 of the Washington Treaty is to be obtained.

A second fundamental point about alliances is that states join them based on their perceptions of national interests and threats posed to those interests. History suggests that alliances have traditionally formed "against" another member of the international system. One might even draw the conclusion that the membership of an alliance is chosen by its opponent(s). This would certainly explain how Great Britain and the United States became the allies of the Soviet Union during World War II. It might even offer some credit to Adolf Hitler for his ill-advised decisions to declare war on the United States and attack the Soviet Union. It could also explain how the United States and Great Britain came to be allied (at least temporarily) with Syria during the Gulf War.

The last fundamental point about alliances is that they do not last forever. Although "national interests" may explain why states enter into alliances, such interests are not static and they are continuously reevaluated. Consequently, the longevity of NATO is both a demonstration of the congruence of national interests as well as the primary reason many observers describe it as the most successful alliance in history. This may be a description that it richly deserves based on the fact that the threat it was created to confront disappeared without a conflict involving the alliance as a whole. Yet throughout its lifetime NATO has been confronted by internal crises that stemmed from conflicting interpretations of the national interests of its members. These crises caused commentators periodically to predict the demise of the alliance. One need only think of Suez (1956), the Yom Kippur War (1973), or the war in the former Yugoslavia. But none of these events proved fatal, and the alliance is neither moribund nor on "life support" systems, as events in Bosnia in 1996 continue to remind us. Yet it is obvious that the geostrategic environment has changed dramatically with respect to the fundamental reasons why NATO came into being and why the alliance continues.

The essence of the NATO relationship is its transatlantic character. The fact that the United States tied its security to that of Europe in the Washington Treaty of 1949 (summarized in the Article 5 security guarantee) remains at the core of the organization. Many alliance supporters are openly concerned about a sense of leadership "fatigue" that America periodically displays towards this commitment. Economic difficulties, internal social problems, regional security threats in Asia or the Persian Gulf, as well as the passing of the generation that created NATO, all contribute to concern over how well Americans perceive their national interest to be furthered by the alliance. In this regard the most important aspect of the 1996 American elections may not be which party wins the presidency, but whether the anticipated dramatic change in the US Senate will result in a body that continues as a staunch supporter of the transatlantic relationship. There can be no doubt that the worst possible outcome for the alliance would be rejection by the Senate of a proposal to admit a new member to NATO. Such a result would not only doom enlargement generally, but might well render the existing organization moribund.

In like fashion, domestic conditions in the other NATO capitals will play a significant role in the final question of NATO enlargement. Serious economic difficulties in Germany, France, and Britain have resulted in public demands for more attention and resources. Throughout the continent political leadership seems to be lacking. In Great Britain the Conservative Party that has controlled parliament for the vast majority of the Cold War is in disarray. France has witnessed the passing of François Mitterrand and his Socialists from power, but the new conservative government is beset by enormous economic difficulties. In Germany, the government of Chancellor Helmut Kohl holds a slim majority in the Bundestag, and the chancellor will eventually pass from the political scene leaving an enormous leadership vacuum. Future German politics will be forced to confront both nagging economic and social problems associated with reunification and the continued splintering of the electorate.

But NATO enlargement will also not occur in isolation from important international factors. Other security dynamics are ongoing that will shape the environment in which the alliance will evolve. The most serious of these obviously centre around future developments in the Russian Federation. Will the future relationship with Russia be characterized by cooperation or confrontation? In answering this question NATO enlargement is seen by some as a cause and by some as an effect. Opponents to enlargement worry that the entry of Central and Eastern European states into the alliance will "poison" the relations of the west with Moscow. Supporters argue that the (at times) apparent antagonism of Moscow toward the west suggests that NATO enlargement should move forward quickly. In addition to NATO, European security architecture may be defined in part by efforts to enhance the role played by the Organization for Security and Cooperation in Europe (OSCE) or the ability of the European Union to define a common foreign/security policy and enlarge its membership.

In concert with the requirement to maintain commonality of interests among the members of the alliance is the need to describe fully the strategic direction of the alliance in a fashion that is supported by current as well as prospective members. By taking a strategic approach to the issue of NATO enlargement, fundamental questions can and should be raised and debated as a necessary prelude to any decision to enlarge the organization. Then, and only then, should the debate turn to questions of who joins, when, and under what conditions.

First, and most importantly, is the essential redefinition of alliance purpose. What is the "end state" the alliance is attempting to achieve, and how does enlargement contribute to that objective? While the collective-defence guarantee of Article 5 was the clearest statement of this purpose during the Cold War, the future security environment suggests that NATO may play a role in resolving intrastate conflicts, problems outside the geographic confines of Europe, or even intra-alliance conflicts. How exactly do we wish to define that purpose and the related strategic objectives?

Second, what are the means available to achieve these objectives? The means would include the resources of the current alliance members (military, financial, political) and those of any potential new members. Are these resources sufficient, and if not, what new resources would be needed? What are the current capabilities of existing and potential alliance members to contribute to these resource requirements? At a basic military level this would include such things as interoperability and complementary command and control systems.

Third, and perhaps most contentious of all, what are the ways in which current and future resources can be brought to bear in order to achieve the desired objectives? This is where the serious work begins. After all, NATO specifically and alliances generally constitute only one possible way in which resources can be marshalled for the tasks at hand. And it is not altogether obvious that NATO is in fact the most appropriate and effective way with which to pursue the objectives. Is NATO to remain a traditional institution of collective defence? If so, what or who is the external threat toward which the alliance is directed? Is NATO to be transformed into a collective-security organization, with responsibility for maintaining stable relations within the ranks of its membership? If so, what are the kinds of threats within the alliance that it should be prepared to address (ethnic and other minority conflicts, political instability in newly formed democracies, economic hardship and instability)? Is NATO to be an international or regional crisis-management organization, with power projection "out-of-area" as its central mission? Exactly how NATO is to marshal and focus its resources is the most fundamental part of this debate, because it ultimately determines exactly what NATO is as an organization. If the alliance does not have an obvious understanding of what it, as an organization, is to be *for,* then any enlargement will be dangerous if for no other reason than NATO will simply not have a clear idea of what it is expected to do when future contingencies arise. Consequently, the political unity necessary for a timely and effective response may be lacking.

Ultimately, the question of NATO enlargement must be answered as a matter of grand strategy. What are the objectives, what is needed to achieve them, and how are the resources to be applied toward the pursuit of those objectives? To date, however, reasons have been offered that are in and of themselves only partial answers to the underlying questions of strategy. Some of the reasons are:

- We have already said that NATO would enlarge and it would be unfair, duplicitous, etc. to reverse that decision now.
- We should reward those countries in Central and Eastern Europe that have been successful in reforming their political and economic systems.
- NATO represents a community of "shared values and interests" and "shared expectations about commitments and responsibilities." By bringing in new members we help to create a broader community in which stability and security can be enhanced through their institutionalization in NATO.
- NATO was used to provide security, democracy, and free-market economies for Europe after World War II, so it can be used to do the same for the rest of Europe after the Cold War.

The first reason alone is no reason at all. It simply ignores the issue whether there exists any compelling strategic justification for enlargement. It runs the obvious risk of compounding previously taken "bad" decisions by refusing to consider the issues. Even if a decision to enlarge is a "good" one, the refusal to confront the strategic issues will make it more difficult for a new NATO to come to grips with its roles and responsibilities (collective and individual). Similarly, rewarding Central and Eastern European countries for successful reforms may be good policy, but is membership in NATO the appropriate reward? And what if that reward comes at a cost to the shared community of values and interests, commitments and responsibilities? Surely we do not want to reward those countries at the very expense of the alliance itself.

While it may be true that NATO helped bring about the successful "democratization" of Western Europe after World War II, there are serious questions about its utility and appropriateness for the "democratization" of Central and Eastern Europe today. A key issue here is one of causality. Did NATO cause democracy and market economies to take hold and flourish, or was it the overriding Soviet threat and concomitant unity of purpose that caused NATO and democratization to succeed? And finally, what do any of these suggested reasons tell us about the pace of enlargement or how to handle potential problems with the Russian Federation? They simply fall short of what a well-reasoned, strategic approach to the issues would provide.

In the end, NATO must be careful to understand that whatever the members determine as its future objectives, they must be based on a sound, careful analysis not only of what the alliance can in theory do, but what it can in practice do successfully. For all of the debate, or lack thereof, one thing remains clear: a NATO that is unable or unwilling to pursue its objectives successfully through a proper application of ways and means contributes little to improved European security and stability. Europe will have less security, not more; it will have more instability, not less. An enlarged NATO that is unable to act will have the deleterious effect of providing a false sense of security to the new members, which in turn may prevent those countries from pursuing more viable courses of action for effectively ensuring their security. And the erosion of confidence that would accompany such a false sense of security could well result in lessened security for the traditional members of the alliance. While it may well be time to reassess and reevaluate the role of NATO in the world, and the ways and means with which it pursues its objectives, the alliance can ill afford to let such a redefinition occur by default. The current members of NATO owe it to themselves and the would-be members of a larger NATO to ask the tough questions and find the best answers on which to base a decision to enlarge. It is an essential issue of strategy.

Walter Lippmann made the following prediction about NATO three days after it was born: "The pact will be remembered long after the conditions that have provoked it are no longer the main business of mankind. For the treaty recognizes and proclaims a community of interest which is much older than the conflict with the Soviet Union, and come what may, will survive it." There is every reason to believe that Lippmann was correct. NATO should successfully weather this new challenge, but the future is not preordained. NATO members must reconsider overall alliance objectives and clearly explain them to their publics in order to insure that enlargement of the alliance is a new beginning and not an untimely end. We trust that the chapters in this book will contribute to the strategic debate that we consider so necessary as a foundation for deciding the future of the most successful alliance in history.

Preface and Acknowledgements

This book had its origins in a Berlin *Kneipe* in early February 1995. The editor and two other contributors to the volume, Jeffrey McCausland and Douglas Stuart, had just attended a NATO symposium held at one of the city's public policy centres, the Paul-Löbe-Institut, and had been rehashing some of the major themes that had arisen during the course of that meeting, including and especially the question of NATO's possible enlargement. It had been an interesting symposium, and as such events do, it seemed to have left participants craving further discussion. Typically, in the case of follow-up sessions over beer, someone eventually raises the question, where do we go from here? I confess to having been that person.

Although I found — and still find — the question interesting, I did not realize how interesting it would be to try to design and bring to completion a research project built around it. This was all the more so as at the outset there was neither a budget nor an obvious institutional sponsor for the follow-on work. Happily, both problems were resolved, and it is a pleasure for me here to acknowledge all those people who played a part in making possible this book.

In the first place, I would like to thank Neil MacFarlane, who succeeded me as Director of the Queen's University Centre for International Relations in July 1995. I discovered what former directors all must learn, namely that it is not so easy to mount a conference when one no longer has access to facilities and other support to which one has grown accustomed. Neil demonstrated a remarkable amount of tolerance in allowing his predecessor to continue to usurp some of the Centre's time and other resources, and I am grateful to him. I hope to be able to return the favour, when I resume directorship of the Centre in July 1996, as Neil moves on to Oxford.

Also at Queen's, I am pleased to acknowledge with gratitude the support provided by the staff of the Department of Political Studies, especially Barbara Murphy, who was nothing short of outstanding in her dedication to the numerous tasks connected with the organization of this project. It has been a treat to work with her, not only on NATO expansion, but on a great number of other things over the past four years in the Department of Political Studies. I extend thanks as well to other Department staff members all of whom, in one way or another, contributed to this effort: Shirley Fraser, Pauline Bettney, Evelyn McCaugherty, and Frances Shepherd. I have stated it before, but never in print, that one of the joys of having headed the Department was the discovery that I had such a wonderful staff with which to work.

As essential as was the help I received in Kingston, this project could not have advanced very far without financial assistance from outsiders. Especially, funding was needed for the workshop at which the volume's chapters were initially presented and critiqued, as well as for subsequent manuscript preparation. I am delighted, in both respects, to note the generosity extended by the following: the NATO Office of Information and Press; the Canadian Department of National Defence's Security and Defence Forum; the Strategic Outreach Program of the Strategic Studies Institute, US Army War College; the Department of Foreign Affairs and International Trade Canada; Hollinger Inc. (in particular Conrad Black); and the Chair d'études militaires et stratégiques of the Université de Montréal (especially Michel Fortmann).

The workshop that directly resulted in this book was held in early December 1995 at the Queen's University International Study Centre, located in a Norman castle set in the Sussex countryside. Herstmonceux Castle provided the perfect atmosphere for debating such an important issue in European security as NATO enlargement, and I wish to thank those associated with the ISC who made it possible for us to avail ourselves of its splendid facilities, in particular Don Macnamara, Sandy Montgomery, and Bernadette Saunders. Ann Fitz-Gerald rendered valuable assistance at the workshop, where she looked after last-minute logistical arrangements.

The project also benefitted immensely from the critiques and other commentary offered by workshop participants Angela Bogdan, Glenn Brown, Ernest Gilman, Gary Guertner, David Jablonsky, Charles King, Steve Kotan, David Malone, Craig Oliphant, Jane Sharp, Reka Szemerkenyi, and Bram Triestram.

Back at Queen's, the book's final production stages were admirably executed by the technical specialists of the School of Policy Studies and its Centre for International Relations. I am pleased, once again, to be able to thank Marilyn Banting, Valerie Jarus, and Mark Howes for their excellent work.

David G. Haglund

Introduction:
The Debate Over Enlarging NATO

David G. Haglund

I

Many, perhaps most, knowledgable readers of this volume will conclude that its title deserves to be faulted on at least two grounds. In the first place, surely the question of the moment is not *will* NATO expand, but how soon, and to which countries? After all, has it not been nearly two years since President Bill Clinton first offered the assurance that it was no longer a matter of whether the alliance would grow, but of when? In the second place, it might be asked, where *could* NATO "go" but east? Those who pose that second question would be in good company, for it is generally conceded that the most likely early admittees to NATO are a trio of so-called Visegrad states: Poland, the Czech Republic, and Hungary. (Some add the group's fourth member, Slovakia, to the select category of front runners.)

Charitably, a few critics might attempt to account for the above-mentioned oddities with the surmise that the editor and some of his colleagues tarried a bit too long in that Berlin *Kneipe* mentioned in the Preface and Acknowledgements. But before such a surmise is made, it might be wise to ponder the volume's subtitle, for it is the editor's view, and that of most of the contributors, that a proper "debate" over NATO enlargement has yet to be held where, ironically, it most needs to be, namely in the courts of public opinion and the halls of parliament of the 16 current alliance members. The latter, let it be recalled, will each have to ratify every new accession to NATO. All of this is not to say that the alliance will not or cannot expand; it is to say that NATO's enlargement is far from a *fait accompli.*[1]

NATO's expansion has become a subject of gathering controversy of late, which is rather surprising in light of the ease with which all 16 allies agreed, at the Brussels summit of January 1994, that enlargement was a foregone conclusion. Not for the first time had a political entity (in this case an alliance) taken a decision on the basis of a restricted discussion among policymakers; and not for the first time would such a decision begin, albeit only after some delay, to stir up opposition. Emblematic of this developing debate within and between allied countries was the most recent Munich Conference on Security Policy (formerly Wehrkunde), where NATO expansion became *the* topic of discussion for most of the conference's two days, and was certainly the single item that attracted the greatest media attention.[2] This contrasts sharply with the mood at the two previous (i.e., post-Brussels) Munich conferences, where NATO expansion hardly registered as a focus of discussion.

No doubt the presence as a panellist of Russia's deputy defence minister, Andrei Kokoshin, contributed to sharpening the dialogue this past February, but it would be misleading to conclude that the only objections to NATO's widening relate to its potential impact upon Russia. It may be that, in the run-up to the Russian presidential elections of June 1996, such have been the most compelling objections; there are, however, a series of other concerns, some related to Russia, some not, that have combined in the past several months to cast uncertainty on the ability of NATO speedily to enlarge.[3]

Some observers are even beginning to doubt that NATO will *ever* expand. One such is Vaclav Havel, the president of the Czech Republic, who worries that unless NATO decides relatively soon to take in new members — among them his country — an opportunity to stabilize Central Europe will have been lost.[4] Yet another prominent figure who thinks that further delay in expanding the alliance may translate into the abandonment of expansion is Newt Gingrich, the speaker of the US House of Representatives, who told a Capitol Hill audience in early March 1996, "I am not sure that this administration is *ever* going to expand NATO." To Gingrich, reflecting on President Clinton's oft-repeated assertion that it was no longer a question of whether but of when to enlarge, it was apparent that the latter word meant more than just a question of timing; it was beginning to mean "whether."[5]

The point of these citations is less to pronounce on whether NATO will actually get around to doing what it says it will do. It is rather to demonstrate that there may be some merit in the claim that the alliance might not, after all, be able to enlarge itself, despite its apparent best intentions and manifold proclamations. If new members are going to be brought into the fold, and they may be, it will not only mean that a way has been found to overcome the growing list of problems that look today to be necessary accompaniments of expansion; it will also likely imply that the very nature of the alliance has altered as its size has increased. It is with those problematical issues that the first part of this book is concerned. In the second part, we examine, through a series of studies focussing on four allied states, the current, incipient state of debate over the alliance's future, as formulated primarily by the political class and other policy élites in the United States, Canada, France, and Germany.

II

In the volume's first chapter, I seek to trace the origins of the idea that NATO should enlarge — an idea that, after all, merely represents a continuation of a well-established alliance trend. In the current debate over enlargement it is sometimes overlooked that growing comes as easily to NATO as it did to Topsy: in 1952 Greece and Turkey joined the original 12, followed in 1955 by the Federal Republic of Germany and, in 1982 Spain. Add to this the expansion of 1990, when the alliance moved eastward by dint of German unification, and one gets the impression that adding members is something NATO does naturally.

Yet there is more to it than simple natural growth, a process that knows no apparent bounds. In the case of the current debate over expansion, there seem clearly to be apparent bounds. There is, as well, a logic, resident both in international relations theories and in the national interest of certain leading allies, that has led the alliance to its current predicament.

While it may be idle if not vain for a political scientist to claim any degree of influence for international relations theorizing in the "real world" of policy, this is precisely what I do in the first half of my chapter. In those pages, I argue that a certain corpus of theory known as "structural realism" has pervaded much of the contemporary discourse on NATO and its future. Specifically, structural realists foresee no great longevity for an alliance whose historical adversary has disappeared. It should not be imagined that the sole "contribution" of theorists comes from the structural realists, for there are a host of competing orientations to international relations whose exponents can and do make compelling cases for the survivability of NATO even without a foe.

Ultimately, one searches the confines of theory in frustration if one seeks certain knowledge about events yet to unfold. The ability to glimpse the future is no more given to scholars than to anyone else; scholars can, however, contribute to setting the context within which policy debates emerge. And so, I argue, it has been with this decade's quest to endow the alliance with an enduring mission in the wake of the Soviet decline and subsequent demise. Within NATO circles, the quest featured prominent milestones — the London summit of 1990, the Rome summit of 1991, the creation of the North Atlantic Cooperation Council (NACC) and the Partnership for Peace (PFP) — on the road to a more inclusive, cooperative approach to security that ostensibly culminated in the enlargement decision.

But the attempt to enlarge and in so doing transform the alliance owed more to the policy preferences of key member states, the United States and

Germany above all, and it is not difficult to detect the presence of scholars and their theories in the formulation of those preferences, at least in the case of the United States. Ironically, it may have been misperception of what the Germans really wanted that led American security analysts and policymakers to decide that NATO should expand (on the basis of their belief that Germany wanted it to, and that Germany was the one ally above others whose wishes required attending). I conclude my chapter with the thought that if Bonn's ardour for enlargement cools (as it seems to have been doing), then so too may Washington's.

Chapter two, co-authored by David Law and Neil MacFarlane, also brings to contemporary policy analysis the contributions of theorists. Specifically, it is the theory of regional security organizations that the authors deploy in seeking to determine whether NATO expansion might be able to make a material contribution to the maintenance of order in the whole of Europe. In this case, it is the goal of projecting stability eastward that is examined, within the context of an inquiry that asks whether regional security organizations might make a better claim to effectiveness than universal ones, and if so, why?

Even claiming that the scattered and diverse lands and societies of the North Atlantic deserved be labelled a "region" could be considered controversial; nevertheless, the authors concede that there is a basis — an ideational one — to something called the "transatlantic community," and that whatever geography might decree to the contrary, one can apply regional theory to the question of NATO expansion. But what, exactly, does that theory suggest regarding the alliance's ability to remedy security dilemmas and challenges on a pan-European basis?

It suggests that there can only be a tenuous basis for believing an enlarged NATO can make a difference by imposing or preserving order in the area between Germany and Russia. While it is true that NATO fares well when compared with almost any other regional organization, and does so in a variety of dimensions, it also suffers the drawbacks of such organizations in at least three areas: 1) there is an asymmetrical distribution of power within the organization; 2) the member states share no common perspective (often quite the reverse!) on the region's security challenges; and 3) the organization is noninclusive, necessarily so.

This is not to deny NATO's strengths, or its attractiveness to countries of Central and Eastern Europe (CEE) that wish to be part of the winning west, for reasons both spiritual and material. Not only might NATO be good for the CEE aspirants to membership, but their aspiration could be a salvational element for NATO, laying to rest, the authors write, "fears that the transatlantic relationship lost its relevance with the end of the Cold War ... [while] ... engaging new generations in Europe and North America in a collective effort to build common security and shared democratic ideals."

But the downside of expansion is also considerable. Significantly, it is not just the Russian question that the authors have in mind. Indeed, expansion to a few CEE states would court the risk of sowing discord among the excluded countries to the east of Germany, while expanding in bulk would threaten to overtax NATO's organizational assets, as well as possibly burden the reform process itself in the aspirant states. As for Russia, it goes without saying that the west's relationship with it will hardly be enhanced if enlargement takes place in opposition to Russian wishes.

Law and MacFarlane conclude that the "expansion of NATO, particularly if it proceeded in an accelerated fashion, would be a costly mistake." They recommend a policy not so much of prevarication as of procrastination, in effect "not deciding to enlarge" instead of deciding *not* to enlarge. In the meantime, NATO could continue to make a difference in Eastern and Southeastern Europe through its good works, offering "limited" security guarantees to CEE states, maintaining the peace in Bosnia, and utilizing the NACC and PFP to erect a "new security community in greater Europe."

Similarly dubious about NATO enlargement, though less concerned with inclusion, is Josef Joffe's chapter, "NATO After Victory." Alliances, Joffe reminds us, are as unlikely to survive when they have triumphed as when they have been defeated. Notwithstanding this historical "iron law," and betraying his own preference that NATO should survive, Joffe proceeds to outline a set of bad and good strategies regarding NATO's future. Analogizing with the experience of firms and drawing on the language and concepts of microeconomics, Joffe argues that the alliance has only four choices. It can close up shop, downsize, develop new products, or try to sell its old products in new markets.

The new product line, an outgrowth of NATO's post-1990 reforms, is peacekeeping and crisis management. Joffe is not optimistic, and this notwithstanding NATO's apparent success in Bosnia with IFOR, that the alliance will turn out to be very adept in performing these functions, and reminds his readers that the secret to NATO's success in the Cold War confrontation with the Warsaw Pact was the fact that it never had to use its military might, but only had to demonstrate it for the purposes of deterrence. "[T]he alliance — like Mount Everest — merely had to *be* there... The objective was simple and enduring: to preserve the status quo."

Nor will the attempt to sell the old product in new markets work, either; this is simply another way of observing that NATO expansion is problematical for a number of reasons. Joffe enumerates the difficulties with enlargement: it will strain NATO's cohesion; it will bring in new members who (with the possible exception of Poland) may not be committed to springing to the defence of their allies, if required; it will be very costly economically; it will complicate the question of NATO's nuclear guarantees; it will leave out of the fold those CEE states that are the most threatened; and it runs the risk of having to appease Russian concerns by altering its fundamental nature.

Instead of contemplating enlargement as a means of adding strategic as-sets to the alliance, Joffe claims NATO is promoting a project that "lacks the punch of compelling interest. The purpose is not to add strategic space and military power but to engage in charity — providing a home for selected 'easties' — where the costs are low." As a result, should it decide to enlarge after all, as it may, NATO will have significantly transformed itself, and downgraded its ca-pacity to serve as a meaningful collective-defence organization.

It will have done so, says Joffe, because enlargement will only proceed with Russian acquiescence, and that can only be obtained under two condi-tions: either the alliance makes the transition from collective defence to collective security; or it withholds its "core product" from new CEE consumers. That core product, he reminds us, is not and never was Article 5 of the Washington Treaty ("a very weakly worded pledge of mutual succour"), but rather consisted in a range of "blood-and-iron" arrangements including forward deployment of allied troops, integrated forces under overall American command arrayed in a "layer-cake" along the former inner-German border, and the presence of US nuclear weapons.

Although enlargement is in general a laudable objective, Joffe worries it is also a dangerous one. "Bringing in new members that seek a home rather than a fort will dilute the compact. Paying the requisite compensation to Russia will more than just dilute; it will destroy." Instead, NATO should "downsize" and con-centrate upon its never-ending mission, which is to balance the weight of Russia, maintain an integrative western structure within which Germany can be fitted, and preserve the American commitment to European security. "[T]he old func-tions, suitably modernized," he concludes, "can still serve as the new rationale for the alliance as it moves toward the ripe old age of 50."

The problems of getting Russian acquiescence in NATO's enlargement or, if that is not possible, the consequences of doing without it, are addressed in chapter four, by Andrei Kortunov. It is important to stress at the outset, insists Kortunov, that for the vast majority of Russians, neither NATO nor its potential expansion is of great concern; for that matter, says Kortunov, even for most of the Russians who take an interest in foreign policy (by definition, a minority of the population) the alliance really is not an issue, since it can "neither resolve immediate Russian foreign policy problems, nor complicate them in a serious way."

The catch, however, is that for the élite with an interest in the alliance — in effect a tiny minority of a minority — NATO's enlargement has come to top the agenda of debate. Those who do follow closely the alliance's announced inten-tions to expand can be lumped into two broad camps, the nationalists and the liberals. To the former, NATO remains what it has always been, a defensive alliance that cannot bode well for Russia. Indeed, many of the nationalists are prepared to see it as an offensive alliance, with sinister designs on Russia, sometimes (to the more conspiratorial) aided and abetted by those who have been wielding power in the Kremlin over the past few years.

The liberals, for their part, regard NATO expansion not as part of some duplicitous plot to subvert Russia, but rather as a result of a "probably not well-conceived reaction to the changing international situation." Liberals stress the role played by ethnic communities in North America in mobilizing support for the early entry of certain CEE states, and they understand that NATO requires a new mission if it is to survive for long in the post-Cold War world. For the liberals, it is not because NATO is considered to be a threat that they tend to oppose the current expansion project; it is rather because Russia runs the risk of being marginalized in European politics as a result of it. "In other words," says Kortunov, "the danger for Russia lies not in NATO enlargement per se, but in the inability of Russia to join the process."

Does it follow that NATO will not expand, because Russia cannot accept it? Not necessarily, he argues. There are four conceivable ways in which Russian leaders might react to the enlargement initiative. They could, for instance, insist upon a "new division of Europe," one in which the Russian compensation for NATO's adding a few of the CEE states would be the erection of an alternative security pole around the Commonwealth of Independent States (CIS). In recognition of NATO's limited expansion, Russia would be granted by the west a "more-or-less explicit endorsement of its role as leader of the European misfits." Although there need be no reason for such a bipolar arrangement to be inimical to western interests, there is reason to believe that, over the long run, such a security structure would degenerate into one of hostile blocs.

A second option would be for Russian leaders to minimize the consequences of an enlarged NATO by minimizing the significance of NATO. This would entail working to secure pride of place for the Organization for Security and Cooperation in Europe (OSCE) over NATO in the new Europe, whose security challenges would be soluble more by collective-security than by collective-defence mechanisms. Again, there would be nothing specifically antiwestern about the emphasis upon the OSCE, especially if it turned out that collective defence could have no meaning absent a great-power threat in Europe; in that event, having strengthened the OSCE would have contributed to the resolution of problems the west wanted solved.

Yet a third option, and by far the one most congenial both to NATO and the wider west, would be for Russia to aspire to membership in the west through partnership with NATO. Special arrangements would be needed to ensure that both sides in the partnership could protect their interests, but to its proponents in Russia (and to those in NATO who favour the idea), Russia would be granted a degree of influence in European security far greater than that possessed by most of the actual members of the alliance, even though it would have to remain outside of it.

The final option, one that has fallen greatly out of favour in Russia save as a "fantasy of radical democrats," would be for Russian leaders to try to obtain full membership in NATO. Its exponents insist that there are in any event different variants of NATO membership, ranging from the tightly integrated Germany to the loosely bound France, and that within such a range it should be possible to accommodate even a country like Russia. Moreover, they say, if integrating Germany was required in the immediate post-World War II decades to bring about a reconciliation between it and its Western European neighbours, would not an integrated Russia have the same effect upon the very countries of Central and Eastern Europe that feel themselves today to be the most insecure?

Kortunov concludes by dismissing the fourth option as incapable of realization, and states that it is unlikely that Russian leaders will make a clear choice between the other three. "Most likely, Russia will continue to fluctuate within the triangle formed by the three more plausible options, gravitating to various angles in response to any number of internal and external factors."

In chapter five, John Barrett approaches NATO's enlargement from a different perspective, stressing that with the Cold War's ending NATO now had, for the first time since its inception, the chance to "rediscover its essence as something more than a collective-defence organization only." Indeed, and reflective of this opportunity, strategic objectives have not been at the forefront of the campaign to enlarge the alliance. Nor can it be claimed that the September 1995 NATO study on enlargement, the so-called "why and how" study, has much to say about strategic rationales.

Barrett's chapter provides a detailed analysis of that NATO study, which he argues does little to provide guidance for the next stage of settling the "who" and "when" of membership, precisely because of NATO's inability to "articulate an agreed *hierarchy* of [the] strategic objectives" enlargement is supposed to serve. Because of this, it will not prove an easy task for the alliance to come to an agreement over which countries should be invited to join, and when — questions that are under intensive study this year, and which are supposed to be meaningfully addressed at the NATO ministerial meetings in December 1996.

Not only is there no emerging consensus on the who and the when, there is no reason to believe that it will be easy to secure ratification of new memberships by the 16 current allies, in the event a consensus could be found within NATO councils. Underlying both these problems is the lack of a compelling strategic purpose to enlargement. "In other words," remarks Barrett, "the most germane question now may not be 'who' or 'when'; it may be 'which.' ... [W]hich objective, if any, will be able to command the consensus needed to open the alliance's doors to new members?"

Nevertheless, strategic goals can be identified and itemized, even if the list must contain mutually exclusive (or at least somewhat contradictory) objectives. Barrett suggests there are four essential strategic aims of the alliance: 1) preserving NATO's effectiveness, 2) furthering the processes of integration

in Europe, 3) preventing the redivision of Europe, and 4) consolidating the democratic reforms under way in the former Warsaw Pact countries. Listed in this
fashion, it is hard to find any country among the current allies that would dispute the merits of the individual objectives. The problem lies elsewhere,
concludes Barrett: "If the alliance is not to stumble into one of its most profound
decisions, then a common, unifying vision must emerge to guide it through the
next steps on enlargement. This vision seems as yet to be absent... The problem ... lies in the fact that the allies are still unsure whether extending membership
will over time weaken NATO, perhaps even endow it with new, ultimately
irresoluble conflicts and instabilities."

III

Part Two of the volume carries the debate away from theory and institutionalized policy settings and embeds it in a series of national case studies, for it will
be, as Barrett's chapter stressed, the alliance members' individual ratifying processes that determine the ultimate fate of the enlargement project. Accordingly,
four countries have been chosen to illustrate the nature of the problem: the
United States, Canada, France, and Germany.

The first of these is the subject of Douglas Stuart's chapter, in which is
posed a critically important question: Will NATO enlargement be an initiative
that enhances or diminishes the American commitment to European security?
There is no little irony in the question, for it has so far been a staple of discussion that expanding NATO is necessary to *keep* America involved in the security
affairs of the old continent. Stuart raises the disturbing prospect that "unresolved issues relating to NATO enlargement are likely to make it harder for the
proponents of a continued US military presence in Europe to argue convincingly their case."

The problem of transatlantic bickering and misunderstanding, so often subsumed under the rubric of "burdensharing" during the Cold War, has not
disappeared in the post-1989 period. To be sure, says Stuart, the Clinton administration has wisely indicated that it wishes the US to remain a major force
in European security affairs. Unfortunately, it has changed direction on the question of expanding NATO, and starting in the summer of 1994, to the surprise of
the allies, it "permitted the NACC and the PFP to be marginalized" and lent its
vigorous support to the CEE states' efforts to join the alliance.

Why did it do this? In large part, says Stuart, because of domestic political
considerations, relating primarily to the 1996 presidential election. Stuart em-
phasizes the reliance of Clinton in 1992 on the electoral vote of those states
with the greatest share of America's CEE ethnic populations: of the 14 largest
such states, Clinton carried 12, and knew that his chances for reelection would

depend in no small measure on maintaining his support with these important ethnic constituencies.

Significantly, the embrace of NATO expansion was not attended by any serious consideration of costs and benefits. Both within the administration and in Congress enlargement was being portrayed in 1994 as an option that involved low costs and high payoffs. This was not, however, the dominant perception of the American military, which has largely been excluded from the discussions on expansion, claims Stuart, who likens the regnant tone of those discussions to "cognitive dissonance."

NATO expansion will have unpleasant implications for defence budgets of the current allies, and it can hardly be counted on to instill a greater spirit of cooperation among the Russians in areas where it is helpful if not essential to have that cooperation. Not only that, but expanding NATO might work against America's desire to see Western Europe carry more of the burden of integrating the CEE countries into European security structures, by "bolster[ing] the position of those factions within Western Europe who wish to establish the EU as an exclusive (and exclusively) 'civilian club' that leaves the messy issues of regional and global security to Washington."

If enlargement cannot be halted, Stuart concludes, it should at least be slowed, both so as to make it "more palatable" to Russia and to ensure that NATO expansion proceeds simultaneously with, and gives encouragement to, the eastward expansion of the EU.

In the other North American NATO member, debate has been occasioned more by the question of the alliance's relevance than by the question of its expansion. As Paul Buteux, Michel Fortmann, and Pierre Martin argue in chapter seven, Canadian policy toward NATO is marked by contradiction: at the political level, there is a tendency to question the ongoing utility of the alliance for Canadian and even transatlantic ends, while at the same time the country's defence and foreign policy remains influenced by decisions taken or not taken in Brussels. Earlier in this decade there was a flurry of interest in the alliance, on the part of analysts and advocacy groups desirous of seeing it converted from a collective-defence to a collective-security organization, but that interest appears to have abated of late.

If the Cold War's ending did not usher in an era of no-threat for Canada, it certainly had the effect of reducing greatly the prospects that the country's physical security could be menaced in the same dire manner it might have been prior to 1990 — that is, by the possibility of a global conflagration touched off by superpower rivalry and involving the use of nuclear weapons. In that sense, Canada *has* become a good deal safer, even if problems have mounted at home on both the economic and constitutional fronts. Because of those problems, Ottawa scrutinizes ever more closely anything that appears to suggest the need to make new security commitments or extend old ones. And defence budgets continue to be chopped.

As the authors argue, "[i]n the present climate of Canadian security discourse it is doubtful that government officials regard regional security problems in Europe as of central strategic or political concern." That being so, it appears on the surface to be surprising that Ottawa should have accepted without demur the expansion of NATO, given that this will almost certainly necessitate some real allocations of scarce economic resources on the part of all the allies. At least, it would have been surprising were it not for Ottawa's "traditional practice [within NATO] of seeking consensus and of supporting any consensus that might emerge." In Canada, as in the United States, there is an eagerness to believe that NATO can enlarge with low risk, and at low cost. Should this prove not to be possible, then it must remain a very real question whether, in the event of expansion, a widening of the fabled "commitment-capability gap" in Canadian defence policy can be avoided, and if so, how.

Ironically, there has been little pressure from the public on policymakers who have been detecting (some say orchestrating) a relative deemphasis upon NATO and Europe in recent years. It is true that support for the alliance has declined somewhat since the Cold War, but NATO remains quite popular with a Canadian society that, for all the demographic, economic, and political transformations of the past decade or so, remains solidly atlanticist. Admittedly, survey data contain little information on the public's views regarding NATO enlargement, chiefly because this issue has, to date, received so little attention in Canada. In this respect, Canada finds itself in the same position as its allies, namely of having embarked upon an interesting initiative without first having discussed it seriously, either within the "political class" or among the broader society.

While there may be nothing newsworthy about Canada working toward, and then supporting, consensus within NATO councils, it really is significant when France falls in line with alliance initiatives, as it has ostensibly done with the enlargement project, even though it was hardly a secret that Paris had been resisting the notion of endowing NATO with an eastern "vocation" almost since the moment the Berlin Wall was breached. It is this puzzle that Pascal Boniface's chapter tries to resolve, for he notes that while there remains much opposition in France to the enlargement of NATO, "no one dares express it officially."

French diffidence stems from three sources. First and perhaps most important of these is the change in the country's relationship with the alliance: no more is NATO seen to be blocking the road to the long-awaited destination of a European Security and Defence Identity (ESDI). Second is the perception in Paris that the momentum of expansion is beginning to lapse elsewhere in the alliance, as the costs and risks of a larger NATO begin to become apparent; if so, why should Paris bring opprobrium down upon itself from CEE states by being seen to be the cause of the failure of the initiative? Third is the conviction that France really could not stop enlargement by itself in any case, so why try?

Boniface sums up the French attitude by paraphrasing Cocteau: "if we cannot prevent disorder from occurring, we can at least pretend to be one of its creators."

French officials do worry as well that if they were seen to be opposed to enlargement it would be taken as (further) evidence that they were opposed to NATO. In fact, argues Boniface, the contrary is the case: France is dubious about enlargement because it perceives much benefit in preserving the alliance. Assuredly, this was not the French outlook earlier in the decade, and certainly not at the time of the creation of the NACC, which was regarded in Paris as evidence that the US was "determined, at any price, to confer new missions on the alliance ... so as to thwart the emergence of the WEU and the Conference on Security and Cooperation in Europe..."

Today, the French have a different worry, not of too much American interest in Europe's security but of too little, and Boniface raises the possibility that NATO's expansion might have a "boomerang" effect on the US commitment to European security, for by stimulating questions about the wisdom of adding new members, the coming enlargement debate might unleash other questions, among them the relevance of NATO itself to American interests. "In this respect," concludes Boniface, "Paris' reluctance to see NATO enlarge too rapidly ... should ironically be taken as the proof of France's attachment, rather than hostility, to the alliance."

Our final chapter, by Reinhard Wolf, explores the evolving German position on NATO expansion. It may turn out that the outcome of the German debate on this issue will be determinative for the alliance. Wolf calls Germany the "doubtful mover" of enlargement, both because the country's defence minister, Volker Rühe, was the first prominent western politician to advocate expanding the alliance and also because while there is a widespread degree of support among the German public that NATO should go east, the support is broader than it is deep. Moreover, enlarging the alliance seems to make intuitive sense, from the standpoint of Germany's own interests, since it holds out the prospect of stabilizing the country's eastern neighbours, advancing the cause of European integration, and cementing the all-important transatlantic relationship by keeping NATO relevant and the North Americans engaged.

Set against these benefits, however, is the Russian question. It is no coincidence that, once Boris Yeltsin spoke out in September 1993 against enlarging the alliance, the enthusiasm of both Chancellor Kohl and his foreign minister, Klaus Kinkel, began to flag. Since that time, Bonn has had to tread carefully over the expansion terrain, in a bid to reassure both the Kremlin and Washington that it is in basic agreement with their sensibilities on the issue. It was an objective, successfully achieved, of Kohl to get the US committed to the parallel expansion of the EU and NATO — not, as some have argued, to stall expansion but rather to take some of the sting out of it for the Russians, by packaging it as part of a broadening of European institutions to the CEE states. Surprisingly, in view of the issue's importance to Germany, there has been little serious debate in the country over NATO expansion. In particular, there has been an unwillingness to ask what must be the most relevant question, namely "whether it is conceivable that Germany might declare war on an aggressive Russia, unless the Federal Republic itself were to come under attack," as a result of security commitments made to new allies? Wolf argues that this question does not get raised because Germans tend to shy away from talking or even thinking about the "national interest" in such a stark manner, preferring instead to take comfort in the shelter of multilateralism and institutionalism, and couching debates on international relations primarily in a normative context rather than in terms of interest or power.

"Compared to their ... western counterparts," Wolf states, "many German experts are still very reluctant to ask whether, to paraphrase Bismarck, the defence of a Central European state could ever warrant the bones of the nation's soldiers." Yet if intergovernmental cooperation is to be successful — indeed if institutionalism is to have a future — it will be incumbent upon Germans to understand more accurately their own interests. "Seen from this perspective," he concludes, "both Germany and the alliance could only benefit from the German debate on NATO's future roles gaining in depth, frankness, and intensity."

Notes

1. A note on terminology is in order here. We shall be employing the terms "expand" and "enlarge" as synonyms. Lest it be thought that there is nothing objectionable about doing this, it must be stated that during the past two years, for reasons that can neither be explained nor recalled, it became considered in official alliance circles the epitome of poor form to use the two terms interchangeably. "Expand," it was said, was too harsh a word, and conveyed the wrong message about NATO's intentions. However much circulation this current terminological politesse may have gained, it is nonetheless silly, since standard English dictionaries will commonly define the one word in terms of the other — as does mine, when it states that to enlarge is to "increase the capacity or scope of; expand." *Random House Dictionary of the English Language* (New York: Random House, 1973), p. 474.

2. Author's notes, 33rd Munich Conference on Security Policy, Munich, 3-4 February 1996. Sample headlines from the German press would include "Vorbehalt Kohls gegen Ost-Erweiterung," *Welt am Sonntag*, 4 February 1996, pp. 1, 3; "Kohl mahnt Westen zur Umsicht," *Die Welt*, 5 February 1996, pp. 1, 4; and "Rußland warnt scharf vor Ost-Erweiterung der NATO," *Süddeutsche Zeitung*, 5 February 1996, p. 1.

3. Theresa Hitchens, "Voices Rise for Slow NATO Growth," *Defense News*, 22-28 April 1996, p. 46.

4. Jim Hoagland, "But Is NATO Ready for Czechs?" *International Herald Tribune*, 9 May 1996, p. 8.

5. Author's notes of keynote address delivered to the forum on "NATO and the Transatlantic Future," co-sponsored by the Hudson Institute and the Progressive Policy Institute, Washington, 7 March 1996.

PART I

THE THEORETICAL AND POLICY SETTING

CHAPTER ONE

NATO Expansion:
Origins and Evolution of an Idea

David G. Haglund

Introduction: The Count Ciano Puzzle

Although John F. Kennedy liked to use the phrase, it is really to Count Galeazzo Ciano, Mussolini's son-in-law and quondam Italian foreign minister, that we owe the thought that, "as always, victory finds a hundred fathers but defeat is an orphan."[1] It may be wrong to conclude that the idea of NATO's necessary enlargement must come a cropper; at the very least it would seem premature so to conclude. Nevertheless, there is something suggestive about Ciano's apothegm when applied to the current debate over NATO expansion. It is at least mildly puzzling that an alliance so willing, at its Brussels summit of January 1994, to embrace the cause of enlargement should today find itself curiously bereft of claimants to the "parenting" honour.[2] Indeed, it might not be too much of an exaggeration to state that after Moscow, the European capital in which one is likely to find the greatest aversion to the concept of NATO enlargement is Brussels![3]

Lest anyone imagine that the Atlantic alliance is breathlessly promoting its early expansion eastward, last year's study into the "whys and hows" of enlargement should dispel any such confusion. Not for nothing has this initial official blueprint for expansion been labelled a "minimalist" document.[4] To be sure, minimalism at this time, especially in light of the upcoming elections in Russia for the presidency, is no mean virtue, all the more so as even a "moderate" such as Boris Yeltsin can be heard to declaim, whether he believes it or not, that expanding NATO to the east "will mean a conflagration of war throughout Europe, for sure."[5]

But it is not just Russian opposition, however inelegantly it gets expressed, that accounts for the allies' current diffidence regarding the expansion project;

even before Russian dudgeon waxed, it was clear that enthusiasm for enlargement was waning in many precincts of the alliance, and this shows up in the NATO enlargement study, particularly when entrance into the alliance is argued to be something that must occur in parallel (though not necessarily simultaneously) with the enlargement eastward of the European Union.[6] What the requirement of parallelism does is to put off the prospects of NATO enlargement for at least the remainder of this decade, as none of the Central and Eastern European (CEE) aspirants to EU membership is, at the moment, close to fulfilling the political and economic criteria for joining, a judgement that seems to have been confirmed by the indifference or outright opposition evinced toward early enlargement by participants at the EU's Majorca meeting in September 1995.[7]

Despite its being dubbed the "why and how" study, NATO's enlargement report is much more thorough in delving into the latter than the former. Admittedly, early on the drafters do touch upon what has to be considered a major desideratum of expansion, namely to "provide increased stability and security for all the Euro-Atlantic area," and by inference one is reminded of the alliance's previous expansions in 1952 (Greece and Turkey), 1955 (the Federal Republic of Germany), and 1982 (Spain) — not to mention 1990 (the former German Democratic Republic). The drafters further imply that NATO might even have a constitutional predisposition to growth, embodied in the Washington Treaty's "Cartesian" Article 10 ("j'existe, donc je m'élargis"), which allows the signatories, "by unanimous agreement, [to] invite any other European state in a position to further the principles of this Treaty and to contribute to the security of the North Atlantic area to accede to this Treaty."[8]

That being said, the observer of NATO affairs who poses the question, "Why has expansion become an issue now?" will find little in the enlargement study to slake his or her curiosity. My purpose in this chapter is to address that question, but to do so in a way that combines an intervention into the realm of international-relations theorizing with an exploration of the perceived "national interest" that some of the major enlargement supporters have argued obliges the alliance to grow. Ideas in international security, after all, do not create themselves, much less do they spring forth from an intellectual void.[9] They may and do "take on life," but it is rarely if ever a life of their own, unconnected with perceptions of "raison d'état" formed by state leaders who must constantly act in an uncertain international environment.

Structural Realism and the Myth of NATO's Necessary Demise

In acting in that environment, policymakers are guided by theory, or at least by theoretical glimmerings, even if they may be loath to acknowledge that guidance.

In this regard, the case for NATO expansion initially began to be made as a means of countering some of the regnant pessimism concerning the alliance's survivability that was being increasingly expressed, in the early post-Cold War years, by many NATO watchers, among whose ranks was a school of theoreticians of international relations known as the "structural realists." It was the sombre but ineluctable message of this school that NATO in the post-Cold War world was dying, for want of an enemy. Though it may be grandiose to claim as many do that this variant of realism has a conceptual stranglehold on international-relations theorizing, it can nevertheless be said to be possessed of some intellectual as well as policy influence. Thus, when the dean of structural realism, Kenneth Waltz, pronounced late in 1993 that "NATO's days are not numbered, but its years are," many could agree, for what, in light both of theory and empirical reality, was the purpose of an alliance without, as Waltz put it, a "worthy opponent"?[10] Josef Joffe expressed the same thought in different words, when he observed more recently that if "you take away its enemy, you will begin to see an alliance looking like a plant without water."[11]

Structural realism can be characterized by a concentration upon the following assumptions: that anarchy is the ordering principle of the international system; that states are everywhere motivated to assure their security as their paramount objective; that self-help is the preferred, and in some cases only, policy injunction; that conflict rather than "cooperation" between states is the norm; and, perhaps most importantly for this discussion, that bipolar balances of power are stable and conducive to peace, while multipolar balances are unstable and conducive to war. In general, and in light of this catalogue not without reason, structural realists are today inclined toward pessimism. They are also inclined to determinism, even though few would admit this, seeking refuge instead in kindlier, gentler constructs such as conditioning, or probabilism.

Curiously, it was their determinism that made structural realists such optimists regarding NATO's prospects from the coign of vantage of the 1980s. Then, and notwithstanding such alliance spats as those occurring over pipelines, Central America, Libya, arcane acronyms such as FOTL, and the sempiternal burden-sharing issue, structural realism's message was a soothing one, perhaps best conveyed by Glenn Snyder, writing a dozen years ago: "It follows that those who see NATO's current crisis as heralding its collapse tend to confuse cause and effect. Although the disagreements have arisen from a variety of proximate causes, they persist largely because the [a]lliance *cannot* break up."[12]

For the structural realists, what structure gives, it also takes away, and this explains their current pessimism about NATO's prospects. It is not simply that the allies lack the common foe once required to assure their common action; it is that the demise of bipolarity guarantees, by definition, the rise of new challengers in the eternal struggle for international power and influence. In this struggle, there can be no reason to exclude, and every reason to expect, at least some of the rising challengers springing from the ranks of today's allies.

Waltz, for instance, envisages three likely rivals to the United States, and two come from the list of America's current allies: Germany (or a future West European federation), Japan, and China.[13] As yet another structural realist, Christopher Layne, explains it, international relations consists in the "same damn things over and over again: war, great power security and economic competitions, the rise and fall of great powers, and the formation and dissolution of alliances."[14]

The Theoretical Case for NATO's Possible Survival

If a consensus characterizes the structural-realist perspective on NATO in the absence of an enemy, eclecticism is the word that best captures the predictive compass of contrasting theories of international relations. Numerous theorists, from a variety of perspectives, will tell you that there is absolutely no reason why NATO must disappear simply because its Cold War antagonist did. Not only is there such a divergence of outlook on the question of NATO's survivability, but there is also a variation in the "levels of analysis" employed by those seeking to provide an answer. Interestingly, some of structural realism's most persuasive critics on the NATO issue can be located at the same "systemic" level of analysis; indeed, some of them are even systemic-level realists!

In this group one finds, for instance, writers of a realist bent who seek to account for system change by referring to the relationship between system leaders ("hegemons") and their challengers. Like structural realists, these analysts are focused upon the balance of power; unlike structural realists, however, they are primarily interested in why and how systems change, and with what consequences. They see change as a resultant of the dynamic of uneven growth as between nations; and for the most celebrated of these writers, Robert Gilpin, the consequences of change are profound, usually entailing major-power war.[15]

But as William Wohlforth has recently explained, realists inclined toward hegemony theory these days need not sound as lugubrious as their contemporary structuralist colleagues, for if it is true that hegemony theorists used to focus upon rising challengers, and were therefore inattentive to the implications of collapsing challengers, they now know better. In short, says Wohlforth, the collapse of the Soviet Union has been an unalloyed good to those who once worried about systemic change producing a great-power war: "[o]nce Soviet power began to decline relative to the United States and its allies, it should have been evident that, absent a reversal of fortunes, no hegemonic war was in the offing. Soviet decline reaffirmed rather than reversed the existing hierarchy of world politics."[16]

It follows, to realists of this stripe, that the Soviet collapse, far from sounding the death knell of the alliance, as the structuralists would have it, can actually be good for NATO. It is good because system change triggers the phenomenon known as "bandwagoning," through which states spurred by the perception of opportunity seek to align themselves with the state or coalition of states held to be in the ascendant, thus capable of bestowing favour and support upon those who seek to clamber aboard the wagon. On this version, the current enthusiasm for joining NATO being evinced by former adversaries in the Warsaw Treaty Organization has less to do with their fear of Russian aggression and more to do with their desire to be included within the institutional embrace of the winning west. Writes Randall Schweller, "[o]ne of the primary motivations for bandwagoning is to share in the spoils of victory. When profit rather than security drives alliance choices, there is no reason to expect that states will be threatened or cajoled to climb aboard the bandwagon; they do so willingly."[17]

Other system-level theorists join the realists above in providing support for the survivability of NATO. For the purposes of this chapter, I shall call them "institutionalists," although it is not uncommon to see them referred to as "neo-institutionalists" or "neoliberals."[18] However we might describe them, institutionalists appear to accept that systemic factors can and do intervene in the affairs of states so as to mitigate the consequences of anarchy for international behaviour: outcomes, in other words, are something other than the aggregation of the interests and actions of individual states. They are resultants that, to one degree or other (and here the institutionalists differ among themselves), have been shaped or conditioned by "intervening variables" at the level of the international system. Those variables might take the form of international organizations (e.g., NATO), of international law, or of the mutual expectation of reciprocity in the creation, application and maintenance of principles, norms, and rules (i.e., regimes). For the institutionalist, what is most important is the conviction that institutions matter, and that they enable the international system to "transcend" the otherwise bleak dictates of the doctrine of "self-help."[19]

All of this is anathema to structural realists such as John Mearsheimer, who argues that "[w]hat is most impressive about institutions, in fact, is how little independent effect they seem to have had on state behavior."[20] Admittedly, institutions can be instruments of states; but it is best not to confuse effect and cause. To Mearsheimer, NATO is a case in point: it did not keep the peace in the post-1949 period, the bipolar balance of power did. NATO was, at best, epiphenomenal, "essentially an American tool for managing power in the face of the Soviet threat."[21] To this kind of claim institutionalists respond with the counterargument that institutions do not necessarily have to accomplish their ends by "independent effects" (though they may); they play a useful role in mitigating the adverse consequences of anarchy and in promoting cooperation both by serving to constitute ideas and values and acting as clearing-houses for their exchange. In these roles, institutionalists say, defensive alliances are no less important than other organizations. Indeed, as the international system becomes characterized by multipolarity in the post-Cold War era, NATO is argued by some to assume more not less importance as a means of rendering intentions more predictable, and thus minimizing the tendency of European states (even Western European ones) to revert to a "nationalization" of defence policy. In the words of Michael Brenner, NATO "should be viewed as an evolving civic community whose pacific relations are the institutionalized norm rather than the calculated preference of states."[22]

Any discussion of intention must soon lead to a discussion of perceptions, and it because of this logical progression that the ostensibly systemic-level of analysis constituted by "institutionalism" inevitably yields to subsystemic (or "second-image") analyses. This is no less true in NATO's than in any other case.[23] At the subsystemic level focusing upon states and their domestic societies, two kinds of claims have been made for NATO's enduring viability. The first relates to what has become known as "democratic peace theory" (or, d.p.t.); the second relates to a rather contrasting perspective, namely classical realism, which unlike its theoretical homologue structural realism, is reasonably if not uniformly congenial to the case for NATO's enduring viability.

Democratic peace theory makes two claims of relevance to the future of NATO. The milder of these claims simply maintains that democracies do not go to war against each other, or even threaten to do so. From this it follows that NATO cannot fall apart, or at least that it will not fall apart because of the reasons adduced by structural realists (or even a few classical realists!), namely the regrettable but necessary implications of balancing behaviour in a multipolar world. NATO may, according to this milder version, lapse into desuetude — for who needs an alliance to keep the peace between liberal democracies? — but it will not shatter into rival blocs of the order foreseen, say, by Conor Cruise O'Brien, who argues that the emerging strategic fault line in Europe will be the Rhine River, as the western allies of the two world wars once again find themselves, sometime early in the coming century, uniting to combat the threat of a powerful Germany.[24]

The stronger of the d.p.t. contentions is that not only does democracy predispose the western allies to peace, it predisposes them to alliance as well. According to this view, NATO is more than a marriage of security convenience between partners possessed of interest-based reasons for cooperation; it is a community of shared values.[25] As such, it can be expected to persist, even if the leadership functions once performed by the United States might attenuate. Notes Mark Boyer, "[w]hatever the motivation for the American role in the formation of the postwar Western alliance system, it is a fair bet that the values engendered in Western cooperation in security affairs will be maintained in the years ahead, based on the assumption that these values have become internalized in the systems of Western alliance nations."[26]

As one would expect, structural realists are, in the main, resistant to the blandishments of democratic peace theory. How could they not be, given their emphasis on the necessity for balancing behaviour to characterize life in an anarchy constituted by security-seeking states?[27] Classical realists, on the other hand, are less dogmatic about democratic peace theory. Certainly, this variant of realism shelters analysts who outdo even the structuralists when it comes to debunking d.p.t. Consider, in this regard, Owen Harries, editor of the *National Interest*, who has argued (not in his own journal) that "the west" is an artificial construction that required a large, collectively perceived threat to be brought into being; in the absence of threat, no common values can be expected to hold it together, and NATO itself runs the risk of dissolution if it heads off, Quixote-like, in quest of new missions and mandates in the post-Cold War world.[28] But other classical realists, even and especially those associated with the *National Interest*, have reminded us that (structural) realists can be their own worst enemies at times, no more so than when they seek to deny that war has all but vanished as a means of conflict-resolution between democracies.[29]

What these classical realists stress is not anarchy, but *raison d'état*, as the motivating force in world politics. Theirs is a less-deterministic vision of international politics than that provided by structuralism, one in which the identification and operationalization of the "national interest" serves to animate statecraft. Clearly, and notwithstanding a predilection for seeking "first causes" in a flawed human nature, classical realism offers more scope for voluntarism than does structural realism.[30] And while there exists no classical-realist party line on NATO's survivability, it is logical to deduce from classical-realist premises that NATO can endure if important states want it to. With equal logic, of course, the opposite deduction can obtain.

This is why it is so important to reiterate that no theory-based prediction regarding NATO can be sufficiently compelling to foreclose the current debate. Theory may be necessary for policy analysis; at least it is impossible to imagine an atheorectical policy analysis that could be worthwhile. But theory, and not just structural-realist theory, should never be thought to be possessed of predictive power. It will have done its job if it has helped us to understand. NATO may "fail," though it need not.

The Alliance's Search for New Missions

It may be one thing to suggest, as the NATO-optimists discussed in the preceding section do, that the alliance has no reason to expire simply because its historic adversary did. But it is another thing to explain how NATO can remain of much use to its member-states, especially its most powerful ones, in the absence of anything for it to do. It is fine to claim that institutions are resistant to cancellation — and even the feckless League of Nations bears at least partial testimony to the claim, surviving as it did the Second World War before being put out of its misery with the founding of the United Nations — but that is really not the point. What is at stake at the moment is not so much whether something we call NATO will endure, it is whether it will matter very much that it does endure. That worry has been on the minds of many, both in Brussels and, as I shall argue below, certain capitals of member states ever since the ending of the Cold War.[31] Even the optimists, it seems, have refused to play the part of Pollyanna. In fact, since for the pessimists NATO is beyond the point of worrying about, it is the optimists who have been most seized of the task of endowing purpose to the alliance. For they too have sensed the truth in at least one structural-realist contention, which is that the historical record does not reveal even a single alliance that proved capable of long outlasting the disappearance of its adversary.[32] However, say the optimists, NATO can confute historicism. If there is no compelling need for collective defence in an era of "no threat," that should hardly prove fatal, for they argue (and have been arguing since 1990) the alliance can be "transformed." And in its transformation, it will find its salvation.

NATO's quest for transformation reflects the concerns of NATO optimists to keep in existence an entity that admittedly may have had an explicit collective-defence purpose, but has also performed an invaluable collective-security-like function. That function, a consequence of the collective-defence mission, was to help the countries of Western Europe overcome their historic rivalries and come together in a regional security community that may not have been (because of the Greco-Turkish dispute) coterminous with NATO's borders, but which was nonetheless a most welcome departure from the previous pattern of interstate competition in Western Europe, and seemed to enshrine lasting peace between that part of the continent's two most important countries, France and Germany. It was certainly the view of Manfred Wörner that the peace of (Western) Europe could not be taken for granted in the absence of the alliance, and there can be no question that this particularly dynamic secretary general had a hand in moving NATO along the transformatory road. Nor was it unusual that, as a German, Wörner should have been sensitive to the alliance's apparent ability to reassure both his country and its neighbours that German energies, whether through a process labelled "double containment" or *Einbindungspolitik*, would never again find outlets inimical to the Western European security community.[33]

Thus, in part because of the ubiquity and plausibility of some theory-derived suppositions that alliances without enemies were tenuous if not outright impossibilities, and in part because of the historical experience of Western European and North American policy élites committed to preserving NATO as a means of preserving Western Europe, the early post-Cold War years witnessed a frenetic search for new roles and missions for the alliance, and it would be this search that would ultimately lead to the apparent (though likely, for reasons I shall explain) shallow consensus on NATO expansion that exists today. Quite aptly has one scholar observed that, with the end of the Cold War, "[f]inding something for NATO to do has become a cottage industry in its own right."[34]

It is important to stress that at this juncture, for NATO to *do* was for it to *be*. The existential quest began with the alliance's London summit of July 1990, which resulted in what at the time looked to be an extraordinary declaration of intent to reach out to the recent adversaries of the Warsaw Treaty Organization (WTO), and in so doing transform NATO from a predominantly military to an increasingly political organization, whose new mandate would stress cooperating with, not containing, the east. In a little more than a year (and an eventful one it was, with the Gulf crisis and war, the CFE Treaty and Charter of Paris, and the Soviet coup and subsequent dissolution) the alliance would seek to give institutional meaning to the cooperative thrust by the creation, at the Rome summit of November 1991, of the North Atlantic Cooperation Council (NACC), which held its inaugural meeting the following month.[35]

Although the NACC sought to foster dialogue and cooperation with recent adversaries in the collapsing WTO, it was clear that the intent would have to be operationalized. That, in turn, has proved less easy than might have originally seemed. Reflecting this difficulty has been the adoption of the alliance's "new strategic concept," another outcome of the Rome summit.[36] Perhaps the most important aspect of this document is its acceptance that the "threat" of yore had been replaced by "risks" that were both "multi-faceted" and "multi-directional." And while the drafters did not see any less of a need for the alliance, they did recognize that now, more than in the past, NATO would have to "frame its strategy within a broad approach to security." Two new security functions in particular were highlighted in the document, dialogue and crisis management.[37]

As we know, both these functions have been the subject of considerable debate within NATO and elsewhere in the nearly five years since the Rome summit. Within a half-year of that meeting, the alliance would embark on a tentative journey into the world of peacekeeping. Alliance foreign ministers, meeting in ministerial session in early June 1992 in Oslo, announced their conditional willingness to assume peacekeeping assignments, on a case-by-case basis, under the responsibility of the Conference on Security and Cooperation in Europe. A year and a half later, dialogue would be given firmer institutional meaning through the launching of the Partnership for Peace. The two undertakings would embroil NATO in a new set of problems as well as contribute, in their own way, to the gathering momentum of 1994 on the alliance's enlargement.

Enlargement Becomes the Issue

There was nothing, in the first three years of the alliance's ostensible transformation, dictating that either dialogue or crisis management need result in, or even require, an expansion of NATO.[38] Indeed, when the Partnership for Peace was announced by the US secretary of defense, Les Aspin, at Travemünde in October 1993 and even when it was officially embraced by the alliance at the

Brussels summit of January 1994, it was widely (and not incorrectly) regarded as a means of putting off the issue of enlargement rather than making it an inevitability. More generally, there was nothing in the alliance's entire transformatory quest that obliged it to take the decision to enlarge to the eastward.

To understand why enlargement would become, by early 1995, *the* issue within alliance councils requires us to descend from the systemic to the unit level of analysis, and to explore the so-called "national interest" of two principal actors within NATO, Germany and the US. For all that separates them, structural realists and institutionalists share a common analytical trait: each group sees the "system" and its workings to be if not a determinative factor in accounting for outcomes, then certainly the one of greatest importance. They may and do disagree on the power of institutions to effect change, with the structural realists holding institutions to be rather less than the sum of their parts, while the institutionalists argue to the contrary. But to grasp fully the origins and evolution of the idea of NATO expansion, we must spend some time examining NATO's "parts."

As several other chapters in this volume will be examining more intensively the national debates (such as they have been) of leading member-states, I will limit myself in this section to some rudimentary comments focused on Germany and the US.[39] A useful starting point, it may be conceded, for the current debate on enlargement is an important address given in the spring of 1993 at the International Institute for Strategic Studies in London by the German defence minister, Volker Rühe.[40] This was not the first time a prominent German political figure had indicated a desire that western institutions (including NATO) be expanded eastward so that, as it was often phrased, the "eastern border of Germany cannot forever remain the eastern border of NATO."[41]

It is not easy to dispute the logic of the postulated German desire to see western institutions extend their sway further to the east; indeed,it would be consummately illogical were the Germans to prefer to look with equanimity on the spread of instability in the countries of Central and Eastern Europe, including the former Soviet Union — lands suggestively lying on the other side of the Federal Republic's own "Río Oder."[42] It betrays a strong German belief in institutionalism's power to alter policy outcomes that Bonn should appear to be so desirous of seeing the pacifying prowess of the EU and NATO work its wonders in the eastern half of a continent whose western half has become peaceful and democratic only thanks to those same institutions.[43]

Just as Manfred Wörner's enthusiasm for NATO's developing an eastern vocation must have reflected his assimilation of recent German historical "lessons," so too has it been for other politicians from Germany, especially in the governing coalition. If *Ostpolitik* could have been, during the Cold War, so useful for advancing a number of German interests, above all its *Deutschlandpolitik*, then it would only make sense that an eastern vocation in the post-Cold War world could be good for Germany. Thus it was no surprise that a political figure so closely associated with regional détente and *Ostpolitik* as was Hans-Dietrich Genscher was should have been, along with his American counterpart James Baker, one of the moving forces behind the NACC.[44]

But before one concludes that German support for an eastern vocation must translate into continued strong backing for the enlargement of NATO, it is well to remember that the dominant, Genscherite, tradition in recent German foreign policy has been characterized as well by what Timothy Garton Ash calls the "politics of *sowohl-als-auch*," meaning that German policy has tried to avoid making hard choices, seeking instead to go in several directions at once. "Fudge," writes Ash, "was the hard core of Genscherism."[45] The foreign minister may be gone, but Ash fears his legacy will live on, and that Germany, when confronted with the need to make a hard choice, will continue to temporize. This seems, in the light of the recent Russian hardening of position on NATO enlargement, to be a safe prediction.

And what of the American interest in expanding NATO? How explain a seeming shift from a policy intended to put off the prospect of enlargement to one ostensibly touting it? Three ways of answering these questions are often encountered. One explanation is that the shift in administration policy reflects nothing so much as domestic electoral expediency, with the president hoping to mobilize the ethnic Central European, mainly Polish, vote during the fall 1994 Congressional elections and afterwards. If correct, this thesis would seem to lend support to two claims about contemporary American foreign policy, namely that the Clinton administration has deliberately deemphasized it in favour of the domestic agenda, and that it has become fundamentally impossible to speak of the "national interest" in an era when the "regionalization of global policy making, the impact of ethnicity on ... foreign policy and the rise of powerful global issue groups" all conspire to produce a "balkanization" of the policymaking process. And this, it is argued, must mean a profound transformation in the way America conceives its place in the world.[46]

Despite its plausibility, there is something wrong with the expand-for-expediency's-sake argument. In the first place, if it is true that the American electorate, and by extension public opinion, is in a "neo-isolationist" mood these days, it is hard to discern the electoral appeal of a claim that America should *expand* its Article 5 commitments under the Washington Treaty.[47] To be sure, such an appeal might win some votes in Chicago or Chicopee, but what of Chattanooga or Chillicothe, or the myriad of other American communities where Polish-Americans are not very numerous? Attempting to make "national" policy by catering to a particular minority is hardly likely to translate into success at the polls, unless of course there are some self-evidently good reasons to make such a policy.

The second problem with the argument that American support for NATO enlargement inheres in domestic political "necessities" is that it overstates the

degree to which foreign policy *has* been deemphasized by the Clinton administration. William Jefferson Clinton the president has turned into someone Bill
Clinton the candidate of 1992 probably would not recognize, for over the past
couple of years he has become, in James Chace's words, the "comeback kid in
foreign policy."[48] Even before the conclusion of the Bosnian peace talks in Dayton,
it was apparent not only that the administration was paying more attention to
the foreign agenda, but that it was doing relatively better with it than with the
domestic one.

More satisfactory are the two answers that are rooted not in domestic but in
foreign-policy soil. The first of these holds that in the post-Cold War era of no
great-power threat, it is incumbent upon NATO, if America is going to stay interested in it, to develop a different profile in international security. According to
this explanation, NATO has to come up with new missions in new regions or
risk a growth in American indifference — or worse — to European security
affairs. In the somewhat minatory words of Pentagon official Paul Gebhard, "[i]f
the Western Europeans are not interested in security beyond their continent,
US interest in working with Western Europe will wane and the US role in its
security will decline, leaving Europe to address alone whatever security problems it faces at home."[49] As Indiana Senator Richard Lugar phrased it more
diplomatically, in a speech to the Atlantic Council in December 1993: "a credible American commitment to an alliance focused on territorial defense against
a non-existent threat ... cannot be politically sustained on Capitol Hill..."[50]

The third answer to the why-expand-NATO question flows from the truth
contained in the above two quotations, only instead of focussing upon security
issues outside Western Europe, it concentrates on strengthening the core of an
alliance still held to be of vital importance to the US by the Clinton administration. In a word, Germany is the answer to the question. By this is suggested that
the Clinton administration has deemed the preservation and strengthening of
relations with Germany to be so critical to its European security policy that it is
showing itself disposed to try to facilitate those projects it believes the Germans regard as essential. Since it is believed, not without reason, that the
expansion of NATO is a German initiative, it is likewise held that expanding the
alliance can solve problems in both halves of Europe, by "stabilizing" Central
and Eastern Europe, and by keeping the Germans happy.[51]

Lending support to the credibility of this third explanation is the fact that the
leading advocates for the expansion of NATO in the US policy community have
had significant experience in Germany and are quite familiar with security debates in that country. One of the earliest articles to shape the American debate
over enlargement was written for *Foreign Affairs* by a trio of senior analysts at
RAND, two of whom have spent much of their careers working on German
issues.[52] Within government, there can be no question that until Richard
Holbrooke became assistant secretary of state for European affairs in the

summer of 1994, NATO enlargement was not a priority issue in Washington. Significantly, Holbrooke's previous assignment was US ambassador to Germany.

One must be careful in accounting for why it is that what one writer calls the "Germanophiles" in Washington seem to be so bent on promoting NATO expansion.[53] Some participants in the debate who have lengthy German experience, Richard Burt for instance (a former ambassador to Germany), may want NATO to expand primarily because they seek to contain Russia. But for the Clinton administration, which has made cooperation with Russia a hallmark of its European policy, it is not so much containing Russia as assuaging Germany that is at issue. In this objective, it could even be argued that Washington is merely continuing with its post-1955 pattern of deferring whenever possible to assumed German sensibilities so as ultimately to safeguard the Western European security community. It seeks and has sought to accomplish this by getting "the west" to embrace and work constructively with Germany, and not as happened after the First World War, to isolate and spurn it. To those who make this argument, the "Versailles remedial," with its injunction to work with not against Germany, remains a powerful socializing factor in America's European policy, and has contributed greatly to the American desire to expand NATO.[54]

Conclusions

From the preceding analysis several conclusions suggest themselves. The first and most important is that a cooling of German desire to see NATO expanded can be expected to have a dampening effect upon American support for expansion.[55] And if both Bonn and Washington reconsider the merits of enlarging NATO, it is hardly likely that expansion will find champions from elsewhere in the alliance.

The second conclusion is that concern about Russian opposition to the enlargement of NATO can be expected to grow both in Germany and the United States. This concern will be especially pronounced in Germany, with its foreign-policy tradition of *sowohl-als-auch*.

The third conclusion is that by its recent show of resolve in Bosnia, NATO has restored a great deal of its "credibility."[56] It would be wrong to credit Operation Deliberate Force exclusively for having been responsible for the chain of events culminating in the Dayton peace accord, and it may be that that accord will eventually prove yet another casualty of the Balkans civil war. But it cannot be denied that of all the international organizations that have tried to end the carnage in Bosnia, only NATO happens to have made a difference. This perhaps is a harsh judgement, but it is an important one to introduce here, for it used to be said, not so long ago, that NATO *had* to expand precisely because it had been no more effective than the UN, OSCE, and EU at halting the blood-shed in ex-Yugoslavia. NATO, it was maintained, needed a victory on the expansion issue to restore its credibility and recoup its losses in Bosnia.[57] With the recent turnaround there, one can expect a diminution in the "credibility"-induced case for enlargement.[58]

Finally, with the latest elections in Poland added to the other developments touched on in these concluding paragraphs, it should no longer be assumed that expansion, when it does occur (as it probably will), must feature among the first new members Poland. It cannot be excluded that enlargement might begin in the southeast, not the east, of Germany, and possibly not even in states that are contiguous with Germany.

Notes

1.   From the 9 September 1942 entry in *The Ciano Diaries, 1939-1943*, as cited in John Bartlett, *Bartlett's Familiar Quotations*, 14th ed., rev. and enl., ed. Emily Morison Beck (Boston: Little, Brown, 1968), p. 1053.

2.   See para. 12 of the "Declaration of the Heads of State and Government Participating in the Meeting of the North Atlantic Council Held at NATO Headquarters, Brussels, on 10-11 January 1994," reproduced as Appendix XII, *NATO Handbook* (Brussels: NATO Office of Information and Press, 1995), pp. 269-75, at p. 272: "We expect and would welcome NATO expansion that would reach to democratic states to our East, as part of an evolutionary process, taking into account political and security developments in the whole of Europe."

3.   I base this on a series of briefings in which I participated at NATO Headquarters in late June 1995.

4.   Joseph Fitchett, "NATO Study Vague on Moving East," *International Herald Tribune*, 28 September 1995, p. 6. (Hereafter this journal will be cited *IHT*.)

5.   Yeltsin made this statement during an 85-minute press conference in the Kremlin on 8 September 1995. Quoted in Steven Erlanger, "Yeltsin Says an Expanded NATO Would Mean War," *IHT*, 9/10 September 1995, pp. 1, 8. On the narrowing chances for reform in Russia, and the growing likelihood that the country will "suffer the fate of Latin America in the 1970s, with weak political institutions, a restive, interventionist army, a devil-may-care attitude of rich to poor, and crippling bouts of hyperinflation," see "Will Russia Reverse Reform?" *Economist*, 28 October 1995, pp. 15-16.

6.   North Atlantic Treaty Organization, "Study on NATO Enlargement" (Brussels, September 1995), para. 18.

7.   Roy Denman, "Central and East European Candidates Will Have to Do Better," *IHT*, 1 November 1995, p. 10; Lionel Barber, "EU Keeps Palace Gates Shut," *Financial Post* (Toronto), 18-20 November 1995, p. 82; Tom Buerkle, "Germany Blocking EU Farm Help to the East," *IHT*, 20 November 1995, p. 5.

8.   "The North Atlantic Treaty, Washington DC, 4 April 1949," Article 10, reproduced as Appendix VIII, *NATO Handbook*, pp. 231-34.

9. On the role of ideas in foreign policy and international relations, see Emmanuel Adler, *The Power of Ideology* (Berkeley: University of California Press, 1987); and Judith Goldstein and Robert Keohane, eds., *Ideas and Foreign Policy* (Ithaca: Cornell University Press, 1993).

10. Kenneth N. Waltz, "The Emerging Structure of International Politics," *International Security* 18 (Fall 1993): 75.

11. Josef Joffe, "Die NATO und Nostradamus," *Süddeutsche Zeitung*, 6 February 1995, p. 4.

12. Glenn H. Snyder, "The Security Dilemma in Alliance Politics," *World Politics* 36 (July 1984): 461-95.

13. Waltz, "Emerging Structure of International Politics," p. 50.

14. Christopher Layne, "Kant or Cant: The Myth of the Democratic Peace," *International Security* 19 (Fall 1994): 10.

15. Robert Gilpin, *War and Change in World Politics* (Cambridge: Cambridge University Press, 1981).

16. William C. Wohlforth, "Realism and the End of the Cold War," *International Security* 19 (Winter 1994/95): 99.

17. Randall L. Schweller, "Bandwagoning for Profit: Bringing the Revisionist State Back In," *International Security* 19 (Summer 1994): 79. An alternative, and perhaps more commonly accepted, usage of bandwagoning holds it to consist in aligning oneself with the source of danger, not of opportunity; for that usage, see Stephen M. Walt, *The Origins of Alliances* (Ithaca: Cornell University Press, 1987), pp. 19-21.

18. See Gunther Hellmann and Reinhard Wolf, "Neorealism, Neoliberal Institutionalism, and the Future of NATO," *Security Studies* 3 (Autumn 1993): 3-43.

19. Paul Schroeder, "Historical Reality vs. Neo-realist Theory," *International Security* 19 (Summer 1994): 119.

20. John J. Mearsheimer, "The False Promise of International Institutions," *International Security* 19 (Winter 1994/95): 47.

21. Ibid., pp. 13-14.

22. Michael Brenner, "The Multilateral Moment," in *Multilateralism and Western Strategy*, ed. Michael Brenner (New York: St. Martin's, 1995), p. 8. Also see Jaap de Wilde, "Reversal in the International System? The Long Peace Debate in the Present," *Working Papers 21/1994* (Copenhagen: Centre for Peace and Conflict Research, 1994), pp. 8-9; and John S. Duffield, "NATO's Functions after the Cold War," *Political Science Quarterly* 109 (Winter 1994-95): 777.

23. Robert G. Kaufman, "A Two-Level Interaction: Structure, Stable Liberal Democracy, and U.S. Grand Strategy," *Security Studies* 3 (Summer 1994): 678-79.

24. Conor Cruise O'Brien, "The Future of 'the West'," *National Interest*, no. 30 (Winter 1992/93), pp. 3-10.

25. For an excellent defence of this contention, see Thomas Risse-Kappen, *Cooperation Among Democracies: The European Influence on U.S. Foreign Policy* (Princeton: Princeton University Press, 1995).

26. Mark A. Boyer, *International Cooperation and Public Goods: Opportunities for the Western Alliance* (Baltimore: Johns Hopkins University Press, 1993), p. 121.

27. For structural-realist critiques of d.p.t., see Layne, "Kant or Cant." Also of interest, though not necessarily part of the structural-realist assault on d.p.t., is David E. Spiro, "The Insignificance of the Liberal Peace," *International Security* 19 (Fall 1994): 50-86.

28. Owen Harries, "The Collapse of 'The West'," *Foreign Affairs* 72 (September/October 1993): 41-53. For a similar stress on the democracies' dependence upon their own negation to flourish, see François Furet, "Europe After Utopianism," *Journal of Democracy* 6 (January 1995): 79-89.

29. Robert W. Tucker, "Realism and the New Consensus," *National Interest*, no. 30 (Winter 1992/93), pp. 33-36.

30. Fareed Zakaria, "Is Realism Finished?" *National Interest*, no. 30 (Winter 1992/93), p. 21.

31. Perhaps as good a date as any for demarking the Cold War's ending is 16 July 1990, when Mikhail Gorbachev met Helmut Kohl in the Caucasus and gave his approval to a unified Germany staying within NATO. See Konrad H. Jarausch, *The Rush to German Unity* (New York: Oxford University Press, 1994), p. 167.

32. Josef Joffe, "Is There Life After Victory? What NATO Can and Cannot Do," *National Interest*, no. 41 (Fall 1995), pp. 19-25. Joffe is one writer whose intellect seems to be pulling him in a direction his heart finds repellent. He worries that the alliance has no basis for enduring in the absence of the enemy, yet at the same time he would lament its passing from the scene.

33. See, for the two terms, Wolfram F. Hanrieder, *Germany, America, Europe: Forty Years of German Foreign Policy* (New Haven: Yale University Press, 1989), pp. 6-11; and Gunther Hellmann, "*Einbindungspolitik*: United Germany and the Promise of Foreign Policy Continuity," a paper presented to the 36th Annual Convention of the International Studies Association, Chicago, February 1995.

34. Jonathan G. Clarke, "Beckoning Quagmires: NATO in Eastern Europe," *Journal of Strategic Studies* 17 (December 1994): 42.

35. William Yerex, "The North Atlantic Cooperation Council: NATO's *Ostpolitik* for Post-Cold War Europe," in *NATO's Eastern Dilemmas*, ed. David G. Haglund, S. Neil MacFarlane, and Joel J. Sokolsky (Boulder: Westview, 1994), pp. 181-94.

36. "The Alliance's Strategic Concept, Agreed by the Heads of State and Government Participating in the Meeting of the North Atlantic Council in Rome on 7-8 November 1991," reproduced as Appendix IX, *NATO Handbook*, pp. 235-48.

37. Ibid., paras. 9, 15, 29, 32.

38. Some writers argue that, its official declarations to the contrary notwithstanding, the alliance rally has not "transformed" itself. See, for instance, Christopher Conliffe, "The Alliance Transformed: A Skeptical View," in *NATO's Eastern Dilemmas*, pp. 23-36.

39. For more detail on those countries' debates over expansion, see the chapters in this volume by Reinhard Wolf and Douglas Stuart. As well, see Peter Rudolf, "The Future of the United States as a European Power: The Case of NATO Enlargement," a paper prepared for the Conference on Engagement and Disengagement: New Directions in US Foreign Policy, University of Maryland, November 1995.

40. This was later published by Rühe under the title, "Euro-Atlantic Policies: A Grand Strategy for a New Era," *Survival* 35 (Summer 1993): 129-37.

41. As Chancellor Helmut Kohl put it, at the "31st Munich Conference on Security Policy," Munich, 5 February 1994 (author's notes).

42. For this image à la mexicaine, I am indebted to Czeslaw Mesjasz, "Assistance for the East in 1989-1993 as Western Security Expenditure," *Working Papers* 3/1994 (Copenhagen: Centre for Peace and Conflict Resolution, 1993), p. 32.

43. Dieter Mahncke, "Parameters of European Security," *Chaillot Papers* 10 (Paris: Institute for Security Studies, Western European Union, September 1993). Also see Uwe Nerlich, "Western Europe's Relations with the United States," *Daedalus* 108 (Winter 1979): 87-111; Karl Kaiser, "Forty Years of German Membership in NATO," *NATO Review* 43 (July 1995): 3-8; Elizabeth Pond, "Germany and Its European Environment," *Washington Quarterly* 16 (Autumn 1993): 131-40; James Sperling, "The German Architecture for Europe: Military, Political and Economic Dimensions," in *The Federal Republic of Germany at Forty-Five: Union without Unity*, ed. Peter H. Merkl (New York: New York University Press, 1995), pp. 359-77; and Ernst Weisenfeld, *Quelle Allemagne pour la France? La politique étrangère française et l'unité allemande depuis 1944*, trans. Jeanne Étoré (Paris: Armand Colin, 1989).

44. See W. R. Smyser, *Germany and America: New Identities, Fateful Rift?* (Boulder: Westview, 1993), p. 92.

45. Timothy Garton Ash, "Germany's Choice," *Foreign Affairs* 73 (July/August 1994): 65-81.

46. This is the thesis of Michael Clough, "Grass-Roots Policymaking: Say Good-Bye to the 'Wise Men'," *Foreign Affairs* 73 (January/February 1994): 2-7. But for the opposing claim that ethnicity can combat "Balkanization" and actually strengthen internationalist tendencies in US foreign policy, see Yossi Shain, "Multicultural Foreign Policy," *Foreign Policy*, no. 100 (Fall 1995), pp. 69-87.

47. For the claim that America is reverting to isolationism, see Arthur Schlesinger, Jr., "Back to the Womb? Isolationism's Renewed Threat," *Foreign Affairs* 74 (July/August 1995): 2-8.

48. Quoted in Martin Walker, "Bill's Head Turned by Foreign Affairs," *Guardian Weekly*, 24 September 1995, p. 6.

49. Paul R. S. Gebhard, *The United States and European Security*, Adelphi Paper 286 (London: International Institute for Strategic Studies, 1994), p. 37.

50. Quoted in Clarke, "Beckoning Quagmires," p. 43.

51. William Pfaff, "Spread the West Eastward, Putting Germany in a United Europe," *IHT*, 8 September 1994, p. 6; Paul F. Horvitz, "With Clinton, Kohl Expresses Support for NATO Growth," *IHT*, 10 February 1995, pp. 1, 6.

52. Ronald D. Asmus, Richard L. Kugler, and F. Stephen Larrabee, "Building a New NATO," *Foreign Affairs* 72 (September/October 1993): 28-40. Also see Idem, "NATO Expansion: The Next Steps," *Survival* 37 (Spring 1995): 7-33. Both Asmus and Larrabee have dedicated much of their careers to the study of Germany.

53. Martin Walker, "Europe Still Divided Along Familiar Lines," *Guardian Weekly*, 14 May 1995, p. 6. Notes another writer apropos the Clinton foreign policy, "[a]n early Russia-first policy now appears to be giving way to expanding NATO eastward." William E. Odom, "How to

Create a True World Order," *Orbis* (Spring 1995): 155. Nevertheless, the postulated rivalry can be overdrawn, for no less an advocate of making Russia the administration's priority than Strobe Talbott has come out in favour of NATO expansion. See Strobe Talbott, "Why NATO Should Grow," *New York Review of Books*, 10 August 1995, pp. 27-30.

54. See the intriguing article by Mary N. Hampton, "NATO at the Creation: U.S. Foreign Policy, West Germany, and the Wilsonian Impulse," *Security Studies* 4 (Spring 1995): 610-56. Also see Risse-Kappen, *Cooperation Among Democracies*, pp. 212-13.

55. By early 1996, it was apparent that Germany was becoming less and less interested in the rapid expansion of either NATO or the EU, and not all of its waning ardour could be ascribed to concern about fuelling nationalist fires in Russia. See Alan Cowell, "Neighbors Knock. Germany Makes Them Wait," *New York Times*, 25 February 1996, p. E:6; Ian Traynor, "Kohl Calm's Yeltsin's Ire," *Guardian Weekly*, 25 February 1996, p. 3; "Vorbehalt Kohls gegen Ost-Erweiterung," *Welt am Sonntag*, 4 February 1996, pp. 1, 3; and "Kohl mahnt Westen zur Umsicht," *Die Welt*, 5 February 1996, pp. 1, 4. Also see the chapter by Reinhard Wolf, this volume.

56. See Rick Atkinson, "Put to the Test, NATO Shows Its Mettle," *IHT*, 20 November 1995, p. 2.

57. See Zbigniew Brzezinski, "A Plan for Europe," *Foreign Affairs* 74 (January/February 1995): 27.

58. Some have even argued a stronger link between Bosnia and enlargement, and suggest that the Clinton administration agreed, in exchange for Russian participation in Bosnian peace-keeping as part of an American multinational division, to shelve the expansion issue for the time being. For this argument, heatedly denied by administration sources, see Peter W. Rodman, "Yalta in the Balkans," *National Review*, 25 December 1995, pp. 23-24; and Idem, "Understanding with Moscow," *Washington Post*, 16 January 1996.

CHAPTER TWO

NATO Expansion and European Regional Security

David M. Law and S. Neil MacFarlane

Introduction

The threat for the deterrence and containment of which the North Atlantic Treaty Organization (NATO) was established evaporated with the end of the Cold War. The relegation of Russia to irrelevance as a factor impinging on the security of NATO member states characteristic of the first years after the end of the Cold War was premature.[1] However, it will be many years before Russia is in a position to pose the kind of continental threat that NATO was designed to forestall. Conventional (structural-realist) wisdom suggests that alliances constructed to deal with specific threats do not long survive the demise of the threat they were meant to address. There is, consequently, reason to doubt the capacity of the organization to survive as a collective-defence organization.[2] However, many in Europe and in North America continue to believe that NATO remains necessary as a means of reducing the possibility of conflict at some point in the future between the core members of the alliance in Western Europe. Although this prospect seems remote, the cooperative ties fostered by the organization and embodied in it may serve to keep it that way.

The dangers of assuming the imminent demise of NATO have been ably presented by David Haglund.[3] Nonetheless, it is easy to appreciate the desire of the organization to outline a new agenda and new functions to replace those that have disappeared. Having a credible mission that justifies continuing investment in the organization will enhance its prospects for survival.

Of the various options available to the organization, that of transforming itself into a provider of the public good of security to Europe as a whole, or at least to that portion of Europe outside the former Soviet Union, has been perceived to be particularly attractive. Although the threat of bipolar conflict has receded, the dangers associated with the political, military, and socio-economic consequences of instability in the recently liberated eastern portions of the continent have become increasingly clear in the disintegration of Yugoslavia and in the tension between centrifugal and centripetal forces within the former Soviet region and within the states that comprise it.[4] NATO is, arguably, the only institution in Europe with the capacity (and — given the implementation plan for the Bosnia-Herzegovina peace concluded in Dayton in November 1995 — possibly the will) to provide stability in the newly unstable Europe. Among the principal arguments for expansion in NATO's enlargement study of September 1995 is the following:

> Projecting stability eastward is now an important NATO function and strategic imperative, possibly the most important such imperative. This can best be accomplished by step-by-step enlargement (as has been the NATO tradition) to subsume and manage these potential instabilities rather than awaiting their inevitable arrival in the present NATO area.[5]

The post-Cold War evolution of the alliance — from the North Atlantic Cooperation Council (NACC) created in 1991, through the Partnership for Peace (PFP) adopted in January 1994, to the decision of the North Atlantic Council in December 1994 to commission the NATO enlargement study — has been one of increasingly ambitious efforts to address this problem.

The chapters in this volume all take specific approaches to this question. Ours relates regional theory and comparative research on the effectiveness of regional organizations in coping with regional threats to peace and security to the question of NATO expansion. It first discusses the nature of the transatlantic region and its normative and organizational outgrowths. It then examines a number of the weaknesses of NATO as an organization in the context of general analysis of capacity and performance of regional institutions, and examines the option of expansion in terms of these weaknesses. Third, it turns to an analysis of the feasibility and merits of expansion. This leads to a number of concluding remarks on the implications of expansion for the organization.

Regionalism and Security

At first glance, the application of the idea of region to the transatlantic area seems (literally) stretched. There is little agreement in the literature on the criteria relevant to the identification of regional identity, or to the weighting of these criteria. Four kinds of variable seem particularly common in analysis of the subject.[6] The first is propinquity, if not contiguity. The existence of a region has an important geographical component, though this is to some extent mitigated by the "shrinking" of distance associated with the revolutions in transportation and communications in the 19th and 20th centuries.

The second is intensity of interactions. The existence of a regional identity is generally considered to imply the existence of a discontinuity at the border of a region with regard to the number and importance of interactions among communities.[7] Third, since these interactions reflect interdependence — sensitivities and vulnerabilities between states — the existence of a region has something to do with the extent to which the decisions of states within an area are affected, positively or negatively, by those who share the contiguous space.[8] The sensitivity and vulnerability of a state to other states in its region are generally deemed to be greater than they are with regard to states outside. The histories of states within a region are, consequently, shared to a greater extent than those with states outside the boundaries. In the realm of security, this is explicit in Barry Buzan's concept of the "security complex," defined as a group of states "whose primary security concerns link together sufficiently closely that their national securities cannot reasonably be considered apart from one another."[9]

Finally, there is an important subjective dimension to the concept. A "region," like any other concept in social discourse, exists in a socially constructed reality. It exists in part because people believe it to exist. This belief may be, although it is not necessarily, linked to a perception of shared cultural heritage and values, to a perception of community.

Although it would be difficult to derive an uncontroversial weighting of these various criteria, it is safe to say that the farther along all of these vectors of analysis an area finds itself, the stronger its regional identity is likely to be. The North Atlantic area appears weak on a number of counts, not least that of geographical proximity. The states of the area are divided by an ocean 3000 miles wide.

In the area of economic interactions among states within the area, the two segments of the transatlantic community have distanced themselves over the past quarter century, and have institutionalized this distance in the creation of two regional economic associations — the European Economic Community, now the European Union (EU), and the Canadian-American Free Trade Agreement, now the North American Free Trade Agreement (NAFTA). An examination of the changing relative weights of intraregional versus transatlantic trade would suggest that the transoceanic economic link is weakening over time in favour of continental associations. Intra-North American and intra-Western European economic ties are growing more rapidly than are transatlantic ones. This appears to be true across the broader spectrum of diplomatic, cultural, and communications transactions as well.

Turning to interdependence, and focussing on security, the American and Western European areas face substantially different situations. Whatever one might make of Canadian neuroses concerning the United States, the two states, since 1817 and more completely since the 1870s, have demilitarized their relationship, while the degree of integration of their economies and societies is arguably unparalleled in international relations. The two countries face no proximate actual or potential threats to their security. The history of relations among Western European states has been less felicitous, while their geopolitical position vis-à-vis potential external threats is less salutary. In these respects, one might consider the transatlantic area to comprise two regions in security terms, their merger being a product of systemic overlay during the Cold War.[10] As this overlay weakens, these distinct security identities tend to reassert themselves.

The Transatlantic Community

One can take these arguments too far. The difficulty that the United States has experienced in remaining out of major European conflict in this century suggests that the two security complexes may be more closely tied than they appear to be at first glance. The evolution of the nuclear balance creates an American tie to the European region that has outlasted the end of the Cold War. These factors are perhaps reflected in the difficulty of articulating the isolationist argument of George Washington and John Quincy Adams in current circumstances in the Euro-American relationship.

The North American members of the transatlantic community are cultural outgrowths of European expansion and settlement. Their history of involvement in international affairs focussed largely on Europe for much of the 19th and 20th centuries. They are linked strongly, furthermore, by a mutual embrace of certain understandings concerning society and politics. Regarding norms, at the unit level, the common ground includes an embrace of democracy and respect for human rights. This does not imply uniformity of domestic systems.

The understanding of democracy in Western Europe is in important respects different from that of the United States. Nor does it imply that the meaning of the concept is constant. We used to think that Canada's comprehension of the concept was closer to that of Europe than to that of the United States. Now we are not so sure. Nonetheless, underlying this variation are certain core propositions, notably that governments should be freely and fairly chosen by their citizens. Likewise, in human rights, although there may be substantial (though perhaps decreasing) differences in weighting of the different (legal/political/economic) individual rights and of individual as opposed to group rights in the societies in question, there would appear to be substantial agreement on a basic set of legal (for example, *habeas corpus* and the right to fair trial), and political (viz. freedom of expression and assembly within fairly broad parameters) rights within the North Atlantic group of states.[11]

Some members have, of course, violated these norms at various times in their history. Portugal was admitted to the alliance as a military dictatorship and remained so until the mid-1970s. Both Greece and Turkey have experienced extended periods of military rule and systematic violation of human rights. Yet these are exceptions. The generalizations hold for the core of the alliance throughout its history. Indeed, one could argue that membership in NATO has had some impact in facilitating the transitions of the outliers towards an embrace of the norms discussed above, while the institutional cooperation embodied in NATO has further embedded these shared norms throughout the community as a whole.

At the level of values relating to interstate interaction, the North Atlantic community reflects a shared sense that war is not an option of policy for the management of relations among alliance partners.[12] The interstate level is linked to the domestic one in the proposition that states embracing democratic values are less prone to war as an instrument of policy.[13] Again, this norm has not been universally honoured over the history of the alliance. Greece and Turkey were near war in 1974 over Cyprus and again in 1987 and 1996 over contested rights and rocks in the Aegean Sea. Their relations have displayed a level of animosity and tension uncharacteristic of the alliance as a whole for much of the post-World War II era.

The perception of common interest and shared norms did not arise spontaneously. It was in large part a result of the hegemonic assertion of the United States in both a classical and Gramscian sense in Western Europe in the postwar era. The American desire to contain the Soviet Union in political, economic, and military terms underlay its commitment to the construction of a democratic Germany and European recovery, and to the institutionalization of security cooperation in the North Atlantic Treaty. American promotion of political democracy and liberal capitalism had much to do with the strengthening in Western Europe of the values discussed above. American military preponderance in Western Europe explains in large part the transcendence of the region's historical contradictions in the realm of national security.

Shared cultural heritage and historical background — coupled with the embrace of common values regarding rights, and social, economic, and political organization — have had important perceptual consequences. The polities and societies of North America believe themselves to be intimately connected to and engaged in the affairs of Europe, particularly in the realm of security, a point reiterated yet again in President Clinton's address on the deployment in Bosnia-Herzegovina of 27 November 1995. Bosnia-Herzegovina is perceived to be important to the United States, because it is important to America's European allies, and the European allies' security interests are perceived to be intimately related to those of the United States itself.

Perception of common interest and shared values, and a consequent sense of community, form the basis for the cooperation in security affairs institutionalized in NATO. The relationship between the institution and the community that it reflects is, however, dialectical. The institution — through its cooperative military structures and the systematic quality of consultation among members —

has created habits of cooperation, strengthening this sense of community and the embrace of its underlying values. It is both a product of, and, in its own right, a producer of community identity.

All of these factors constitute important reasons to qualify the analysis of emerging continental identities provided above. They also provide some grounds for viewing the North Atlantic area as a whole as a region for purposes of political and security analysis. However, the evolution of the international relations of the area — notably, the weakening of strategic overlay and the disappearance of the common external threat, the erosion of American preponderance, and the gradual emergence of subregional political and security identities — does raise doubts about the survivability of this identity and the institution that embodies it. It is this concatenation of circumstances that informs the effort to define new roles for the organization.

NATO as a Regional Security Organization

NATO historically has had two principal purposes. First and foremost, it was a collective-defence organization, designed to counter a specific threat emanating from outside the region. Second, it sought to stabilize the historically troubled relations of its members. The link across the Atlantic to the United States and Canada served both of these purposes. As the external threat has diminished in credibility, the principal organizational function has arguably become the maintenance of stable peaceful relations among its members. In this respect, the organization has come to focus more clearly on collective security.[14]

However, this is not the full story. The traditional focus of collective security has been on interstate relations among members. The evolving role of alliance forces and command structures in the former Yugoslavia and changes in NATO doctrine suggest that the alliance may be more willing than in the past to involve itself in out-of-area operations and in essentially substate conflicts in peacekeeping and peace-enforcement roles. This indicates acceptance of a broader organizational mandate to preserve and to enhance stability in the European region outside the former Soviet Union, on the assumption that interstate disputes and substate conflicts outside the NATO area could have serious implications for members of the alliance. NATO is frequently considered to be more suited than other European institutions (e.g., the OSCE and the WEU) for these tasks, given its financial and military resources, and also its accumulated experience of collaborative military activity. Expansion is perhaps the logical strategic conclusion to such an evolution in thinking, on the presumption that negative externalities can be more effectively addressed or defused by internalizing them.[15]

Since this evolution involves a gradual embrace of tasks associated with regional security organizations, it is appropriate, before evaluating the merits and demerits of expansion, to situate NATO in the larger context of the comparative literature on regional organizations as purveyors of the public good of regional security. Such an enquiry is also suggested by the recent emphasis on regional organizations as possible subcontractors for the UN in dealing with threats to international peace and security. Recent work in this area has identified a number of widely shared strengths and weaknesses of regional organizations.[16] NATO compares favourably to many organizations in this category in terms of the resources (financial, military, and bureaucratic) available to it, in the development of habits of cooperation among its national members, in the absence of serious conflict among them (with the exception of Greece and Turkey), and in the underlying consensus on values characteristic of the organization.

In three areas at least, however, NATO shares the weaknesses of most other regional organizations. The first lies in the asymmetrical distribution of power within the organization. Although the existence of an hegemonic power may conduce in a general sense to cooperation, comparative research suggests that insecurities associated with such asymmetries complicate the development of cooperative approaches to regional instability. This may be particularly relevant in instances where the position of the hegemon is perceived to be declining. In such circumstances, those whose position is improving relative to that of the preponderant power may be less willing to defer.

Second is a lack of consensus on issues relating to regional security that results from conflicting agendas on the part of member states. Regional states are those most likely to have interests that are affected by local conflicts. Hence, they have stronger incentives than extraregional actors to involve themselves in regional problems. However, there is no guarantee that the perceived interests of the members of a regional organization will coincide on the issue in question. In fact, to the extent that regional actors line up on opposing sides of local conflicts, they may directly contradict each other. In this respect, regional organizations may have greater difficulty in responding to problems of regional security than do extraregional actors.

Third is the noninclusive character of organizations. Membership in regional organizations by regional states tends to be incomplete. Indeed, many regional organizations (e.g., the Arab League, the GCC, and the OAS) were founded or have evolved to address threats emanating from excluded regional actors. This makes them unreliable instruments in the process of conciliation of such actors. The fact that the offending outsider has no place at the table within the organization makes it difficult for the organization to play a central role in the management and resolution of the problem in question.

The distribution of power in the Atlantic alliance is uneven in at least two relevant respects. First is the great disparity in military power between the US and the rest. Recognition of the consequent disparity in contribution to NATO's overall military posture has been reflected in the command structure of the alliance and in the claim of a right to lead on the part of the United States. This has occasioned significant tension within the alliance typified by the long-term strain in the Franco-American relationship within NATO, in France's attitude towards participation in alliance military structures (although that attitude may, as Pascal Boniface's chapter argues, be changing), and in the challenge posed by France in particular to the transatlantic identity.

The problem of power asymmetries has a second aspect in the uneven development of the European powers themselves. Although Germany has been careful to avoid clear manifestation of its growing relative weight within Western and Central Europe in its approach to cooperation in NATO, this trend risks reactivation of historical sensitivities in relations between Germany and its neighbours.[17] Such factors tended to be suppressed by the strategic overlay and common threat of the Cold War. With the disappearance of this constraining impact, it is an open question whether the 40-year suspension in Western European security relations has been sufficient to put these questions to rest. To judge from the uncoordinated NATO and EU response to the disintegration of Yugoslavia, there remain significant potential problems here.

In this instance, the German government pushed for the rapid recognition of the new states claiming international status after the collapse of the federal state in the face of substantial opposition from France, among others. Some have speculated that one reason for France's unhappiness with rapid recognition was its concern that German power and influence were likely to expand rapidly in Central and Southeastern Europe and that German policy on this issue was a reflection of such an aspiration. The result was a lack of Western European consensus on what was perhaps the most critical decision in post-Cold War Europe, and a successful German effort to force its allies' hands through unilateral action.

The Yugoslav example is illustrative of the second issue as well. The major European players in the decision to recognize had longstanding historical connections with particular actors on the different sides of the conflict. This disparity of perceived interest was reflected in the community's decision process. Matters were also complicated by the fact that the United States perceived itself to be less engaged in the issue and was, consequently, willing to allow the Europeans to take the lead. The result was bad policy and a three-year delay in mounting an effective NATO response while the contending players within the organization sorted out their disparate positions on the question.

One might conclude that the disappearance of overlay removes an important constraint not only on the implications of power asymmetries in the European and transatlantic theatres, but also on the expression of disagreements on concrete security issues. In both respects, the regional identity of which NATO is the institutional expression is likely to become more fragile as the Cold War recedes. This would suggest a degree of prudence in subjecting it to new strains. Expansion may well produce further disagreements among key members of the alliance and, if it does proceed, would introduce an entirely new set of potential disagreements among members. This question will be taken up in the next section in the discussion of alliance management.

The final point here concerns exclusivity. NATO obviously has very partial coverage in Europe. Most of Europe's current and potential security problems occur outside the NATO area. Their protagonists are not fully represented at the table. Moreover, as the Russian position suggests, the exclusive character of NATO membership, when coupled with the institution's history as an organization of collective defence (or, as the Russians would put it, a Cold War alliance), draws into question the legitimacy of its claim to status as the central pillar of a cooperative structure of regional security in Europe. This complicates the effort to prevent, manage, and resolve regional instabilities. In this respect at least, NATO is less well placed to assume such a role than is, for example, the OSCE. This brings us to a more complete discussion of the expansion project, since, if it addresses nothing else, it should at least address this deficiency in NATO.

Enlargement and NATO's Role as a Regional Security Organization

In this section, we examine the issue of NATO expansion in the context of European regional security. As already noted, the concept has certain attractions, both in terms of NATO's perceived need for a new role beyond that of collective defence, and in terms of its potential contribution to the stability of Central and Eastern Europe. First of all, we examine the case for expansion. We then examine its weaknesses. Finally, we relate the discussion to the previous analysis of the regional identity of the North Atlantic area and its organizational manifestation in NATO.

There is little doubt that NATO membership would mitigate many of the security concerns of Central European candidates for admission. The countries of this region face, as do those they would join in the alliance, the panoply of "postmodern" security headaches, and more. There is the still largely theoretical fear of nuclear blackmail from a predator state or piratical group beyond, or quite possibly within, the European perimeter. There is the very real danger of being sucked into the maelstrom of ethnic violence. There is the never-ending threat of the ambitious neighbour. There is the abiding fear of oneself, the authoritarian temptation, the attraction of ethnic majoritarianism as the great simplifier, the dangerous disconnection between ambitious élites and disaffected populaces, each propelled by the arithmetic of material survival.

There is also an important subjective, or perceptual, dimension in the Central and Eastern European (CEE) drive for membership. The quest for alliance membership is as much about recognition, acceptance, and sanction of policies undertaken as it is about anything else. Whole communities strive to be acknowledged as belonging to the western civilization from which they were forcefully cut off for so long. Élites seek outside approval of their efforts at reform — and what better proof of their success than to be invited to become a member of a club that brings together many of the world's most developed democracies?

NATO has no really serious competition as an organization that may satisfy these concerns. Despite the very real pains it has been experiencing in growing into its new post-Cold War roles, it stands head and shoulders above other institutions as a security provider in contemporary Europe. These considerations have been very much at work in NATO decisions to create the North Atlantic Cooperation Council, to establish the Partnership for Peace, and to proceed with the enlargement project.

In particular, alliance outreach activities have been motivated by the belief that the 16 can demonstrate an extremely successful record in multilateral security cooperation, and by the expectation that this experience can be emulated elsewhere. The allies operate under the assumption that multilateral security cooperation is in itself stabilizing, in that it has a pacifying effect on the relations among participating countries and can provide reassurance to third parties. They further assume that countries that cooperate closely with the alliance can come to enjoy the same kind of benefits as NATO member countries have historically enjoyed, including the:

- development of a tradition of fruitful and fair politico-military cooperation between countries of different strategic weight (e.g., on the model of the US and Luxembourg which have the same voting rights at NATO);
- establishment of cooperative relationships between former enemies (e.g., France and Germany);
- containment of regional rivalries (e.g., Greece and Turkey);
- encouragement of regional integration (e.g., the EU); and
- nurturing of a security environment conducive to the development of rule of law, prospering economies, and democratic institutions.[18]

Beyond this, the argumentation put forward by members of the enlargement camp has an almost deterministic quality to it. While NATO continues to refuse to allow itself to be drawn into a public discussion of names and times, the leading candidates for enlargement have not changed since the early 1990s. Moreover, the overall approach to enlargement described in the September 1995 study has evolved remarkably little from the planning that was originally done in the NATO international secretariat in the middle of 1993.[19] The key elements largely were, and remain, the following:

- institutional expansion is essential if the security needs of at least some CEE states are to be met;
- enlargement will enhance security in Europe as a whole and it will not create any new dividing lines;

- enlargement will not proceed in one but in several steps; as it does, sufficient reassurance can and will be provided to those slated for membership later, or not at all, to safeguard against instability;
- enlargement will not undercut the attractiveness of NATO's existing programs of cooperation with CEE states, namely the NACC and PFP;
- the OSCE should be "further strengthened" as a means *inter alia* of providing reassurance to nonmembers;
- NATO enlargement can and should unfold in a way that is complementary — approximately, if not precisely — to that of the EU and the WEU;
- while the membership of no European state will be excluded a priori, Russia and Ukraine (and presumably all other former Soviet republics, with the exception of the Baltic states) are unlikely ever to become members; NATO can, however, compensate for the exclusion of the two pivotal post-Soviet states by developing special relationships with them;
- the promise of membership will effectively counteract the threat of new instances of intra- and interstate ethnic conflict prior to accession; thereafter peer pressure and the growing sensitization to alliance security culture will suffice;
- enlargement will be an affordable process, both for current and new members;
- finally, enlargement will be a manageable process that can unfold without any debilitating strains upon the alliance's core defence functions, strategic posture including nuclear profile, or its ability to take decisions quickly and efficiently — in a German word, its *Konsensfähigkeit*.

Institutional widening is further seen as a way of putting to rest fears that the transatlantic relationship lost its relevance with the end of the Cold War and can, at the same time, serve as a way of engaging new generations in Europe and North America in a collective effort to build common security and shared democratic ideals. From this perspective, extending alliance membership to CEE countries is the logical next step in NATO's evolution, whereas not to do so is to accept that the transatlantic security partnership has outlived its usefulness. In short, to widen the ranks of the alliance is to fulfill the organization's historical destiny.

The Case against Enlargement

Notwithstanding the powerful arguments and interests marshalled in favour of NATO's institutional widening, it is possible to make the case that enlargement would be detrimental to the security interests of all the major players, particularly the current and prospective members of NATO, thus producing a result diametrically opposed to that intended by the champions of enlargement. The following sections examine the downsides of the expansion project from the vantage points of sociology, alliance management, and strategy. We start with sociology.

Institutional widening is sociologically unsound for a number of reasons. First and foremost, notwithstanding the alliance's determination to avoid drawing new dividing lines in Europe, enlargement would ineluctably do just that. As the September 1995 study intimates, NATO does not intend to embrace all OSCE states or to incorporate all aspiring members at one time. It would thus create new lines of demarcation in the undivided Europe that NATO members were supposed to have sanctified with the Charter of Paris. The alliance would thereby suggest that certain states were more deserving of privileged security status — through NATO membership — than others, or that certain communities were justifiably being included while others were not. In short, enlargement would not resolve the problem of exclusion mentioned earlier, but might well exacerbate it.

A "mini" or phased enlargement might prove less of a difficulty if criteria for deciding "who is in and who out" could be developed that enjoyed a certain credibility in both NATO and non-NATO countries. As it is, NATO has by its own admission no fixed criteria, nor any intention to devise them. From an internal alliance perspective, this is more than understandable. Article 10 of the Washington Treaty, which the enlargement study identifies as the operative clause for the enlargement process, stipulates only that a new member must be a European state, be in a position to further the principles of the Treaty and to contribute to the security of the North Atlantic Treaty area, and be invited to join by virtue of a consensus decision. For those left on the outside looking in, inclusion of their neighbours on this basis would be difficult for élites, and even more so for populations, to accept. A rationale for any enlargement decisions will be expected and will have to be provided by governments, parliaments, and publics in NATO and non-NATO countries alike. Article 10 alone will simply not suffice as that rationale.

This is especially true in view of the last parliamentary and presidential elections in Hungary and Poland. Their results make clear that there is no qualitative distinction between electoral patterns there and in the rest of the CEE region. The same is true of the socio-economic situation in the area in general. Differences there are, and often quite dramatic ones, but they are not sufficiently profound to build a case for some countries being more "deserving" than others of alliance membership.

In an orderly world, the prospect of a staged expansion of the alliance to all aspirants might well suffice to limit the negative aspects of a mini-enlargement. But in the Europe of the 1990s, uncertainty reigns. Thus, promises of inclusion in a second or third phase would be taken at less than face value. For the publics in countries not making the first cut, if not for their leaderships, this would be interpreted as a vote of nonconfidence both in their countries' overall direction and in their "defensibility." As such, this interpretation would be judged as tantamount to their abandonment by the west.

Much has been made of the feelings of rejection and hostility that enlargement would engender in Russia. But feelings of estrangement would by no means be limited to it alone. For example, noninclusion would prove particularly difficult for the Baltic states, but not solely because of the way this would be interpreted in certain Russian circles. For NATO to bring Poland on board but not Lithuania would likely be received as an affront among the latter's population. It would confront its Polish minority with a further psychological barrier to normal cross-border interaction with the larger Polish community. NATO in this event would not have diminished but inflated the significance of borders, and in the process strengthened those political forces that stress the esoterics of identity and shy from the exigencies of reform. Domestic forces that felt closer to the old order in the Baltics than to the new would be emboldened.

Nonadmittance of other CEE states participating in NACC and PFP would produce similar phenomena there. For example, if, as seems likely, Hungary were included in an initial enlargement, this would create greater feelings of isolation among the two million or so Hungarians in Rumania, exacerbate ethnic tensions there, and complicate the traditionally tenuous relationship between Budapest and Bucharest. At the same time, Rumania's relative feelings of geographical and political solitude would be reinforced, and its already weaker reform movement jeopardized.

There is no shortage of nationality issues that could be adversely affected. An enlargement process that brought in Poland, the Czech Republic, and Hungary but left out Albania, Bulgaria, and Slovakia would not be helpful in fostering cooperative approaches to ethnic concerns. It would do little good, but some harm, to Albanian-Greek, Bulgarian-Turkish, Slovak-Czech, and Slovak-Hungarian relations. There are then several arguments against enlargement beyond its specific impact on Russia. But clearly the implications of alienation in the latter case are potentially far more serious than they would be in any other country and deserve special consideration.

In sum, although expansion as envisaged goes some distance toward addressing the problem of exclusion identified in earlier sections, it would not resolve it. To the extent that enlargement were likely to include those states that have moved farthest in the areas of economic and political reform — namely those CEE states least affected by the fissiparous tendencies of the region — it would sidestep the problems of instability and incipient conflict that it is apparently intended to forestall, leaving the most prominent sources of regional instability outside the alliance framework. Indeed, by drawing new lines of inclusion and exclusion, it could generate different sources of regional instability. For all of these reasons, even without consideration of Russia, the expansion project faces serious problems.

Yet Russia is the most serious potential problem in this area. The alliance has stated that Russia should have no veto over its decisionmaking. This is fully justified if only because NATO has none in Moscow or anywhere else in the CIS. At the same time, no potential new member of the alliance can have a serious interest in a deterioration of NATO/Russian relations. This is recognized in the enlargement study, and in general NATO has bent over backwards to reassure Moscow and to keep it abreast of developments on the enlargement front. "No surprises" is the catchword. NATO has stated that enlargement is not directed against Russia. It has suggested that NATO's defence posture in any new member state would be nonthreatening. It has worked to develop a special relationship with Russia beyond its participation in NACC and PFP, which would include a framework for cooperative political and security relations. Moreover, it has partly been to assuage Russian concerns that NATO has been prepared to hold high the veto power of the UN Security Council and to commit itself to further strengthening of the OSCE. Both are bodies in which Russia is on an equal footing with the United States. Still, this approach fails to take into account the sociological realities of Russia.

The country's political élites are currently preoccupied with survival, more often than not at one another's expense. There is enough brute power at the centre to organize military actions such as that in Chechnya, but the decisionmakers and their entourages have thus far been too divided to be able to mobilize behind any "grand idea." On the issue of cooperation with the west, there are essentially two, very loosely constituted, camps. One camp has no long-term future in a successfully transforming Russia; its antiwestern reflexes run deep. But it has been prepared to cooperate with the west insofar as this has kept resources flowing in their country's, and their personal, direction. A second camp sees a future for itself in a reformed Russia. Its cooperation with the west is not tactical but strategic, although there is sympathy within this group for policies designed to win favours in western capitals by Russia playing "hard to get" in dealing with such issues as the former Yugoslavia and disarmament.

These Russian westophiles *cum* modernizers fear that NATO enlargement could indeed, as President Yeltsin has warned, spark a Cold Peace, discrediting those who have been demonstrably in favour of cooperation with the west and isolating them from life-giving sources of political and material support. This camp does not believe in a military threat from the west, not now or in the event of enlargement. But it is concerned lest enlargement be utilized to mobilize a majority behind policies that might keep the new "old guard" in power, at least for a time. In an environment where short-term survivalism dominates, this is a cause of no little concern. The westophiles *cum* modernizers are particularly apprehensive about the propaganda value at street level of an "anti-Russia enlargement" in a country that has been invaded no fewer than four times in as many centuries from a westerly direction, and whose collective mindset is thus receptive to warnings that history could repeat itself yet again.

What does our second camp do in the face of such considerations? It has essentially two choices, neither of them of much comfort. One is to subordinate its concerns about enlargement to its fundamentally prowestern orientation and to fight a battle it is condemned to lose in view of the prevailing political winds in Russia. The other is to join forces with those groups within the élite that are politically (and perhaps even genetically) predisposed to being antiwestern, on the assumption or the hope that this would provide the best opportunities for survival and damage limitation.

NATO enlargement, if it does come, could easily compromise those forces in Russia that have advocated close relations with the west and in the process precipitate a dangerous shift in the domestic balance of power. The exclusion of Russia from dominant security structures in Europe is already a problem. Enlargement carries a substantial risk of deepening Russia's alienation, despite the alliance's efforts to contain it.

A related difficulty concerns Russia's relationship with other CIS states and, in particular, the impact of NATO enlargement on the ongoing debate within the élites of Russia and other republics of the former Soviet Union concerning bilateral and multilateral relations, and the shape of regional security arrangements. Western policy in regions such as the Caucasus and Central Asia is sorely restricted not only by a lack of will and resources but by regional circumstances. Most of these countries have experienced very little reform and a great deal of instability. Their leaderships' options are few and they have increasingly tended to favour a perpetuation of close ties with and dependence on Moscow. Here the issue is not membership in NATO sooner or even later; rather, it is the means by which western countries can keep open lines of communication and influence, even if it may only be under a future generation of leaders that these lines can be utilized in any meaningful way. But to make a demarcation suggesting that the Caucasians and Central Asians do not belong to the Euro-Atlantic zone is to encourage them to feel that they must choose between Russia and isolation, and to encourage neoimperialist forces in Russia to believe that they can pursue with impunity their traditionally hegemonic objectives in these areas.

The most critical relationship in the former Soviet Union is that of Russia and Ukraine, for which the prospect of enlargement raises a number of questions. What would be the impact of a NATO enlargement that excluded Ukraine? Would it strengthen or weaken the forces in favour of strategic accommodation with Moscow? Would it be likely, in either case, to propel Ukraine towards reconsideration of its nonnuclear stance? Would NATO enlargement go down in history as the development that triggered a reinforcement of the CIS? This is indeed what Yeltsin seemed to be suggesting in a speech in September 1995.

The point is less whether such an effort could ultimately be successful than whether it would be attempted, and the consequences for international stability even, as seems likely, were it destined to fail.

Enlargement and Alliance Management

There are a number of difficulties associated with enlargement that belong to the domain of institutional manageability. One problem concerns NATO's ability to manage the more complex decisionmaking environment that would result from even a mini-enlargement. The NATO environment already consists of a complex array of full members, NACC participants, countries that do not participate in NACC but are involved in consultations on peacekeeping, and countries that participate to varying extents in PFP activities. Enlargement would create additional categories of actual and potential membership. An already complex managerial hierarchy would become even more cumbersome.

A second problem concerns the interaction between alliance activities and those of NACC and PFP. The top candidates for early membership in NATO are among the most enthusiastic participants in NATO's cooperation programs. There is a possibility that their elevation to alliance membership would jeopardize the survival of NACC or PFP, or both.

Third, enlargement would place additional burdens on the alliance's ability to reach quick and credible decisions, putting at risk its *Konsensfähigkeit*. Interests within an alliance stretching from Alaska to Anatolia are by definition diverse. As already noted, they have become much more subject to regional pressures since the end of the Cold War. These can be expected to be even more apparent in any decisionmaking about enlargement.

Fourth, enlargement will be messy. Spain, the last new member of NATO, required four years from its original decision on accession to the holding of a referendum to confirm the decision and the terms of its membership, after which another four years were required to elaborate and approve the six coordination agreements to govern the Spanish/NATO military relationship. It is possible that the process would be similar in respect of certain new member countries.

Fifth, if NATO were to enlarge to include all aspirants to membership, its roster would come very close to resembling that of the OSCE. This would further blur the boundaries between European security institutions.

Sixth, there is a real danger that institutional expansion would tend to deflect NATO energies from "real-life" contingencies, in particular the ongoing conflict in the former Yugoslavia. In fact, it may have been the very difficulties encountered in dealing with this situation that originally helped fuel the enlargement option in the alliance context. (Likewise, a successful role for NATO in implementing the Dayton Agreement could serve to calm enlargement passions.)

To summarize, there is little reason to believe that enlargement would address in any helpful way the problems of diversity within the existing North Atlantic identity. On the contrary, there are numerous reasons to believe that it might weaken that identity further.

Strategic Implications of Enlargement

Several strategic implications flow from the sociological and organizational considerations reviewed above. An enlarged NATO would tend to accentuate contradictions between states that have been historical rivals and which, in the era of ethnic politics, would find themselves on opposite sides of the new strategic fence an expanding NATO would ineluctably erect. At the same time, the number of states that were hostile or potentially hostile to NATO would be augmented. The organization would have made the transition from having one all-dominating enemy to having no enemies to having several enemies, entertaining varying degrees and kinds of opposition to NATO. In some cases, NATO would serve only as a welcome scapegoat for a reform effort gone wrong or as a pretext for slowing the pace of reform. In other instances, real tensions could (re)appear.

In parallel, enlargement would tend to encourage efforts to consolidate CIS cooperation in the domains of defence and foreign policy. Enlargement would furthermore push into the public domain issues associated with NATO's and Russia's strategic posture that the two sides have effectively managed to keep sublimated during the post-Cold War era. NATO has attempted to deemphasize its nuclear role and continues to do so in the enlargement context, as its study on the project makes clear. But again, if the experience of NATO's last new member, Spain, is anything to go by, enlargement will not only be messy and time-consuming, it will rivet public attention upon a series of sensitive strategic issues, in particular the role of the integrated military structure and nuclear weapons in the post-Cold War world.

In sum, enlargement would likely translate into a security minus, not a security plus, for old and new members alike, as well as for nonmembers. At a minimum, enlargement would probably lead to a renewal of some of the geopolitical and ideological "atmospherics" that, it was thought, had disappeared with the end of the Cold War in Europe; spark increases in defence expenditure; and, at a time when the Euro-Atlantic states without exception are experiencing relative resource penury, deflect attention from the domestic restructuring tasks that require their attention. Beyond that, there is always the risk that the processes enlargement might set in train could evolve in a manner impossible to control, with long-term negative consequences difficult to predict.

Conclusion

In the second section of this chapter, we explored the nature of NATO's geographical, historical, and perceptual identity as a regional organization. In this regard, we found its greatest strength in the post-Cold War strategic context to be the community of shared values and expectations that it embodies. In the third section, we situated NATO in the general context of regional organizations as purveyors of regional security, and found that it shared many of the common weaknesses of such organizations. Asymmetries in the distribution of power, coupled with inconsistencies in perceived interest among members, complicated cooperative action in coping with regional threats to peace and security. In addition, as with many other organizations, NATO's effectiveness in dealing with regional security issues outside its own area was constrained by the exclusive character of its membership.

This led us into an extensive analysis of the expansion project. In our judgement, it fails adequately to address the issue of inclusiveness since it will again leave out the most conflict-prone areas of the European region. Moreover, it recreates the problem of exclusion in new forms, and it risks alienating more deeply those left out. Given that the integration of Russia in particular into Europe's security "architecture" is perhaps the most pressing problem facing the old continent's security planners in the aftermath of the Cold War, an expansion that risks such alienation is imprudent, particularly when, as in Bosnia-Herzegovina, Russian cooperation is essential to successful management of out-of-area security issues in Europe. There are few compelling counterarguments suggesting that expansion might improve the security of Europe. As Senator Sam Nunn once put it, "NATO's announced position is that the question of enlargement is not whether, but when and how. Somehow I have missed any logical explanation of why."[20]

For all of these reasons, the expansion of NATO, particularly if it proceeded in an accelerated fashion, would be a costly mistake. Indeed, the likely negative effects of enlargement are so compelling that it is difficult to imagine that it was sober strategic calculus that originally set the enlargement process in motion. Be that as it may, the disadvantages are such that it seems reasonable to assume that there is every likelihood that when — or rather if — push comes to shove, the 16 votes required to forge a NATO consensus will simply not be forthcoming.

This would raise serious problems for the alliance — problems that could prove almost as serious as those that would be engendered by the "successful" pursuit of the enlargement project. The first is that Russia would be seen to have won the enlargement war. If Yelstin remains president of the Russian Federation or is succeeded by a "democratic, centrist" alternative, this is a battle that the west can safely afford to have lost. If, however, the next president belongs to a communist or nationalist fraction, nonenlargement could well encourage the then prevailing antiwestern reflexes.

The second problem is that nonenlargement in the face of hostile rumblings from Russia translates into a significant loss of credibility in Central and Eastern Europe, replete with all the imaginable, and largely understandable, populist rhetoric about a second Yalta that would follow.

There is no easy fix in these circumstances, but there are a number of possible initiatives that might help ease the situation. The first would be frustratingly *diplomatesque*, but, in the right combination with other measures, no less useful for that. NATO should continue its consultations on enlargement but effectively postpone any decision in the matter until the *Greek Calends.* The purpose would be to keep the Russian foreign policy debate off balance at the same time as would-be members in Central and Eastern Europe were given time and space to adjust their rhetoric and retool their approaches.

Not deciding to enlarge is actually easy to imagine, in view of the complexity of the issue and the reservations that will be harboured in more than one alliance capital, and need not be the subject of an actual decision. The danger here is that indefinite postponement might impede the development of alternative structures of security cooperation in Central and Eastern Europe. The flanking measures that would be required to compensate for this effect by underscoring NATO's continuing commitment to CEE security would be rather more challenging for the decisionmaking process.

First and foremost, NATO might envisage a limited form of security guarantee for CEE countries. A blanket guarantee is not necessary; nor would it be advisable in view of the questionable purposes to which it could be put in certain bilateral struggles. Indeed, even though such a guarantee still exists between and among the NATO 16, it may no longer be strategically realistic even there. A conditional guarantee could commit NATO to the principles of sanctity of borders and the negotiated change of frontiers on an ad hoc and time-limited basis. It could be stabilizing, for example, in the event of a deterioration of Hungarian-Rumanian relations if it were known that NATO had the capacity and the will to interject itself between belligerents on either side attempting to move territorial/communal goalposts by force.

Intimately related to this point is the importance of ensuring that IFOR and related western initiatives in Bosnia succeed in suffocating the flames of conflict there and paving the path to a lasting peace. Nothing NATO says or does in the post-Cold War period will have any resonance if it fails in Bosnia. However, successful IFOR involvement in the former Yugoslavia can show that, ultimately, security does not depend on institutional status, but on whether and how members and nonmembers work together in causes of common concern.

Thirdly, NATO must continue, and reinforce as necessary, its efforts to build a new security community in greater Europe based on ad hoc cooperation around the alliance's core. NACC and Partnership for Peace, suitably supported by the current membership, are adequate tools. These may not be the tidy, fixed relationships of the Cold War, but they can be sufficient responses in an era that must put a premium on flexibility in evolving new relationships between former foes and erstwhile allies.

Notes

1. On this point, see S. Neil MacFarlane, "The Deperipheralization of Russia," in *The Centre-Periphery Debate in International Security*, ed. David G. Haglund (Clementsport, NS: Lester B. Pearson Canadian International Peacekeeping Training Centre, 1996), pp. 29-41.

2. See David G. Haglund, S. Neil MacFarlane, and Joel J. Sokolsky, "NATO and the Quest for Ongoing Viability," in *NATO's Eastern Dilemmas*, ed. Haglund, MacFarlane, and Sokolsky (Boulder: Westview, 1994), pp. 11-22.

3. David G. Haglund, "Must NATO Fail? Theories, Myths, and Policy Dilemmas," *International Journal* 50 (Autumn 1995): 651-74.

4. See, for Yugoslavia, Karsten Voigt, "NATO Enlargement: A Holistic Approach for the Future," *SAIS Review* (Summer-Fall 1995): 122; and for the former Soviet Union, Giorgio Napolitano, Karsten Voigt, and Tamas Wachsler, co-rapporteurs, "The Enlargement of the Alliance," Draft Special Report of the Working Group on NATO Enlargement (Brussels: North Atlantic Assembly, October 1995), p. 1.

5. Napolitano, Voigt, and Wacshler, "Enlargement of the Alliance," p. 3.

6. For a similar analysis, see Bruce Russett, "International Relations and the International System," in *Regional Politics and World Order*, ed. Richard Falk and Saul Mendlovitz (San Francisco: W. H. Freeman, 1973), p. 187.

7. However, as was pointed out long ago by V. C. Finch, this discontinuity is generally muted and regional borders consequently are difficult to define. See his "Geographical Science and Social Philosophy," *Annals of the Association of American Geographers* 29,1 (1939): 14.

8. This is clearly related to the concept of "mutuality" articulated by Barry Buzan in *People, States, and Fear: An Agenda for International Security Studies in the Post-Cold War Era* (New York: Harvester Wheatsheaf, 1991), p. 194.

9. Ibid., p. 190.

10. On the concept of "overlay," see ibid., p. 198.

11. For an impressive discussion of the community of values in the North Atlantic area, and its implications for interstate relations, see Thomas Risse-Kappen, *Cooperation among Democracies: The European Influence on American Foreign Policy* (Princeton: Princeton University Press, 1995), pp. 24-41, 195-209.

12. In this respect, it resembles Karl Deutsch's concept of the "pluralistic security community." See Deutsch et al., *Political Community and the North Atlantic Area: International Organization in the Light of Historical Experience* (Princeton: Princeton University Press, 1968), p. 5.

13. See Michael Doyle, "Liberalism and World Politics," *American Political Science Review* 80 (December 1986): 1151-69.

14. That is to say, a structure of security whereby the group of members commits itself to a collective response to an act of aggression by any of its members against any other member. For a useful discussion of the meaning of collective security, see John Ruggie, "Multilateralism: The Anatomy of an Institution," *International Organization* 46 (Summer 1992): 569.

15. This logic is similar to that imputed by Edward Luttwak to the Roman Empire. His conclusion with regard to the overstretching consequences of such expansion does not foster enthusiasm. See his *The Grand Strategy of the Roman Empire from the First Century A.D. to the Third* (Baltimore: Johns Hopkins University Press, 1976), *passim.*

16. See S. Neil MacFarlane and Thomas G. Weiss, "Regional Organizations and Regional Security," *Security Studies* 2 (Autumn 1992): 6-37.

17. Many German political figures take the view that embedding Germany in cooperative European and transatlantic structures is necessary to reassure neighbouring European states in the context of the growth of German power.

18. David Law, "Widen or Whither: The Challenge of NATO Enlargement," paper presented to interparliamentary conference at the Polish Sejm, Warsaw, May 1995.

19. This assessment is based on the personal observations of co-author David Law, who headed the policy planning unit of the NATO International Staff between 1992 and 1994, and was directly involved in this process.

20. Sam Nunn, "The Future of NATO in an Uncertain World," *Vital Speeches of the Day*, 15 July 1995, pp. 583-86.

CHAPTER THREE

NATO After Victory:
New Products, New Markets, and
the Microeconomics of Alliance

Josef Joffe

Introduction: The Curse of Victory

Alliances die when they win and when they lose. That defeat spells death should be obvious. An alliance routed is an alliance ruined. Defeat is the end because it proves that the coalition could not live up to its purpose, which is the aggregation of military power for the sake of defence or aggression. And so, surrender dissolves both bonds and obligations. No coalition in this century has survived capitulation — neither Germany's alliances in two world wars nor the Soviet bloc of the Cold War. But alliances also die when they win — from the anti-Napoleon coalition of the 19th century to the anti-Hitler alliance of the 20th.

Nor is this deadly disease a mere accident of history; for victory, too, robs coalitions of their raison d'être. When the great threat disappears, so does the mighty glue that binds states in alliance. As the pressure weakens, so does the force that harnesses disparate national interests. Worse, once partners no longer need to worry about their common enemy, they begin to worry about one another: How will yesterday's comrade-in-arms use its unshackled power tomorrow? Rivalry resumes as the victors face no other powers but themselves. Recall Britain after 1919, as it turned once more to balancing against France. The most dramatic instance of this truth is of course the case of the United States and the Soviet Union. Hardly had they vanquished Nazi Germany when they turned against each other.

True, NATO seems to defy this iron law of history. Years after victory in the Cold War, NATO is still alive and poised to move into the 21st century. No member has moved to dissolve, none has even intimated a desire to abscond. Indeed, there are more countries clamouring to join than NATO can — or wants to — accommodate. But then, the anti-Napoleon coalition did not die in 1815, either. It took at least seven years before Britain, its maritime mastermind, began to detach itself from the continent. But whatever the historical analogies, NATO, like all victorious alliances, has a deadly question hanging over it: What is its reason for being if the threat that spawned and sustained it is gone?

The problem may best be described in the language of microeconomics. NATO finds itself in the position of a firm that suddenly faces a severe downward shift of the demand curve for its classical wares. In NATO's case, the problem is the drastic decline of the strategic threat, and hence of the demand for its two best products: deterrence and defence. Faced with an ailing "cash cow," what does such a company do?

There are four, and *only* four, basic choices:

1. The firm sells its assets, distributes the proceeds to its shareholders and closes up.
2. It downsizes *pari passu* with the decline in demand in order to regain an equilibrium between costs and benefits and to keep shareholders from defecting.
3. It develops *new products* in order to replace yesterday's "cash cow" with new "shooting stars."
4. It tries to conquer *new markets* for its old product.

The last two — marketing a new product and conquering new markets — are precisely the strategies NATO has pursued since the beginning of the 1990s. What has been the record, what are the prospects for the future?

"Out of Area or Out of Business"

The new product has been peacekeeping and peace-enforcement in Europe, i.e., in Bosnia. Hardly had the Cold War ended with Moscow's capitulation[1] when a vast new market opened up in Southeast Europe. Demand for the new product emerged with Serbia's intervention against Croatia and Slovenia in 1991; demand leapt upward with the tripartite war that broke out in Bosnia in 1992 between Serbs, Croats, and Muslims.

Did NATO deliver on the supply? The record was miserable until the summer of 1995. Prior to that time, it looked as if the few newly designed goods might somehow satisfy the demands of the Bosnian security market. NATO bombed a bit, and the Bosnian Serbs retracted a bit — symbolically in both cases, as it turned out.

For by the spring of 1995, a murderous gap had opened between the meagre security supply trickling off NATO's production lines and the burgeoning demand generated by the escalation of Serbian violence. Instead of intimidation, NATO reaped retaliation and provocation. An American warplane was shot down, UN forces were taken hostage, Tuzla was attacked in the most gruesome manner, with 71 civilians dead. In July, the ultimate provocation occurred when Serbian forces, taking UN soldiers prisoners on the way, broke into Srebrenica, a UN-designated safe haven for 40,000 inhabitants and several thousand refugees. Yet NATO did not act. In short, what NATO had to offer in the way of defence and deterrence was woefully inadequate to the demand. The explanation for the failure of NATO's new product came in three parts — in rising order of importance and generality.

First, by acting as "subcontractor" to the UN, NATO had imposed on itself an absurd chain of command, ending at the Security Council, where the lack of unanimity nipped any real military option in the bud. Or more accurately, *because* NATO did not want to act, the alliance willingly put itself in thrall to the Security Council where the presence of Russia (and, to some extent, China) would *guarantee* stalemate.

Which leads to the second level, Russia. After a brief period of retraction, even subservience to the west (e.g., during the Gulf War, 1990-1991), Russia began to act as not-so-tacit protector of the Serbs. Having emerged from the shock of defeat in the Cold War, Russia began to reemphasize rivalry and the quest for advantage in its mixed relationship with the west. In the Balkans, the signal was that Russia would not allow the west to dominate a region where competition had been the rule since the last third of the 19th century. Faced with taking on Russia, which it still wants to "socialize" into a cooperative relationship, the west granted Moscow a tacit veto power in the Bosnian war.

The third, and most general, reason why NATO did not excel with its new product line derives from the very nature of this alliance. To get to the root of the problem, we must first ask: Why was the alliance so successful in the past? Whence came its unprecedented longevity? There is a simple answer: because it did not have to *do* anything. In the affairs of men and nations there is a world of difference between a passive as opposed to an active, a negative as opposed to a positive, and a deterrent as opposed to a compellent, posture.

NATO's classic strategy withstood the test of time because it was passive, negative, and deterrence-dominated. It was "negative" in the sense that NATO was designed to *prevent* something: an attack on its members. It was "passive" in the sense that the alliance — like Mount Everest — merely had to *be* there; the 12, later 16, members did not have to decide on their common purpose as the sun rose every day. The objective was simple and enduring: to preserve the status quo, and the means was deterrence rather than compellence. The name of the game was *having* military power, not using it. NATO was like a mutual-savings society that never had to decide — and do so unanimously — on how to *spend* the money, a task at which sovereign states rarely excel.

The basic point need not be laboured. For countries in alliance it is vastly more comfortable to agree on the status quo than to concur on its change. Staying in place is easier than blazing a new path, especially when down that road lurk the incalculable risks of unleashing force now and facing escalation later. Above all, NATO was built around a single interest that was powerful, permanent, and all-embracing: the deterrence of Soviet aggression.

In Bosnia, however, the reverse was true on all counts. There, NATO was asked to assume an active, positive, and compellent posture. And this made all the difference in the world. Now, the alliance *had* to decide what to do with its money in the bank. Now, it *had* to contemplate real risks and costs. Now, it *had* to create a consensus anew each day. And now, the members quickly realized that their interests were *not* alike. The drama of divergent interests began in 1990/91 when reunited Germany (with Austria in tow) took on the United States, Britain, and France over the recognition of Croatia and Slovenia. The drama continued with the opting out of two key members, America and Germany. While Germany claimed that its history and constitution forbade out-of-area operations, the US was only too happy to hear from the EU that it would go into the Bosnia business on its own.

The third act commenced in the winter of 1994, when NATO's attempt to open up a new branch for out-of-area business rocked the very core of the company. As Congress threatened "lift and strike," Britain and France stridently began to accuse the US of betrayal and abandonment. Lifting the embargo, London and Paris claimed, would expose their UN contingents to murderous crossfire — making extraction impossible without American intervention. Yet the US, so they alleged, would add betrayal to injury by refusing to cover the retreat. There was a whiff of "Suez" in the air, recalling America's abandonment of its two oldest allies in their war against Nasser's Egypt, followed by their ignominious retreat and enveloped in one of the worst crises in NATO's history.

These three years of supply failure should be kept firmly in mind, as we peer into a future that now seems to be marked by the very opposite of the record I have just described. In the late summer of 1995, NATO abruptly switched course. Following the bloody bombardment of Sarajevo, NATO unleashed a sustained and sophisticated bombing campaign that, along with the Muslim-Croatian advance on the ground, sobered up the Serbs and drove them to the bargaining table in Dayton. Thereafter, the alliance shed the chains that had bound it to the Security Council and proceeded to field a force of 60,000 to enforce the Dayton peace.

Had NATO, then, at last delivered the appropriate supply of security? Doubts are in order. Fundamentally, it had not been NATO that acted, but the United States. It was the US that had discharged three critical tasks. First, Washington harnessed a coalition of the willing to prosecute the air campaign. (Significantly, Germany, the second-most important NATO member, refused to accept a combat role.) Second, it held off the Russians with a mix of suasion and deterrence. (Significantly, the commander of the Russian contingent reports not to NATO, but to IFOR's American commander qua American.) Third, it was the US, in the guise of the assistant secretary of state, Richard Holbrooke, that bludgeoned the warring tribes of Bosnia into an agreement of sorts.[2] Fourth, it was Washington that provided most of the military power in IFOR. In short, this was a Balkan version of the Gulf War coalition rather than an *alliance* peace-enforcement operation.

And like the Gulf Coalition, IFOR was, for *intrinsic* reasons, badly positioned to win the peace (as opposed to merely carrying the day on the battlefield). All peacekeeping is saddled with a fundamental dilemma: its commitment must be open-ended — like the allied occupation of Germany after World War II. For, by definition, *enforcement* implies that intervention has not removed the original causes of conflict. If the commitment is not open-ended (IFOR's mandate has been limited to 12 months), the contestants on the ground will simply bide their time and prepare for the day when the guardians will have departed.

Nor is it a sheer accident that IFOR's mandate was limited in time. The coalition of the willing was not held together by powerful national interest but by a vague commitment to "stability" and/or humanitarian duty. Domestic support for the mission was thin everywhere, and nowhere thinner than in the United States. Likewise in Germany, a country that decided to get out of harm's way *ab initio* by providing only logistical and medical support one step removed (in Croatia). There was also a joker in the pack, namely Russia, which insisted on having its own sector of "occupation," as it were. There was another, lesser, joker by the name of France, a country forever torn between its inability to lead on its own and its unwillingness to submit to the United States for any length of time.

And so, neither the bombing campaign nor the insertion of IFOR could (yet) prove the critical point: that an alliance built around deterrence and defence is capable of shifting to an active, positive, and compellent posture. Peace-enforcement in a peripheral theatre does not make for a compelling interest that sustains long-term involvement, let alone the sacrifice that *real* peace-making, i.e., combat, entails. "Somalia" remains the watchword for any operation that lacks the binding glue of convergent national interests on the part of the many, and reliable leadership on the part of the one country, the United States, that is alone equipped to provide it.

"Grow or Die"

What about Strategy 4, selling the old product in a new market, that is, enlarging the realm of security and deterrence to the new democracies in the east?

Though by the mid-1990s all principal members of NATO were talking as if enlargement were only a matter of "when," and no longer of "whether," NATO, *as we know it*,[3] will not be extended eastward. If it does enlarge, it will not be the "Real Thing," but a sweetish concoction that will only faintly resemble "Classic Coke." There are three sets of reasons for this dour assessment: one pertains to the nature of the would-be members in Central and Eastern Europe, the second to the strategic implications of enlargement, and the third, and most weighty one, to Russia.

The Candidates

To begin with, any alliance must think coldly and ask whether enlargement actually yields a net gain in security. These considerations will move to centre-stage as NATO approaches the moment of truth defined by the "when" and the "who." The costs are certainly impressive. To list but a few:

- With 20 or more members, NATO will lose cohesion, no matter who joins. But in alliances, numbers do not necessarily beget strength. Cohesion in a single-member veto system declines geometrically with the increase in numbers. The more national wills to be harnessed to a single purpose, the less likely will be a consensual outcome. In the NATO case, the specific candidates will simply add to heterogeneity by dint of their domestic systems which range from postcommunism in Poland to creeping authoritarianism in Slovakia.
- It is not clear whether these prospective members (with the exception of Poland) truly relish the idea of "all for one, and one for all" when it comes to the use of force. At a minimum, there is a pronounced ambivalence on the part of Hungary and the Czech Republic. (At a 1995 meeting in Washington, the Czech ambassador was heard to muse whether his country would really want to go to war for Turkey.) These countries do not feel threatened by Russia; if they do, they do not articulate these fears in the open. They have other concerns at the top of their agendas. Above all, they want to be part of the western democratic and economic club; with the exception of Poland perhaps, their main quest is not for military security and the onerous obligations that entails.
- Who will pay the tens of billions of dollars required for bringing the new armies up to NATO standards? The new democracies do not have the money, and the old ones do not relish the prospect of exporting eastward what they are saving in the speedy rush to disarmament.
- What about tangible guarantees, especially nuclear guarantees? Will NATO move troops into a forward position on the eastern border of Poland? We cannot look forward to the Article 5 debate in the US Senate.

Strategic Issues

What about those states — the Baltics, Ukraine — that are threatened most but will be left out? Curiously, the more security problems a would-be member has, the less sympathy NATO displays for its entreaties. That paradox is easily resolved by looking backward. In the late 1940s, the US was downright zealous to extend NATO eastward, that is, into West Germany, the most exposed country in Europe. Why? Because the Federal Republic represented an enormous strategic asset, providing additional geographic depth and an impressive reservoir of manpower. Those new resources dwarfed the risks of extending the alliance all the way to the confrontation line with Soviet forces *in situ.*[4]

Today, this logic does *not* apply to the Baltics and Ukraine because these assets are dwarfed by the risks of a renewed contest with Moscow. NATO, in other words, wants to enlarge only where such is possible "on the cheap." From this we ought to conclude that the enterprise lacks the punch of compelling interest. The purpose is not to add strategic space and military power but to engage in charity — providing a home for selected "easties" — where the costs are low. As in the affairs of men, the charitable impulse of states does not make for steadiness and determination. Concretely, by pursuing enlargement on the cheap, the west has turned the project into a hostage to Soviet demands, be they for a veto or for compensation (which I discuss below).

Nonetheless, the strategic issues must not be ignored. For whatever new line NATO does draw in the east will tacitly mark off new areas of influence. Indeed, to draw a new line is to issue a silent signal, nay, an invitation to Russia to absorb the rest — from the Baltics to Bulgaria — into *its* sphere of power. That, of course, militates fiercely against the very premise of NATO enlargement, which is to enlarge its house of stability across the entire continent.

Currently, the contest over influence in Central and Eastern Europe ranges from the implicit to the subtle. Expanding NATO's sway in a formal way will leave those in the cold who need it most and then recreate, though in a different guise, the very blocs Europe has sought to transcend in the wake of the Cold War. Worse, enlargement might regalvanize precisely the power contest between the west and Russia the end of the Cold War had presumably laid to rest.

The Russian Veto

Ever since late 1994, Russia has flung down an ever more strident "nyet" to NATO enlargement. With equal insistence, the west has intoned, mantra-like, that nobody shall have a veto over its strategic choices, that enlargement is no longer a matter of "whether" but of "when." Unfortunately, the seemingly categorical difference between "whether" and "when" can be quite small in the world of practical policy. Such dates may well recede into a very long distance. To put it most brutally, as long as there is the shred of a possibility that Russia *can* be socialized into the community of responsible great powers, the west will act on the tacit premise that Moscow is more important than Prague, Bratislava, Budapest, and Warsaw, let alone Riga or Kiev. And when that last shred ever disappears, it will be too late. In a neo-Cold War setting, one of explicit and harsh rivalry, nobody in the west will dare enlarge. Changing the geopolitical status quo on the brink constitutes too incalculable a risk. At worst, then, the answer to "when" might become "never."

What if NATO, driven by past commitments, bureaucratic momentum, and CEE pressures, enlarges nonetheless? If NATO does move east, it will not purvey the "Real Thing," the security community that it has so successfully marketed in its traditional realm of business. Why would this be so?

Russia's consent is only conceivable under two circumstances. One is "dilution-*cum*-transcendence." Under that scenario, Russia would concur — indeed, happily — if NATO as a whole closed down its core business: its deterrence and defence structure arrayed against the one country, that is, has been, and remains too "big" for Europe. The west has known Moscow's price for decades. Whatever the guise — from Stalin to Yeltsin, from "disengagement" to the "common house of Europe" — the proposals all boiled down to exchanging a collective-defence system (A plus B *against* X) for a collective-security system (A plus B *with* X, the enemy not being predesignated and a member of the set).

The new Russia's policy is not that different from that of the old Soviet Union. The basic thrust is to dissolve the Atlantic alliance in an "overarching" structure for the sake of amity, cooperation, and understanding. Yet apart from the fact that collective security never works when needed,[5] such system is the very opposite of alliance. It lacks the commitment and the certainty that makes for cohesion. We might call it "NATO," but if Russia is a member, whether tacit or formal, it will be but the name attached to a new thing under the sun.

The other and more recent scenario revolves around Russia's demand that the alliance's core product not be sold in the new eastern market. What is the "core product?" It is *not* Article 5, which actually contains but a very weakly worded pledge of mutual succour. The "Real Thing" is the blood-and-iron arrangements on the ground that turned verbal pledges into tangible guarantees: the forward-deployment of troops, the "layer cake," the integration of forces under an American SACEUR, and the insertion of US nuclear weapons into the deterrence equation.

All of these features signaled a credible and enduring message. An attack on one would be an attack on all, and since all (or most) would be embroiled in the fighting *ab initio*, the chance of abandonment (the oldest bane of alliances) dwindled toward nil. American nuclear weapons in a forward position added extra punch to the deterrent proposition, as they forever threatened to erase the distinction between a small, regional war and a large, global one.

In 1996, Russia executed a subtle tack by placing its ancient demand for an "overarching" system on the back burner and by softening its insistence on a straightforward veto. Instead, Moscow began to signal conditional assent. First, enlargement had to be limited to a few candidates, presumably the "usual suspects" — the Czech Republic, Hungary, and Poland. Second, there could be "no nukes and no troops." Western forces must not be shifted forward from Germany, nor could the alliance extend its nuclear umbrella to the new members.

If accepted, such conditions will defang the entire enterprise and withhold precisely the one NATO good the would-be joiners crave most: tangible guarantees. Poland certainly remembers from 1939 that covenants without swords are just words. And the others will also recall the hapless experience of Poland after 1 September 1939. But then, does it matter if the alliance, by accepting Moscow's conditions, could kill two birds with one stone? After all, in one fell swoop, the west would garner the consent of the Russians as well as of those NATO countries that are not too eager to shoulder onerous new obligations.

It does matter because such course will have consequences. For one, it will dilute the alliance by dint of status differentials. True, France (no integration), Norway (no nuclear weapons), and Spain (neither of the above) had long ago claimed special status for themselves. But add three, four more à la carte members to the alliance, and we will end up with two different animals in the same barn. In one corner will be the "real" alliance, in the other a *soi-disant* alliance, states with second-class membership. And that will not be NATO as we know it, a system where all or most members bear the same obligations and enjoy the same succour.

Moreover, what do countries do that are situated on the most exposed flank of the alliance and do not enjoy full and credible security guarantees? They labour under two temptations, neither of which is conducive to the health of alliances. One might be to *force* full membership by engaging in provocative behaviour that turns small crises into big ones and thus sucks their allies into a forward position on their own soil. Such an outcome would put the senior members into an excruciating position. Either they move and risk unwanted escalation; or they do not move and risk humiliation for themselves and the alliance as a whole.

The second temptation is the obverse of provocation, namely propitiation. Knowing they cannot count on real security guarantees, the second-class members will strike side-deals with their most powerful potential foe (i.e., Russia). Unable to count on western succour in the moment of truth, they might act as quasi-neutrals or advocates of Russian interests in times of crisis. Or they might simply oppose from the inside whatever course of action the alliance seeks to hammer out when a contest of wills is at hand. Like the first temptation, such a course, a classic resort of smaller powers, does not add to alliance cohesion.

Let us make the basic point by returning to the company analogy. In the real business world, conglomerization — adding new branches to the parent company — is not a guarantee of higher profits or resurgent growth. The expected synergistic effect frequently comes out negative because knowledge gained in the traditional sector does not travel well to unfamiliar ones; absorbing new firms, especially shaky ones, subtracts resources from the core business. It is no accident that many companies both in America and Europe who had gone on a mad acquisition binge in the 1980s shed their subsidiaries in the 1990s.

How does this apply to NATO? Enlargement is a noble goal, but its underlying thrust has little to do with the alliance's traditional business. The driving idea is to spread the blessings of democracy and market economics to the east; the would-be members want, and we want to extend, a home and a community to them. These are laudable and important objectives, but they militate against the imperatives of cohesion and credibility. Indeed, the critical problem of enlargement is that NATO will take on tasks that are not only alien but also noxious to the purposes of alliance. Bringing in new members that seek a home rather than a fort will dilute the compact. Paying the requisite compensation to Russia will more than just dilute; it will destroy. Whatever the nature of the deal — à la carte or second-rate membership for the ex-satrapies, or an inside role for Russia — NATO as we have known it will not survive enlargement.

Conclusion: Downsizing for Survival

If the new product (peace-making) falls short of the long-term demand, and if the new market (enlargement) holds out more poison than profit, what is left for the alliance as it faces a downward-shifting demand curve for its traditional wares?

There are still Strategies 1 and 2, folding up and downsizing. Strategy 1 can be dispatched most easily. That the west ought not to close up shop should be self-evident. First, there is the residual risk by the name of Russia that requires a well-oiled defence machinery. Second, pulling down the production lines will require start-up costs in the next round that will overwhelm upkeep expenditures here and now. Third, NATO has bequeathed an enormous tradition of cooperation — social capital, to use an expression of the day. Dismantling this going concern will necessarily entail the renationalization of western defences — perhaps even the return to the older game of nations that has brought so much grief to Europe in the past. And so, NATO continues to have a powerful claim on the future.

What then about Strategy 2: downsizing — that is, producing what NATO has done best, but on a lower scale tailored to the reduced demand? This approach, though neither valiant nor inspiring, holds out the best promise.

What is NATO's classic product? Again, we might invoke the immortal phrase of Lord Ismay, its first secretary general: "Keep the Russians out, the Americans in, and the Germans down." These three functions, suitably modernized of course, still deliver a potent rationale for the alliance. Let us take them in turn.

Keeping the Russians Out

Russia will be neither democratic nor pacific for a long time. Russia is trying to reconstitute the former Soviet empire — peacefully where possible, violently where necessary. But beyond its domestic constitution, Russia is simply too "big" for Europe; it has been — and will continue to be — a problem in the European balance. So a downsized NATO with a rapid reconstitution capability remains a critical weight in the equation. Indeed, the better NATO's shape, the more it can radiate security into Eastern Europe, even to those nations that do not become members, without sparking a new, explicit power contest.

Keeping the Americans In

This role, too, remains vital. Even with a reduced strategic threat, it is not at all clear whether there can be European security without Atlantic security. Europe has flourished because the United States has essentially become a European power — and Europe did not flourish in this century when American power was not part of the balance. Moreover, everybody from Lisbon to Lodz wants the Americans in — even the cranky French who, deep in their heart, want to secure the American presence as a counterweight to German and Russian power.

Keeping the Germans Down

Evidently, that function long ago changed to "keeping the Germans integrated." But even in the new setting, this function has not lost its claim on the future. Germany, though the model of a liberal democracy, is once more sovereign, larger, and in the middle. It is again too big to be left alone, and not big enough to go it alone. The comforting thing about the latest unification is that the Germans know this. Multilateralism and community remain unwritten articles of their constitution. The Germans understand full well that NATO and the US reassure everybody else by shortening the shadow of German power. To remain integrated, to produce security collectively, is good for Europe and good for Germany, and the Germans will accept, nay, cherish, such a setting as long as it is available.

Let us generalize the argument. Deep in their hearts, all the Europeans dread the "renationalization" of their defences. The Atlantic alliance has spared the Europeans the need for an autonomous defence policy, historically the most powerful cause of conflict and war. They know that nonautonomy, the integration of their defence policy under a powerful outsider, provided the benign stage on which they could forget their ancient rivalries and link hands in economic and political community. And deep in their hearts, the Europeans suspect that they may not live as harmoniously in the absence of Big Brother from across the Atlantic.[6]

In conclusion, the old functions, suitably modernized, can still serve as the new rationale for the alliance as it moves toward the ripe old age of 50. But people in middle age should not do more than their constitution permits. The attempt at new products and new markets has not really recapitalized the company we know of as NATO. Those who point to the new product — the bombing campaign and Dayton — must not forget the conflicts of interests that had paralyzed the 16 shareholders in the preceding three years. And those who want to extend the old product to a new market must not ignore the pitfalls that enlargement entails, especially the compensatory demands of Russia which signal dilution or subversion. Since closing up shop is the worst course, a downsized product line plus a rapid reconstitution capability mark out the best strategy as the alliance faces the 21st century.

Notes

This chapter builds on the author's "Is There Life After Victory? What NATO Can and Cannot Do," *National Interest*, no. 41 (Fall 1995), pp. 19-25.

1. The best single date is probably 16 July 1990, when Mikhail Gorbachev accepted German reunification within the west. Since the Cold War broke out in earnest over the issue of who would control Germany, it is only fitting that its end should be marked by that date. To give away the GDR, the Soviet empire's easternmost strategic brace, meant to yield the rest. Alternatively, one might choose 25 December 1991, the day when the Soviet Union was dissolved and the white, red, and blue flag of Russia was hauled up on the Kremlin.

2. Though celebrated as a "peace," Dayton really marked the grudging tripartite consent to the de facto partition of Bosnia into a Serbian component and a "Muslim-Croat Federation."

3. The critical features of "Classic NATO" were four-fold: an integrated force and command structure; an American supreme commander; US nuclear weapons in a forward position; and the "layer cake," the presence of many national forces in the most likely sector of confrontation.

4. As a result, revisionist historians have argued that it was precisely the incorporation of West Germany that rendered the Cold War explicit, unavoidable, and long-term.

5. For an elaboration, see the author's "Collective Security and the Future of Europe: Failed Dreams and Dead Ends," *Survival* 34 (Spring 1992): 36-50.

6. For an expanded version of this argument, see Josef Joffe, *The Limited Partnership: Europe, the United States, and the Burdens of Alliance* (Cambridge: Ballinger, 1987), ch. 5.

CHAPTER FOUR

NATO Enlargement and Russia: In Search of an Adequate Response

Andrei Kortunov

Introduction

Of the numerous issues in international politics that separate Russia from the west, the enlargement of NATO to the east has to be among the most sensitive and politically explosive. One must recognize, however, that today this is a purely élitist issue in Russia. The overwhelming majority of Russians do not care much about NATO. Neither do they care much about foreign policy in general. Foreign policy has always been an élite sport in Russia; it is even more the case now given the immense domestic problems that the country faces. Foreign policy has very little to do with day-to-day lives of ordinary people, who find it difficult to trace a direct causal relationship between their own situations and international politics. The country is clearly inward-oriented and the average Russian in the street will definitely not put the enlargement of NATO on top of his or her priorities' list, ahead of such really burning problems as continuous inflation, unemployment, organized crime, or corruption among state bureaucrats.

Who in Russia Cares about NATO?

Even for the minority of Russians who do care about foreign policy, NATO remains mostly irrelevant. Such matters as obtaining visas to Baltic states, going through customs at the Russian-Ukrainian border, getting shipments of consumer goods from Turkey or China, accommodating relatives and friends coming from Tajikistan or Armenia seem to be much more practical and immediate than does the rather remote and unclear prospect of NATO's enlargement. The Atlantic alliance, no matter what it does or says, will not stop the war in Chechnya or prevent illegal Chinese immigrants from infiltrating the Russian Far East. At the same time, even an enlarged NATO will continue to be a relatively minor factor in bilateral relations between Russia and Kazakhstan, or Russia and Ukraine. In short, NATO can neither resolve immediate Russian foreign policy problems, nor complicate them in a serious way.

The so-called "new Russians" (the emerging business community of the country) have their own foreign policy agenda: they watch very carefully the changing rates of the US dollar, the price lists of foreign consumer goods, the customs duties imposed by Moscow and its trade partners in the west, and so on. Their businesses can be directly affected by the next IMF credit to Russia, by the decisions of the G-7 group, or even by new interest rates set by the *Bundesbank*. The growth of the European Union is an important matter for them, because it has had and will continue to have a serious impact on their business practices in Europe. However, NATO enlargement is rarely on the radar screens of these "new Russians."

No matter what politicians or political scientists might have to say about it, Russian society remains (or rather has become) pragmatic, consumption-oriented, and very difficult to mobilize. The record of the past few years indicates that a single event — no matter how dramatic it might look — can hardly knock Russian society off balance. It paid little attention to German unification, stoically survived Soviet disintegration, and has stayed mostly indifferent to the war in Chechnya. There exist no empirical, sociological data to suggest that the enlargement of NATO would cause radical shifts in the general Russian public's attitudes, much less engender a psychological trauma sufficient to cause the triumph of radical nationalists, militant revanchists, or the like.

The psychological impact of a possible NATO enlargement upon Russian society is also limited by the fact that it would not constitute such a clear-cut and sudden change in international politics as to make the world different, literally overnight. (In this respect, it could not come close to rivalling the dissolution of the Soviet Union.) If enlargement happens at all, it will be a long, drawn-out process, with many setbacks and interruptions — a process, in short, that would be incapable of gripping the imagination or making the blood freeze in the veins of an ordinary Russian.

As other chapters in this volume have indicated, there exist numerous uncertainties about how the decision to enlarge is going to be implemented and what mode of participation is envisioned for the new members. There are no easy answers to many key questions, which are of crucial importance for Russian national security. When will new members be admitted? Which Central European countries will be asked to join?

Will all new participants be fully covered by Article 5 of the North Atlantic Treaty? Will the joint military organization of NATO expand its zone of responsibility to all of Eastern Europe, extending to the very borders of Russia? Will all new members participate fully in the joint military organization of NATO? Will foreign bases and facilities be established in Eastern Europe? Will foreign troops be permanently stationed there? Will nuclear weapons be deployed? What kind of military strategy will NATO need to adopt as a result of enlargement?

Given all these uncertainties and the current vagueness of the enlargement concept, it is very difficult to sell the "new NATO threat" to the general Russian public or even to politically concerned individuals. But political and military élites in Moscow do take the NATO-enlargement issue much more seriously. One might accuse them of hypocrisy when they refer to the "Russian people" in justifying their own opposition to NATO's going east, but nobody can deny that this has become a top-ranking question on the country's political agenda.

NATO enlargement is more than just visible in editorial columns of Moscow dailies, on the podium of the State Duma, and at numerous academic conferences and seminars. For the top "ten thousand" of Russia's decisionmakers and opinion shapers, the issue is a crucial litmus test foreshadowing the future of relations between Russia and the west. True, there are other litmus tests — to name but three: START-2, Bosnia, and IMF credits — but no other single issue better captures the myriad dimensions of Russian-western interaction in the post-Cold War period.

The opposition to Boris Yeltsin's leadership in Moscow, nationalist and liberal alike, tends to interpret the "expansion" of the Atlantic alliance, with Russia being left on the outside, as one of the most serious defeats, if not *the* most serious defeat, of the Yeltsin-Kozyrev foreign policy during the past four years. It is the ultimate proof that Russian policy since 1991 has been based on profoundly incorrect assumptions, which have led the country down a blind alley.

It is well known that Moscow welcomed the January 1994 NATO decision to launch the "Partnership for Peace" (PFP) program, which implied some possibilities for military cooperation between NATO and Russia, and looked like being an alternative to the alliance's expansion. Moscow, however, was very slow to negotiate specific terms of its participation in PFP. Foreign Minister Andrei Kozyrev's appeal for a special status for Russia was rejected by the west, which interpreted it as a demand for a "veto power" over admittance of new members to NATO.

In the eyes of many in Russia, PFP seemed designed to prepare the ground for an early enlargement of NATO while, at the same time, excluding Russia from new European defence arrangements. In early December 1994, NATO reached a decision in principle to admit some Central European countries into the alliance. While the exact terms, conditions, and timing remain to be determined (issues covered in John Barrett's chapter), apparently the Czech Republic, Poland, and Hungary will be among the first new members. Other former Warsaw Pact countries may follow later, and Baltic states and other former Soviet republics will at some point also be considered among the candidates.

Yeltsin himself has been unable to close his eyes to NATO's enlargement, even if he may not consider it to be a real security challenge to Russia.[1] He has already committed himself to opposing enlargement, and never misses a chance to raise the problem in bilateral negotiations and multilateral fora. The obvious unwillingness of the west to take into account Russian objections forced Yeltsin at the very last moment to reverse the decision to sign the documents on Moscow's participation in the PFP. And at the CFE summit in Budapest, Yeltsin discovered that Russia's proposals to turn the newly created Organization for Security and Cooperation in Europe (OSCE) into the cornerstone of European security would be discounted by President Clinton and other western leaders. Angered, Yeltsin had to concede defeat, but not without warning the west that the Cold War might be replaced by a "Cold Peace."

The following May, Russia did decide to join PFP, but the importance of NATO-Russian military cooperation was at the time overshadowed by the major political dispute gathering momentum over NATO's enlargement, which was interpreted by all major Russian political groups as an unfriendly gesture. It seemed that the west had decided to consolidate its victory in the Cold War and fill the "vacuum," or buffer zone, created between Russia and NATO as a result of the withdrawal of Russian troops from Central and Eastern Europe through the absorption of former Soviet satellites and the isolation of Russia. No matter how NATO enlargement might influence the security problems of Russia in practical terms, the issue has acquired major symbolic significance, turning into a matter of principle that no political party or movement in Russia can ignore or downplay.

Enlargement of NATO: The Nationalist Interpretation

The nationalistic position on NATO enlargement, now shared by most communist and neocommunist groups alike, boils down to the general presumption that Russia is being pushed out of its traditional sphere of influence at the same time that a potentially hostile bloc is being erected closer to its western borders. Nationalists, as a rule, underscore that despite all its soothing and even "Russia-friendly" rhetoric, NATO remains a defensive alliance and thus its main purpose must remain that of any such alliance, to oppose a common enemy. Except for Russia, NATO members do not have such a common enemy and it seems highly unlikely that they might acquire one in any foreseeable future. (They may have other threats and challenges, but these are threats and challenges to particular NATO states or groups of states, not to the alliance at large.) Russia remains the usual suspect, and the expansion of NATO is a logical step that allows NATO (or even the west in general) to obtain geostrategic advantage over Russia in the event of possible conflicts in the future.[2]

Furthermore, classic international relations theory stipulates that a military alliance can only serve three specific functions: defence, deterrence, or aggression. Since, as nationalists argue, Russia does not and will not have in any foreseeable future a military potential capable of threatening the west or even Central Europe (the Chechen experience is an explicit example of the current poor state of the Russian army), the idea of NATO as a defensive structure against a resurgent Russian imperialism makes little sense. Therefore, NATO is left with two other functions: deterrence and aggression. If it is not planning a direct aggression against Russia, it can employ its military might, enhanced by its eastward expansion, for the purpose of political pressure, even blackmail.

Even if NATO does not harbour any immediate hostile intentions toward Russia, its evident conservatism in changing strategic plans and patterns of operation (e.g., the reluctance to adjust radically its nuclear posture) is a clear indication that NATO today and in the future will not be a partner, but rather an opponent, of Moscow's. Nationalist-minded Russian generals like to stress that — judging from NATO's current training programs, procurement policies, deployment patterns, and field manuals — the alliance is still planning to fight a large-scale conventional (and offensive) war in Europe. This "traditionalism," in the view of Russian nationalists, can hardly be explained by bureaucratic inertia or the lack of imagination on the part of NATO officials in Brussels; it must have deeper roots. NATO wants to keep its powder dry not to counter a new Saddam Hussein or to prevent Islamic fundamentalism from triumphing in Turkey, but rather to contain Russia.

Finally, nationalists claim that NATO's current enlargement plans are not an improvised reaction to pledges made to a number of Central European states; they are a step in a more general, and long-term, western strategy that includes paving the way for a gradual revision of the neutral status of such countries as Austria, Sweden, and Finland, while being intended to deny to Russia the opportunity to consolidate around itself the other former Soviet republics.[3] Given the perceived unwillingness of Washington to let Russia into the emerging pacific community of states, the enlargement of NATO is held to be an important component of a new "encirclement policy" allegedly being directed by the west toward Russia.

NATO enlargement is analyzed by Russian nationalists in the broader framework of the alliance's activities during the past few years, which include, among other things, the Gulf War and military involvement in the former Yugoslavia. The Gulf War is considered to be a very clear signal that NATO intends to engage itself in out-of-area operations policing the Third World. The bombing of Bosnian Serbs is interpreted as being even more threatening to Russia, as a signal of NATO's intention to impose its will on the whole of Europe by direct application of military force.[4] Some civilian and military experts go further, suggesting that strikes against Bosnian Serbs are nothing less than a "dress rehearsal" for possible NATO aggression against Russia itself.[5]

The enlargement of NATO is considered in this context to be something more sinister than just an opportunistic or forced move. Nationalists accuse the west, and in particular the US and Germany, of violating some tacit understandings with, and commitments to, the former Soviet Union.[6] Yeltsin and Kozyrev are accused by nationalists of having been too slow to realize this threat from NATO, and of allowing themselves to be misled by the general talk of a "strategic partnership" between Russia and the United States.

Of course, more radical nationalists argue that the Kremlin policy was not just a naïve and romantic attempt to "join the west" based on a number of misperceptions and false assumptions, but rather a planned conspiracy of prowestern subversive forces in the Kremlin who knew perfectly well exactly what they were doing. The conspiracy theory interprets the last ten years of Soviet/Russian foreign policy as a chain of deliberate actions (including such deeds as the unification of Germany, withdrawal from Central Europe, the CFE treaty, and the START-1 and START-2 treaties) whose intent is to weaken Russia, deprive it of its great-power status, destroy its military might, and subordinate it to the west. Boris Yeltsin and, especially, Andrei Kozyrev are perceived as the masterminds behind this process.

Enlargement of NATO: The Liberal Interpretation

The liberals' criticism of Yeltsin's policies toward NATO, as well as their interpretation of the reasons for and consequences of the possibility of enlargement, are very different from the nationalists' views. Russian liberals claim that the inconsistent and passive approach of the Kremlin to NATO has been compounded by an inability to come to terms with rapidly changing European political developments. Further complicating factors have been hysterical nationalistic outbursts by the Russian leadership, and attempts to solve difficult political problems through military force (such as the storming of the Russian Parliament by Yeltsin in October 1993, or the war in Chechnya launched in December 1994), which combined have pushed the west into a corner. Despite all good intentions toward Russia, and almost contrary to their own long-term interests, the United States and its Western European allies have had to yield to the pressure of the Visegrad group and accelerate the latter's political and military integration with the west.

The decision to enlarge, as Russian liberals understand it, was in no way part of a sinister master plan of the west's aimed at weakening and isolating Russia, but an improvised and probably not well-conceived reaction to the changing international situation. Liberals also tend to emphasize the role of domestic politics in such NATO countries as the United States and Canada, where powerful ethnic communities from Central Europe launched an active lobbying campaign for the prompt admission of "their" countries to NATO. Finally, many liberals in Moscow believe that the primary reason for NATO's enlargement is the desperate need for the alliance to find a new mission for itself after the end of the Cold War, and they understand that the dilemma facing the alliance today is "to enlarge or to perish."

Russia, in the view of its liberals, failed to make full use of the opportunities that were opened to it in the framework of the Partnership for Peace program. Russian reactions to PFP were slow and unimaginative. Russian diplomacy either tended, for a long time, to slight the CSCE/OSCE as a potential counterweight to NATO in the field of European security or, in the opposite sense, proposed such radical plans for reforming the CSCE/OSCE that most of the European states did not even care to discuss them. What is even more important, liberals argue, is that Yeltsin's leadership failed to start any meaningful military reform, and instead desperately tried to preserve all the worst features of the Soviet army: *inter alia* its size, structure, insularity, overbureaucratization, corruption, and immunity from any real civilian control. The Russian army in its current state is simply not compatible with NATO forces and Moscow has been doomed to lose the race to join the west to its more dynamic and reform-oriented CEE neighbours.

Most liberals appear to believe that the enlargement of NATO will not strengthen the alliance, but will weaken its military capabilities. Among other things, they see enlargement undermining the credibility of US strategic guarantees to Europe, complicating the decisionmaking process within NATO, and creating the need for escalating investments aimed at the modernization of Central European armies, training, and infrastructure. Therefore, they find no reason to speak of a "new threat from the west." Besides, a liberal approach to the west and its values assumes that democratic countries in any case cannot present a threat to other democracies, by virtue of their political institutions, traditions, and procedures; no matter how strong NATO might become, a liberal and democratic Russia will have nothing to fear from it.[7]

In general, Russian liberals tend to look at NATO not as a classic defensive alliance, but as a mechanism for foreign and defence policy coordination among western democracies. That is why the liberal approach dismisses the nationalists' fears and concerns rooted in traditional international relations theory. This logic also implies that the enlargement of NATO can even be a positive development for Russia because it will widen the "global democratic space" and bring political stability to Central Europe. Moreover, Central European states anchored to the western security system will find it easier to overcome their historic animosities and prejudices toward Russia, and will therefore be in a better position to develop a more balanced and constructive relationship with their eastern neighbour. In fact, the concept of NATO enlargement has been interpreted by liberals rather broadly — not only in the military-political sense but also in terms of history and philosophy. NATO is regarded as a mechanism that is instrumental in modernizing societies, overcoming nationalistic aberrations, and conditioning the thinking and behaviour of new political élites.[8]

Russian liberals argue that the reason why it has proved possible to avert ethnic and international conflicts in Western Europe is because the former adversaries there managed to develop a relationship of confidence and partnership. In its turn, confidence within the NATO framework was a "spin-off" of the cooperation achieved by the members of the bloc in the military field, with the probability of war between allies being, as a rule, in inverse proportion to the level of military integration between them. (The example of the Greek-Turkish rivalry appears to confirm this relationship: although both countries were integrated into basic NATO structures by the mid-1970s, the level of *bilateral* Greek-Turkish military integration remained extremely low.)[9]

Responding to the nationalists' criticism of NATO enlargement, liberals also argue that it will be a long and precarious process with only remote practical results that might theoretically affect Russia in a negative way. Territorial extension of NATO will definitely involve substantial financial responsibilities — rearmament, retraining of personnel, and most of all, creating new operational and logistical infrastructure. The overwhelming share of these expenses can be covered only by Western European governments. It seems very easy to conclude, argue the liberals, that it is the Western European voters and taxpayers who will ultimately decide the fate of such expenditures, and therefore of NATO expansion.

As is noted in several other chapters in this volume, a thorough discussion of NATO extension and its expected consequences has hardly begun in the west. When it does, four allied countries will likely be among the most vociferous. Spain, Portugal, Greece, and to a lesser extent Italy all face certain problems in accelerating their pace of modernization and in surmounting their economic model of "dualistic growth." NATO extension is even now being interpreted by some interest groups in Southern Europe as a diversion of resources vital for economic and social transformation in their region. Thus, from a liberal view point, even if the enlarged NATO at some point in the distant future were to consider turning into a genuine defensive alliance aimed at Russia, it would encounter very serious problems in generating adequate resources and political will.[10]

On the other hand, a number of Russian liberal-minded experts on the Central European countries assume that even Hungary, Poland, and the Czech Republic will have second thoughts about their full integration into NATO structures once they get a fuller understanding of the financial, political, and other commitments they will have to make and the standards they will have to meet. Given their desperate need for resources in such fields as the environment, education, health care, and culture, it is very unlikely that parliaments in these countries will readily vote for purchases of expensive western military equipment, or the modernization of their defence infrastructure.

However, the exclusion of Russia from an emerging system of European security that has NATO as its cornerstone, from a liberal point of view, will have significant negative political implications for Moscow. Russia will become marginalized in European politics, and be reduced to a semi-European, peripheral country with no more than limited access to pan-European affairs.[11] In other words, the danger for Russia lies not in NATO enlargement per se, but in the inability of Russia to join the process. Liberals are concerned that the enlargement of NATO will bring to life the old Russian complex of inferiority that, in turn, can make it more difficult to integrate Russia into western political, economic, and security structures.

The idea of using NATO as the embryo of a new European security order is attacked by Russian liberals from yet another angle. There is a lack of clarity about the stages of integration of the states of Central Europe, and equally about the criteria for the selection of candidates. Should the states of Central Europe be admitted to NATO in the first stage, the FSU republics would have good reason to consider themselves discriminated against. Should Ukraine, Belarus, and the Baltic countries join the alliance in the second stage, then Russia could find itself in a rather vulnerable geostrategic position. Should the dominant criterion for admission be the measure of progress toward both democratization and the market economy, the political landscape of Europe would begin to resemble a disassembled children's mosaic. Furthermore, it is often argued that a "selective" involvement of the CEE countries in NATO might disrupt delicate subregional balances in Europe. For example, if Hungary becomes a member but Rumania does not, Budapest will undoubtedly be tempted to take advantage of its new status to pressure Bucharest over the issue of Transylvania. The selective inclusion of some republics of ex-Yugoslavia in NATO could also change the power balance in the Balkans with possible negative consequences.

One of the most immediate negative consequences of NATO enlargement, as liberals see it, will be the inevitable erosion of the entire arms-control regime between Russia and the west. It would be practically impossible for Russia not to revise START-1 and START-2, as well as the CFE and INF treaties, given the completely new geostrategic situation in Europe. On this point, liberals basically align themselves with nationalists, though they might have very different assessments of the genuine challenge that NATO might pose to Russian security.[12]

Finally, even those Russian liberals who demonstrate full understanding of NATO's enlargement dilemmas still point out that the timing of the move — no matter how symbolic it might be and how limited the impact it will have on Russia's security — is extremely ill-chosen. They argue that the decision to take in new members coincided with a change of political moods in Russia, and with growing frustrations over the country's inability successfully to introduce market reforms and liberal democracy as well as to join the community of western states. NATO turned out to be insensitive to the difficulties of the domestic political transition in Russia, thus strengthening the cause of anti-western and anti-reform forces.[13]

This insensitivity was exacerbated, in the thinking of liberals, by the alleged unwillingness of NATO to consult Russia on other issues or to take into account Russian concerns and interests.[14] Though liberals do not interpret NATO's neglect as a purposeful strategy aimed at humiliating Russia and pushing it out of Europe, they do insist that the scant respect the alliance has accorded to Russian positions on a number of international issues could not but boost anti-NATO feelings in the country.

Alternative Russian Responses, I: Redivision of Europe

On the basis of their very different perceptions of NATO in general and, in particular, of the motives and goals of the enlargement project, Russian nationalists and liberals suggest varying responses that Russia might consider, under the circumstances. One can single out at least four such options for Russia in case enlargement can be neither stopped nor slowed down.

The first option can be labelled the "new division of Europe." The decision to enlarge is interpreted in this context as a tacit proposal to Russia, from the west, to split Europe into "spheres of influence." Since the former Soviet republics (with the possible exception of the Baltic states) are not perceived in the west as serious candidates to join NATO in any observable future, they will by default remain within the Russian strategic zone of influence. Russia has to recognize and honour the fact of NATO expansion as a result of the "western victory" in the Cold War. It should also accept the fact that Central Europe (at least, the four Visegrad states) will gravitate to the western cultural, political, and economic space and that this movement cannot be stopped.

However, in exchange for such recognition the west for its part should recognize the "special role" of Russia on the territory of the former Soviet Union and, perhaps, also in the larger eastern and southeastern corners of Europe that will be left outside of the expanding NATO. In other words, Russia should get from the west a more-or-less explicit endorsement of its role as leader of the European misfits.

The "new-division" option touches upon a question that transcends the Russia-NATO relationship. The core of the problem discussed here is how to define Russia's rights and responsibilities in respect of the other independent states — that is, the FSU republics. Does Russia have the right to a "sphere of influence" on this territory, and if it does, how can Russian neoimperialism and collisions with western countries be precluded? Is Russia committed to supporting the neighbouring states economically (for example, by supplying them with power resources on soft terms and keeping its markets open to their goods) and if it is, how can it be made to honour these commitments and refrain from blackmailing economically the other post-Soviet republics? What, in general, must be accomplished to get those other republics to expect no potential threat from Russia and to prevent the latter, in turn, from feeling isolated?

Within the framework of current political debates in Moscow, the "new division of Europe" might suggest the following avenues for Russian policy:

- aggressive promotion of a "collective-security system" erected on the territory of the former USSR (i.e., Russia should push hard to forge a practical mechanism for implementing the Tashkent Treaty on Collective Security of 15 May 1992);
- active bilateral diplomacy within the CIS (above all, new efforts to supplement the existing strategic alliance with Belarus by similar arrangements with Ukraine and Kazakhstan and, if possible, also with Georgia and Armenia; if and when necessary Russia should use economic sticks and carrots as well as a whole spectrum of political means at its disposal to make the above-mentioned countries more cooperative);
- attempts to reach a CIS consensus position toward the PFP program and develop coordinated CIS positions on NATO in general; negotiate with NATO on a "division of responsibilities" in peacekeeping, which would imply an explicit or implicit recognition by the west of the leading role of Russia in the CIS;
- clear and unambiguous renunciation by Russia of the CFE treaty as being outdated and in contradiction of the new strategic situation in Europe; development and implementation of a new Russian military doctrine that would provide for adequate capabilities to play a "leading security role" on the territory of the former Soviet Union;
- demands that NATO not extend its activities to the territory of the Baltic states and that it preserve the status quo regarding the Kaliningrad region;
- getting a western commitment written into OSCE documents not to bring CIS states into military-political alliances potentially hostile to Russia, in exchange for a Russian pledge not to interfere in the internal affairs of its closest neighbours.

The "new-division" option is not necessarily hostile to the west. Its proponents believe that the west is in any case not interested in projecting its influence to places like Ukraine or Belarus or, at least, that the west is not ready to commit the political, military, and economic resources needed to integrate former Soviet republics into its civilizational space. Therefore, Russia is allegedly perceived by western politicians to be the dominant power in the region; the only question remaining is whether its domination takes less benign or more benign forms.

According to this logic, redividing Europe would mean nothing more than a formal acceptance of existing realities. In particular, it would imply that the west should not try to extend NATO into the territory of the former USSR or to feed any illusions in some of the former Soviet republics that they will some day qualify for NATO membership. The future security architecture of the European continent would be based on two equal pillars — NATO and the CIS — each being responsible for stability in "its" part of the continent. Naturally, this option would require some form of institutionalization of the CIS-NATO relationship, so that the former could enjoy its proper status within the new architecture of Europe. Agreements between the two institutions should settle the principles and directions of NATO-CIS cooperation in order to safeguard international security while not duplicating the future CFE-2 treaty.

Such a solution, say its proponents, could lessen the possibility of a clash of interests between Russia and NATO over the CEE states and would make the situation in that region more stable and predictable. At the same time it would limit the possible manifestations of neoimperialism on Russia's part, preventing Moscow from adopting a "Monroe doctrine" of its own in respect of the neighbours next door. The "Finlandization" of FSU republics could, some have suggested, be accompanied by a Russian undertaking to act as an economic counterbalance for Eurasia, forswearing excessive practices in trading and monetary relations in a manner similar to that of Germany in the European Community. Finally, Russia could make itself principally responsible for the maintenance and development of the region's infrastructure, including for instance its transport and energy system, and its information and telecommunication channels.

On the other hand, should the west not "behave," the new division of Europe could lead to a mini-Cold War occurring on the continent. Russia would then have to consolidate its sphere of influence even if the west were opposed. In that case, the division of Europe might take more confrontational forms, with two military blocs opposing each other and a new "iron curtain" separating them.[15] A tough Russian response to NATO enlargement also implies a renewed accent on nuclear weapons, with new NATO members chosen as prime targets for Russian missiles.[16] Some argue that Russia should not stop even at violating the existing nuclear arms-control treaties in order to meet the new challenge of NATO, and should as well avoid making any additional commitments in this field.[17]

Needless to say, radical nationalists who have always been suspicious of the west and confident of a "special place" for Russia in global civilization, would clearly prefer the confrontational outcome. Among other things, a new confrontation with the west would allow them to justify both a new emphasis on defence and security and a shift toward authoritarianism in domestic Russian politics.

However, even in its most moderate form the idea of a "special relationship" between NATO and Russia raises a whole series of fundamental objections. First, the recognition of a new division of Europe would be viewed by conservative American politicians and certainly by the leadership of the country's respective ethnic communities as constituting nothing less than a betrayal of the interests of the newly established states and a de facto surrender of them to Russian control. Most of these states are believed to regard Russia, first and foremost, as the main threat to their security, and, indeed, to their independence and sovereignty, and therefore would never settle for a "new Yalta."

Second, the concept of a "new division of Europe" is based, in the opinion of liberal analysts, on the implicit premise that the interests of Russia and those of the west in this part of the world would materially diverge and even clash. Yet this kind of opposition is not obvious at all. In particular, the Yeltsin-Kozyrev policy of 1992 through 1994 toward the countries adjoining Russia aroused no particular criticism in the US. As to the involvement of the new states in military-political alliances, this question has not even been raised in practical terms so far; the countries of Eastern Europe seem to have been virtually denied admission to NATO. In this sense, implicit mutual understanding between Russia and the west is preferable to any formalized agreement.

Third, it has been noted that any "new Yalta," no matter the form it might take, would bind both Russia and the west, one way or another, and lead to an artificial disruption of Europe's common security space, now in the making, notably the OSCE mechanisms. Moreover, in the event of any dramatic turn in Russia's foreign policy, a "new Yalta" could even goad the new states of the region into forming an anti-Russian alliance (for instance, a Ukrainian-led one) to create their own regional balance.

Fourth, political instability in Russia itself and the uncertainty of the prospects ahead for its foreign policy call in question the value of any arrangements aimed at long-term strategic compromise. Such arrangements could be disavowed or modified unilaterally by a new team of Russian leaders.

Fifth and finally, it is still an open question to what degree Russia can turn itself into the centre of gravity for post-Soviet political space. Assessments made in 1992-93 (both in Russia and the west) of the performance of the CIS and of its future prospects can be regarded as a species of indirect criticism of the very concept of a Russian "special responsibility" in the FSU zone. These assessments were, for the most part, distinguished by their extreme criticism. The Community was originally expected to exist for just a few months, being, as a matter of fact, no more than a makeshift structure to dismantle the Soviet Union, but that view gave way to another that held the CIS could actually survive for a relatively long span of time — precisely because of its institutional weakness and political nullity. The fragility of the CIS was interpreted, notably, as a sign of weakness of Russia's positions, and as evidence that the centrifugal trends on FSU territory still prevailed over the centripetal ones. in this context, a "Finlandization" of the republics immediately bordering on Russia appeared practically unrealizable. Even less practical seems the idea expressed by President Yeltsin that CIS could be turned into a counterbalance to NATO.[18]

Alternative Russian Responses, II: OSCE versus NATO

The second option is that of pitting the OSCE against NATO. This implies that Russia still has opportunities to prevent NATO from monopolizing the security agenda in Europe. Since NATO is not an all-European structure (for even should it grow by another four or five states, it will still represent a minority of European countries), the bloc cannot claim legitimacy and unconditional support from all European states. The OSCE, on the contrary, is a truly pan-European forum comprising as well the United States and Canada. Consequently, an OSCE decision can be considered "legitimate" for Europe, while any NAT0 decision may be challenged by states outside the bloc.

Moreover, it bears noting that the CSCE (the predecessor of the OSCE) was conceived from the very start as a mechanism of collective security in Europe, while NATO was formed in the clamant Cold War environment to discharge functions having nothing to do with collective security. NATO's record in settling conflicts that have arisen between its members can hardly be unequivocally defined as successful. No way has been found to stop the conflict between Greece and Turkey, and the problem has been passed on to the United Nations. Neither was the dispute between Great Britain and Spain over Gibraltar resolved in Brussels, NATO preferring to qualify the problem as an issue of bilateral Anglo-Spanish relations. The point is that most of the probable international conflicts in Eastern Europe can be likened precisely to the Greco-Turkish or the Gibraltar problems rather than to any far-fetched breakthrough by Warsaw Pact tanks to the Channel — which is of course what NATO was structured to oppose for decades. In other words, to turn NATO into the bedrock of a collective-security system in Europe would require a revision of the very foundations of this aliance, while for the OSCE such a transformation would be a matter of natural evolution.

As a NATO outsider, Russia should concentrate on building the broadest possible coalition of states interested in promoting OSCE mechanisms. The prime goals of Russian policy in this regard should be the following:

- to make sure that all the peacekeeping problems in Europe fall under the exclusive jurisdiction of the OSCE; that NATO deprived of any broadly defined or ambiguous mandate on peacekeeping operations on a bloc basis (as was allegedly the case in Bosnia); to promote a more active role of the OSCE in peacekeeping on the territory of the former Soviet Union and Russia proper — even if this role looks annoying and uncomfortable for the Russian military in cases such as Chechnya;
- to use the OSCE mechanism in order to revise the CFE treaty on a new non-bloc basis (the new CFE-2 treaty should replace the bloc ceilings with national ones); to turn the OSCE into the all-European arms-control mechanism and to prevent NATO from substituting the "first basket" of the OSCE process with its own institutions and mechanisms;
- to make sure that Russia enjoys a preferential status within new, enhanced OSCE structures (e.g., Russia would get a permanent membership on a European Security Council with a veto right similar to the one it has in the UN; as well, Russia receives a number of votes in OSCE bodies that reflect its size, power, and stature in European politics).

In a way, the "OSCE-vs.-NATO" option can be regarded both as liberal and relatively favourable to the west. Moreover, it looks preferential, in the sense of forging new relations between Russia and Central European countries that bring benefit to the latter. In a historical context, Central Europe's "manifest destiny" is to reemerge as a kind of geopolitical bridge connecting Western and Southern Europe with Russia, enabling it to exploit to the fullest its geographical centrality and permitting it to recapture the very capacious Russian market. The attraction of this for the CEE states inheres in the obvious difficulty they will experience in integrating into Western European institutions. Economic cooperation based on vital mutual interests should ultimately displace deep-seated anti-Russian fears and prejudices in the region. Most certainly, the process would solidify psychological confidence and a sense of personal and collective security among the Central European countries. But to lay the political foundation for such an economic interaction between Russia and its immediate western neighbours, an all-European institution is needed, one that would bring Russia and Central Europe together, not draw them apart.

As for the security concerns of the Central European countries and their desire to "join Europe," NATO is not the only instrument capable of satisfying both. A viable alternative is to be found in a rapid admission of the Visegrad states to the EU and the WEU, while decoupling WEU membership from membership to NATO.[19] Indeed, if the west is so concerned about democracy and market reforms in Central Europe, why should it not concentrate on the enlargement of the European Union instead of NATO? After all, the EU will have a much deeper and more comprehensive influence on the development of Central Europe than will NATO.

On the other hand, if the Western European allies of the US are not even ready to make relatively moderate economic sacrifices to accommodate their eastern neighbours within an enlarged EU, it is doubtful that they could be truly concerned about stability in Central Europe, no matter what their leaders might have to say on that topic. Moreover, the evident unwillingness of Western Europeans to fight domestic protectionism on behalf of Central European producers must put into question an assumption that Western Europeans would ever fight a real war for the sake of Central Europe. In any case, the enlargement of NATO as a "cheap" substitute for the enlargement of the EU is logically untenable.

Despite all its surface attractiveness, an OSCE-centred security order in Europe looks much less realistic than the "division-of-Europe" option. First, the claim that there can be an efficient collective-security system is regarded with utmost skepticism by many experts, in Russia and the west alike. They point to numerous historic failures to introduce such a system — from ancient Greece to Europe between this century's two world wars. The principle of consensus as a core mechanism of the OSCE imposes a major limitation on its functioning, especially given the large number of countries that joined the organization after the disintegration of the Soviet Union and Yugoslavia.

Second, even if such an order could be achieved, it seems highly unlikely that Russia would ever be entitled to any kind of special status within it. Most of the European states would oppose all attempts to replicate in Europe the UN Security Council, with its tiny élite of permanent members. On a more general note, the very idea of a United Nations for Europe can hardly look attractive, in light of the recent experience of the UN itself.

Alternative Russian Responses, III:
Membership through Partnership

This option seems to be the one most favourably disposed both to NATO and the west. It implies an active and consistent Russian policy aimed at strengthening and deepening the country's cooperation with the alliance. The idea is that if cooperation takes root and covers areas of crucial importance for both Russia and the west, at some point the entire matter of NATO expansion to the east will become irrelevant. Even though formally outside the alliance, Russia would be in a position to exercise substantial influence on NATO decisions that might directly or indirectly impinge upon its interests. In many ways Russia would be more important to NATO than those smaller Central European states that would formally join the alliance. In particular, proponents of this option suggest that Russia should concentrate on the following:

- to get NATO's commitment not to take any military decisions that could have a negative impact on Russia's security (as a first step, Russia should insist upon a formal confirmation of the alliance's currently stated intentions — e.g., not to deploy nuclear weapons on the territories of new members, not to build major military bases in Central Europe); NATO should also commit itself not to conduct military activities on the territories of the Baltic states and other former Soviet republics;[20]

- to promote further evolution of military-technical and operational plans and postures of NATO in a direction favourable to Russia;
- to negotiate with NATO nondiscriminatory access of Russia to European (and other) arms markets, including a "fair share" for Russian defence industries in the forthcoming modernization of Central European armies (optimists even believe in a single American-European-Russian arms and military-technology market, within which Russia and Ukraine would occupy a worthy place. Such a market would imply standardizing the major types of armaments, lifting restrictions on access of the post-Soviet republics to western military technologies, adopting common rules of competition for producers within that single market, devising a system of supervision over the export of military technologies to developing countries, and so on);
- to insist upon a qualitatively new, higher-level cooperation between Russia and NATO in the area of defence conversion and coordination of military-industrial policies in general;
- to work out and put in practice a mechanism for ongoing, high-level political and military consultations between Russia and NATO.

The "Membership-through-Partnership" option assumes Russian-NATO cooperation on the basis of profound compromise, with each side doing its best to recognize the legitimate security interests of the other, so that there could be no question of concessions coming only from the Russian side. The key elements of this approach are to put the existing political understanding between Russia and the west on a legally binding basis and to institutionalize the relationship by creating a network of structures for joint decisionmaking and cooperative implementation of decisions. Proponents of the third option argue that Russia has a great deal to offer in exchange for NATO's good will. Russia can provide guarantees, for example, that it will not build up its conventional forces near neighbouring states to the west, or use military threats against any neighbouring state; it can also pledge to continue the denuclearization process.

Yet another advantage stressed by the champions of this model of integrating the post-Soviet republics into western security structures is that NATO is now beginning to diversify its functions. In addition to planning for traditional military-political objectives, NATO and its various bodies are trying to make their contribution towards resolving problems related to the conversion of military production and to the environment; as well, NATO endeavours to coordinate the industrial research policies of its member countries. This is to say that "linking up" with NATO becomes a matter of particular value to the FSU republics, while NAT0, for its part, would get further important leverage on the foreign policies and defence strategies of the new states.

Opponents of this option usually refer to one of two arguments, depending on which political camp they inhabit. Nationalists argue that Russia cannot possibly trust NATO. The alliance's leadership, squeezed between Russian concerns and pressures from Central Europe, may well promise almost any kind of "special relationship" with Moscow in order to get the latter's consent to enlargement. However, the political and legal content of any such agreement would by definition have to be inferior to the agreements governing new members' acceptance. In a sense, Russia would become hostage to its special relationship with NATO, for the west could employ the threat of revising or abrogating the agreement at its own discretion when and if it considered Russian behaviour to be inappropriate.

Liberals argue that it is Russia, not the west, that is not ready for a special relationship. Without meaningful military reform in the country, all attempts to coordinate defence-conversion or defence industries in general are doomed to failure. Likewise without such a reform Russian producers will hardly be in a position to become integrated into a common western international arms market. Furthermore, in order to interact with NATO, Russia will need to take a "more responsible" stand on many international issues transcending the security problems of Europe.

Alternative Russian Responses, IV: Getting Russia into NATO

The most radical option is to try to get Russia into NATO as a full-fledged member. This option was very popular a half-decade or so ago, when Russian liberals in Moscow were trying to enter every western international institution the Soviet Union had formerly opposed. Even President Yeltsin stated that to enter NATO was a strategic goal of Russia's. The idea has never taken on any practical form; it lost most of its original supporters between 1993 and the present, and survives as more or less a fantasy of radical democrats. However, from time to time the option is revisited by serious scholars and politicians seeking to break out of the vicious logic of traditional arguments exchanged between Russia and NATO.

There could be said to be four historically established models of integration of individual states in the political and military mechanisms of NATO. The first is the "German model," which presupposes the complete integration of a state's armed forces in NATO structures. The second is the "French model" that, to the contrary, is limited to political cooperation while leaving intact the member's military independence — without, however, precluding consultations and interaction on specific military matters. The third model applies to the majority of the other European NATO countries, and it implies subordinating most of their national contingents to the unified NATO command in the event of war or acute crisis, while preserving the autonomy of military planning and management in time of peace. Finally, the fourth, the "American model," means putting the unified NATO command in control of a smaller proportion of one's national forces (those deployed in Europe), while pledging to place under that command about half the country's forces deployed in other parts of the world.

Which, if any, of these models might be applicable to Russia? The most conservative assumption holds one to be the most practicable, at least in the short to medium term, namely the "French" model. Any other model would require too much painful reshaping within NATO. Besides, as the advocates of this model point out, Russia is not prepared at this time for closer association with NATO; like the France of the 1960s and 1970s, it has yet to live through a period of unalloyed, but apparently unavoidable, nationalism (albeit in a moderate, not aggressive, form) — notably in its foreign and defence policies. Only in a decade or two might it be right and proper to speak of Russia's comprehensive integration into NATO's political and military institutions. The "French model" for Russia is rather popular among moderate liberals in the State Duma, where it is supported, for example, by the chairman of the defence committee, Sergey Yushenkov.

The "American model" also has some supporters. They note a certain symmetry of America's and Russia's position in relation to the European continent. Since Russia is not a purely European power and its strategic interests extend to other regions, it is hardly worthwhile insisting on full "geographic" integration. On the other hand, neither would the current (and, perhaps, new) NATO members be keen to assume any automatic obligations regarding the defence of the southern and eastern borders of the Russian Federation.

At the same time, an "American" or a "French" solution to Russia's integration could well prove insufficient from the standpoint of strategic and political stability on the European continent. After all, the main problem for Russia's foreign policy in Europe is not the inadequacy of political links with the west but the fact that most of Russia's westerly next-door neighbours — whether from among the former Soviet republics or in Central Europe — view the Russian Federation as, at least, a potential threat to their security and even to their existence as independent states. How much ground there is for such fears, and whether it is right to consider Russia as a direct descendant of Soviet statism, remain debatable. But there is no denying the mistrust and suspicion in the capitals of the neighbouring states with regard to Moscow's policy.

In this sense, the problem of Russia's integration into the western security order has very much in common, indeed, with West Germany's integration into NATO in the 1950s. Germany after the Second World War engendered, just as Russia does today, mistrust and suspicion on the part of its closest neighbours.

In fact, this is what made it imperative to work out a special "German model" of integration. It was precisely the most complete integration of Germany into the Atlantic alliance and the melding of the Bundeswehr with NATO structures that made it possible to overcome the anti-German fears and suspicions of Western Europe.

It is hard to presume that the "German model" of the 1950s could be carbon-copied by Russia in the 1990s, if only because Russia is not a vanquished and occupied country whose sovereignty has been limited and military machine destroyed. But if there can be any involvement of Russia at all, it will be politically worthwhile only if comprehensive and far-reaching. The more "internationalized" the Russian armed forces are, the easier will it be for Russia to resolve its political problems with its next-door neighbours.

Conclusion

It is precisely because the Russia of today is not the Germany of 40 years ago that Russia's hypothetical integration into NATO, attended by the "internationalization" of its armed forces, would be impossible, if attempted unilaterally. To integrate Russia, the current members of the alliance would themselves have to achieve a fundamentally higher level of integration than they now enjoy. Yet the political willingness of both the US and its Western European partners to do this is and must be open to question.

Given the highly volatile character of contemporary Russian politics, and in view of the numerous uncertainties the country faces, it is hard to imagine that Moscow will soon make a decisive choice among the first three options I discussed above — viz., those of redividing Europe, trying to secure prominence for the OSCE over NATO, and achieving membership through partnership. As for the fourth option, this seems to be too radical for any Russian government to countenance in the near-term future. Most likely, Russia will continue to fluctuate within the triangle formed by the three more plausible options, gravitating to various angles in response to any number of internal and external factors. Needless to say, western policies are going to be crucial in defining the particular accents and nuances of Russian attitudes to NATO.

Notes

1.   One of the indications suggesting that Yeltsin at the beginning did not pay much attention to NATO enlargement was his blunt statement in Warsaw, in August 1993, that Russia would have no objections if Poland joined NATO. Shortly thereafter, however, Yeltsin's position on the issue changed radically.

2.   Even on the official level, statements are made interpreting NATO's enlargement as a continuation of traditional, long-term, anti-Russian, and anti-Soviet approaches on the part of the west. According to Andrei Kokoshin, first deputy defence minister, the enlargement of the Atlantic alliance is a "containment" policy, one whose target this time is not communism, as was the case during the Cold War, but Russia as a great power and even as a certain type of civilization. See Vadim Yegorov, "Plans for NATO Expansion: Russian First Deputy Defence Minister Sees Them as a Historical Mistake," *Nezavisimaya Gazeta*, 21 October 1995, p. 2. (Unless otherwise noted, all translations from Russian sources are the author's.)

3.   "An eastward expansion of the NATO bloc obviously is inevitable and is planned in several stages. In the first stage (over two or three years) Poland, Czechia, Slovakia, and Hungary will be accepted into NATO. In the second stage (tentatively by 2000) it is planned to accept Slovenia, Rumania, Bulgaria, and possibly also Lithuania, Latvia, and Estonia. The inclusion of Finland and Austria in NATO is likely in this same stage. Finally, the acceptance of Ukraine into NATO is not excluded in the third stage (approximately in 2005). But Russia will not be accepted into NATO under any circumstances." Institute for Defence Studies (INOBIS), "Conceptual Provisions of a Strategy for Countering the Main External Threats to Russian Federation National Security" (Moscow, October 1995), p. 6.

4.   "NATO's undeclared war against the Serbs means that it has already gained practical experience, schooled the world public, and mentally prepared NATO soldiers for conducting combat operations against Slavs with impunity," remarks the former commander of the Black Sea fleet, Admiral Eduard Baltin. Quoted in Zhanna Kasyanenko, "Black Sea Fleet Commander: Velvet War Has Been Lost," *Sovetskaya Rossiya*, 31 October 1995, p. 3.

5.   Russian Major General Viktor Gomenkov concurs: "NATO's muscle-flexing policy, the arbitrary expansion of the bloc's zone of responsibility, the policy of eastward enlargement, are primarily spearheaded against Russia. Moreover, the North Atlantic Alliance, as a result of its intervention in the Balkan events, has obtained first-hand experience in conducting offensive operations on foreign territory. It has tested the effectiveness of its troops and armaments on an enemy, which uses Soviet-type tactics and armaments. All this shows that NATO is not our possible partner but a direct threat to Russia's security. It does not ensure Europe's security." Interview with *ITAR-TASS*, 21 November 1995.

6.   Liberals are not immune to this line of logic either. Writes Vyacheslav Dashichev, a liberal scholar from IMEMO: "The everyday assertions that NATO is accommodating the Central European countries seeking protection against a new Russian danger beneath the bloc's umbrella appear clumsy. The question of an expansion of NATO and of the United States filling the military-political vacuum in East Europe after the departure from this region of the Soviet Union was raised back in 1990 by influential American politicians of the Kissinger type representing the geopolitical school of Realpolitik. We would recall that this question — together with the military-political status of the future Germany — occupied a central place at the Two Plus Four negotiations. Both President Bush and Secretary of State Baker, as well as Chancellor Kohl, assured Gorbachev at that time that the North Atlantic alliance would not expand eastward. In the treaties signed in September 1990, the NATO leaders undertook not to deploy foreign military forces even on the territory of East Germany after the withdrawal

therefrom of Soviet forces. This has now been forgotten." Vyacheslav Dashichev, "European Tragedy," *Nezavisimaya Gazeta*, 10 October 1995, p. 5.

7.   "Do the adversaries of the North Atlantic alliance allow of the possibility, say, even in the event of the East European countries being admitted to NATO, of this organization launching combat operations against Russia? And of one fine day American aircraft, following the ex- ample of the impertinent German boy Rust, landing in Red Square and, simultaneously, at other strategic points of Russia also? Or, having forgotten about nuclear parity, commencing the bombing of our cities and villages? I believe that such operations of the NATO-ites, and they are possible only with the full consent of all the countries with a democratic form of rule that are members of this organization and whose presidents and generals are under the control of society, are possible only in the excited minds of some of our hysterical types from the field of politics. The prospect of a military clash between Russia and NATO can be ruled out by definition." Boris Orlov, "What's Behind the Talk About NATO's 'Aggressiveness'?" *Nezavisimaya Gazeta*, 25 November 1995, p. 4.

8.   This is not literally the case. The record to date of linking authoritarian states to the security systems of democratic ones (e.g., the integration of Greece and Turkey, and also Portugal and Spain, into NATO, the CSCE and the EC) shows that democratization is, as a rule, primarily associated with the economic, rather than military-political, aspects of international cooperation. If there have been any external factors that played a certain part in implanting democratic institutions in the authoritarian regimes of noncommunist Europe, these were, above all, attributable to the EC, not NATO. There is scant reason to expect any fundamen- tally different dynamic to apply in postcommunist Europe. For the postcommunist states, the primacy of economic interests over military-political ones is abundantly clear, and will inevitably tell on their foreign policies.

9.   This contention, however, is also vulnerable to criticism. The military integration of independ- ent states is a rather long and painful process. It has taken several decades to achieve it even in Western Europe, and this notwithstanding all the urgency of the Cold War situation, complete with serious breakdowns and crises. The integration of Central European countries into NATO, under the most favourable conditions, would take even longer. There- fore, NATO will hardly be in a position to resolve the security problems of Central Europe in the short and, indeed, even in the medium term.

10.   According to some Russian experts, the enlargement of NATO to Central Europe would cost at least US $100 billion, which is not easy to mobilize. See "Russian-American Relations: The Test of Choice" (Moscow: Institute for US and Canada Studies, 1995), p. 28. These assessments are not much different from western calculations of costs related to NATO en- largement, which are put in the range of US $50 to $100 billion. See, for example, Richard L. Kugler. "Defense Program Requirements," in *NATO Enlargement: Opinions and Options,* ed. Jeffrey Simon (Washington: National Defense University Press, 1995), p. 192; and Joseph C. Kun, "In Search of Guarantees: The Elusive NATO — Is Enlargement in Sight? *Potomac Papers*, November 1995, pp. 1-13.

11.   Writes Alexei Pushkov, liberal columnist for the weekly *Moscow News*: "NATO is preparing not simply for the admittance of several new members but for a radical geostrategic shift, which would make this bloc an undoubted dominant factor in world politics. For Russia this would mean that the doors to full participation in European affairs would be practically closed to it. Within the NATO concept all European countries that are not at this time members of the bloc are divided into two categories — likely candidates for membership and countries that will never become members of the bloc. Russia, naturally, is in the second category. And inasmuch as the enlargement of the bloc is closely linked in time with the admittance of new members to the EU and the Western European Union, Russia would at the start of next year

be dealing with an expanded and consolidated Euro-Atlantic community in which there would be no place for it. The new Europe would stretch not from the Atlantic to the Urals, as Charles de Gaulle once proposed, but from San Francisco to Brest. The bloc's expansion would preserve and strengthen the American presence in Europe, simultaneously supplanting Russia, which belongs to Europe geographically." Aleksey Pushkov, "NATO Begins the 'Eastern Game'," *Moskovskiye Novosti*, no. 67, 1-8 October 1995, p. 11.

12. Andrei Kokoshin, civilian first deputy of defence and one of the token liberals in the defence ministry, argues that "many spheres of arms limitations and reduction would be severely and maybe mortally affected by NATO expansion to the east." Rick Atkinson, "Russian Official Assails NATO Expansion Plans, Warning of Sharper Conflict," *Washington Post*, 4 February 1996, p. A30. This statement is echoed by a similar remark of Gennady Zyuganov, leader of the Russian Communist Party. The expansion of NATO, in his opinion, jeopardizes the START-2 and CFE treaties: "If one speaks about NATO's enlargement then it is necessary to sum up all countries that will join the alliance... [NATO enlargement] ... violates the balance of conventional forces, destroys the achieved agreements, and raises the issue of how to compensate for this." Remarks reported by Interfax, "NATO Enlargement Threatens START-2 Ratification," 29 January 1996.

13. A "certified" liberal, Yeltsin's former press secretary, Vyacheslav Kostikov, argued that the "expansion of NATO through the addition of new members from the group of countries reasonably close to Russian borders would evoke a negative reaction in Russian public opinion, would foster the development of unwanted moods among civilian and military circles and in the final analysis could lead to military/political destabilization." *Segodnya*, 3 January 1994, p. 1.

14. The most evident case was the failure of NATO to inform Russia about its air strikes in Bosnia. Former Foreign Minister Andrei Kozyrev recalled: "In February 1994, when the situation around Sarajevo once again became critical, NATO decided to bomb the positions held by the Bosnian Serbs. Russia was presented with that decision as a *fait accompli*, despite its active participation in the efforts to settle the Bosnian crisis and its traditional influence on one of the conflicting parties." Andrei Kozyrev, "Partnership or Cold Peace?" *Foreign Policy*, Summer 1995, p. 10.

15. As Anton Surikov, of the Institute of US and Canada Studies, has stated: "In case the Baltic republics are included into NATO, the Russian armed forces will be sent to the territory of Estonia, Lithuania, and Latvia. Any attempts of the alliance to oppose it by force can trigger a world nuclear catastrophe." He also argues that Russia may deploy tactical nuclear weapons on its border with Poland and in its southern regions to counterbalance NATO expansion to Poland, the Czech Republic, and Hungary. *ITAR-TASS*, 2 October 1995.

16. According to media accounts, the general staff of the Russian Federation (RF) was already, in the autumn of 1995, considering nuclear countermeasures to a possible NATO enlargement. "Among Russian military analysts, few doubt that our former Warsaw Treaty allies are prepared to place their military facilities at the disposal of the North Atlantic union immediately, even if they are not members of the bloc, in the event the situation in the European theatre of military operations worsens. The RF defence ministry knows that specialists of the US Army geodetic service have already carried out the necessary work and assessed, for the use of NATO joint armed forces, the airfield and road networks of not only Poland, but also of the Baltic countries. The general staff proposals envisage that in the event the Czech Republic and Poland are integrated into the North Atlantic union's political and military structures and NATO nuclear weapons are deployed there, the coordinates of targets found on Czech and Polish territory will be entered in the flight plans of Russian ICBMs. In practical terms, and in line with existing concepts, this means that in passing from a theoretically

possible military conflict between the RF and NATO to the nuclear stage, the sides would at first exchange limited missile strikes at deployed troops of the first operational echelon without committing to action the main strategic forces. What can this entail for Prague and Warsaw? Easy to imagine!" Igor Korotchenko and Mikhail Karpov, "Russian Nuclear Missiles Will Be Retargeted at Czech Republic and Poland. Such a Proposal Is Being Prepared by RF Armed Forces General Staff in the Event of NATO's Real Expansion toward East," *Nezavisimaya Gazeta*, 7 October 1995, pp. 1-2.

17. If NATO expands, argue two top nuclear specialists at Arzamas-16, Russia will have to deploy "nuclear air defence and sea defence weapons on its western borders, as well as tactical and operational missile systems, including Pioneer [SS-20] and Oka [SS-23]" — weapons banned under the INF agreement. The two also proclaim that if NATO enlarges Russia will not sign a comprehensive test ban. *ITAR-TASS*, "Banned Missile Would Counter NATO Expansion," *OMRI Daily Digest 1*, no. 62, 27 March 1996, p. 2.

18. "The president's idea that Uzbekistan and Kyrgyzstan will help us in a confrontation with NATO cannot be attributed to anything but emotion. Especially since there is no point in counting on Ukraine's involvement in a new military alliance." Aleksandr Lyasko, "Doctrine Is New, But Looks Old," *Komsomolskaya Pravda*, 29 September - 6 October 1995, p. 2.

19. As a reputable security expert from the Yabloko party, Alexei Arbatov, argues, "EU/WEU membership will much better correspond to the proclaimed goals of Visegrad states [than] joining NATO: integration into Western Europe (in contrast to the Atlantic alliance); domestic stability and territorial integrity; capital investment; and market access and incentives for economic cooperation. As for security commitments, those of the WEU are quite strong, actually more binding than NATO Articles 4 and 5, and are anyway strongly coupled to NATO guarantees through Article 5 of the modified Brussels Treaty." Alexei Arbatov. "Waking Up to A Post-Euphoric World," a paper prepared for the conference "Rethinking Russian-American Relations," Carnegie Moscow Center, 10-11 May 1996, p. 7.

20. This last point seems to be especially sensitive for Russia's political and military establishments. Even those who may be ready to accept in principle the inclusion of the Visegrad group into NATO become hawkish when the discussion gravitates to the issue of the Baltic states' or Ukraine's possible participation in the alliance. Writes Pavel Felgengauer, a reform-minded defence analyst in Moscow: "Russia's future reaction to any attempt to deploy foreign troops near its border (including such a move under the guise of conducting maneuvers) is quite predictable. It will be exactly the same as Washington's reaction in 1961, when our troops landed in Cuba. First there will be blockade (if the geographic location of the future conflict allows it), then an ultimatum demanding an immediate withdrawal, and, if the ultimatum is not complied with, a preventive strike that would deprive the adversary of offensive capabilities." Pavel Felgengauer, "NATO Expansion: An Unsuccessful Compromise," *Segodnya*, 28 September 1995, p. 3.

CHAPTER FIVE

NATO's Year of Study:
Results and Policy Implications

John Barrett

Introduction

The end of the Cold War presented NATO governments with an unexpected luxury in the form of opportunities never before considered, let alone encountered. This was not a material benefaction, in the manner of the ever-elusive "peace dividend" that was to result from wide-ranging cuts in defence budgets and armed forces. Rather, it was an opportunity to take unforced decisions on the future of the alliance, on its new roles and missions, and on the possibility of opening its membership to countries that had recently been adversaries.

Regarding the last of these — namely, enlarging NATO's membership — the allies were in the enviable position, for the first time since the North Atlantic Treaty was negotiated back in 1948-49, of being able to set out the requirements of membership on criteria *other* than those of strategic containment alone.[1] That was a luxury not permitted by the collective-defence imperatives imposed by the Cold War. With the reunification of Germany, and the collapse of the Soviet Union and the Warsaw Pact, it was now possible for NATO to rediscover its essence as something more than a collective-defence organization only.[2]

Not all would share this optimism. Doubts have been cast about the capacity of NATO (or any other alliance, for that matter) to continue to exist after the disappearance of the initial threat.[3] The editor of this volume has elsewhere examined the issue of NATO's survivability in light of divers, and competing, theoretical approaches in international relations.[4] All such enquiries must cover a much broader range of issues than the specific policy decision to open the alliance to new members.

The impact of NATO enlargement on the alliance's future will be characterized differently according to the theoretical approach adopted. Of course, the theoretical approaches identified by Haglund — structural realism, hegemonic realism, institutionalism (including neo-institutionalism and neo-liberalism), democratic peace theory, and classical realism — are concerned with the broader issue of the alliance's survival after the Cold War and not with NATO enlargement per se. But he adds that while theory may help us to understand, the real factors at work concerning the alliance's future have more to do with how NATO "resolves its two most urgent policy issues, relating to the Balkans and to the former Warsaw Treaty Organization states."[5]

The latter point is really about the admission of states of Central and Eastern Europe (CEE) into NATO. In essence, what the theoretical approaches address is the "why" of NATO enlargement. Is it being sought to contain possible security threats, including that of a resurgent Russia? To promote stability in Central and Eastern Europe, either as a collective-defence organization or some future kind of pan-European collective-security entity? As a means of rebalancing between the US and the Europeans shared burdens of providing security? To reaffirm US interests as well as interest? Or is NATO enlargement simply the latest stage of an inclusivist and integrationist process under way in Western Europe since the 1960s and now spreading wider to states hitherto excluded by the exigencies of Cold War ideological confrontation?

In this chapter, the focus will be policy description and analysis. In the section immediately below, I describe the policy framework guiding the NATO enlargement process. Following that, I query why the process of NATO enlargement appears — certainly in the view of many Central European states as well as many parliamentarians and publics in allied countries[6] — to be taking so long.

I will argue that the rationale, or the "why," of enlargement does not yet rest on a shared understanding of the *strategic* objectives of taking in new members. The assumption underlying this argument is that NATO is, and remains, a strategic alliance. But allies individually appear to assign different priorities to what the enlargement process is trying to achieve. This in turn will have different implications for the other three questions of "how," "who," and "when."[7] Even though there may be widespread acceptance of a number of key strategic objectives, placing any of them ahead of others or trying to achieve them simultaneously will continue to have the effect of forestalling consensus on the "who" and "when." The inability to articulate an agreed *hierarchy* of strategic objectives is what lies behind the difficulty in naming candidates for alliance membership. In this sense, it is reflective of the debate itself among the informed publics in many NATO countries.

NATO'S Enlargement Study

Much ink has been spilled on the subject of NATO enlargement, including specu-
lation on how the decision was reached and the identity of the players
instrumental in making it happen.[8] My objective in this section is not to enter
the discussion of the path towards the decision itself, but rather to describe the
subsequent development of the policy framework.

At the NATO Brussels summit of January 1994, allied heads of state and
government took the decision in principle to open the alliance to new members.
The exact wording stipulates that allied leaders "would expect and welcome
the expansion of NATO to other European democratic states as part of an evolutionary process, taking into account political and security developments in
the whole of Europe."[9] In endorsing the principle of enlargement, they stressed
that admission of new members to the alliance was not to be an end in itself;
rather, it must contribute to Europe's wider security and stability. This, in a nut-
shell, is the strategic objective of NATO enlargement implicit in the Brussels
Declaration.[10]

One would have thought that, in taking this momentous decision, NATO
governments would have previously engaged in a full analysis and wide debate, with their publics involved, of the "why" of enlargement. However, much of
the rationale was only spelled out later, in the internal NATO study on enlargement, initiated at the fall ministerial meeting of the North Atlantic Council on
5 December 1994, almost 11 months after the Brussels summit.[11] The study's
mandate was to analyze how NATO should enlarge, to determine the principles
to guide this process as well as the implications of the eventual inclusion of
new members for the alliance and for possible new members. It was completed
in September 1995, following which collective and individual briefings on its
conclusions were given in Brussels and in a number of capitals of partner
countries.

The six chapter headings of the study show the range of the approach
taken by NATO in addressing the enlargement issue. The first chapter is entitled the "purposes and principles of enlargement"; the second is on "how to
ensure that enlargement contributes to the stability and security of the entire
Euro-Atlantic area, as part of a broad European security architecture, and supports the objective of an undivided Europe"; the third examines how the North
Atlantic Cooperation Council (NACC) and Partnership for Peace (PFP) "can
contribute concretely to the enlargement process"; the fourth asks how to ensure that "enlargement strengthens the effectiveness of the Alliance, preserves
its ability to perform its core functions of common defence as well as to undertake peacekeeping and other new missions, and upholds the principles and
objectives of the Washington Treaty"; the fifth seeks to explore the "implications
of membership for new members, including their rights and obligations," as well

as the preparations they must make to qualify for membership; and the sixth concentrates upon "modalities according to which the enlargement process should proceed."

The study stopped short of setting specific thresholds or criteria that potential members would first have to satisfy before being invited to join. One reason for this omission was mentioned earlier — that is, the natural limitations imposed by a generic study. Further refinement would require case-by-case consideration; but to gain such precision would in turn necessitate having the specific circumstances of a given country in mind. Politically, this would preempt the decisionmaking on identifying the candidate members for admission. At the very least, it would raise the expectations of any country so mentioned. Also, some aspects of alliance structures, modalities, and procedures are not easily quantifiable.[12] And if quantifiable thresholds or criteria were to have been stated, they might wrongly have been taken by candidate countries to be more "essential" than they actually were. For example, achieving a level of interoperability is not tantamount to "passing the test" of admission into NATO.

Nor did the study attempt to identify any "front-runner" candidates or set a timetable for alliance decisions on enlargement. Rather, it functioned more as an exercise in clarification, where all aspects of the alliance — such as the obligations and commitments of members, or the nature of their participation in military structures and collective-defence arrangements — are described in detail. The goal was to remove any possible misunderstanding over the fundamental political nature of the alliance, its strategic objectives, and the way in which military forces (including nuclear) are organized, deployed, and subordinated to higher political authority. It benefitted the allies also, for after its release, no member-state could say that it had not anticipated or thought through carefully enough the possible implications of accepting new members.

Utility of the Enlargement Study

Rather than recapitulating the study chapter by chapter, it may be more useful here to identify several points that will likely guide future decisionmaking on the enlargement process.[13] Despite the study's level of generality, some useful direction signs do emerge. They can be subsumed under eight general categories.

First, new members will enjoy all the rights and assume all obligations of membership under the Washington Treaty. Any thoughts of possible "associate" memberships or "second-tier" security guarantees are thus out of the question. Also banished is any idea of a modification of the Washington Treaty for those who do join.[14]

There is also a strong statement concerning the "extra-alliance" obligations that potential new members must adopt, even before they accede formally to it

— namely, to settle ethnic, external territorial, or internal jurisdictional disputes by peaceful means, in accordance with OSCE principles. As the study underlines: "Resolution of such disputes would be a factor in determining whether to invite a state to join the Alliance."[15] Concern by existing members over possibly importing new instabilities into the alliance as a result of enlargement lies at the root of this political requirement. It will undoubtedly figure more prominently in the enlargement process as interested partners make progress on fulfilling other requirements (notably military-related ones needed for interoperability with NATO forces).

Second, NATO enlargement — as the study notes — will have a significant impact on the European security environment and will have implications for all European countries, including those that do not join NATO early or at all. Maintaining active cooperative relations with these states will therefore be particularly important "in order to avoid divisions or uncertainties in Europe and to ensure broad, inclusive approaches to cooperative security."[16] The NACC and Partnership for Peace are key means of preventing the sort of divisions in Europe that some "enlargement skeptics" believe will be provoked by enlargement.[17] Thus, the vitality and credibility of NACC/PFP for countries unlikely to join NATO early or at all will become increasingly important. Implicit here is also the sense that PFP must not be regarded by partners as little more than a "waiting room" for NATO membership.

Third, an "eventual broad congruence" of European membership in NATO, the EU, and the WEU would, according to the study, have "positive effects" on European security. More importantly, the alliance "should at an appropriate time give particular consideration to countries with a perspective of EU membership, and which have shown an interest in joining NATO."[18] With these words, the study has produced the first substantial indication on the importance of a congruence of NATO, EU, and WEU memberships — or what some would see as the need for coherence of the "common European security space." It also has implications for the "when" of enlargement, for it could mean that the separate processes should be more congruent in timing as well. But more importantly, it suggests that those countries with "Europe Agreements"[19] would have a head start on other countries aspiring to NATO membership.

Fourth, according to the study there is no governing rule on whether countries would be invited to join sequentially or several simultaneously. Either case could apply when the time for deciding "who" and "when" is reached. However, a situation could arise where a new member might "close the door" on subsequent admissions.[20] What is recognized here is that if a new member has all the rights of existing members, then it also must have the right to withhold its agreement to the continuation of the enlargement process. The 17th member of NATO could, in this scenario, also be the last one. In order to avoid such a situation, there may be a requirement for "specific political commitments in the course of accession negotiations."[21]

There is also the strong desire to ensure that NATO remains open to further accessions.[22] One possible way would be to offer to certain countries a political commitment to accept them, with the precise timing and details of accession being a matter of subsequent negotiation and decision. In EU parlance this would be called offering a "perspective" on membership. Although such a proposal is not made in the study, it could be the basis of an approach that would reaffirm politically and procedurally the alliance's openness to further accessions.

Fifth, the study points out that new members will not be required to achieve full interoperability with NATO before joining. However, they will need to meet certain minimum standards. In fact, an important element in new members' military contributions will be a commitment in good faith to pursue the objectives of standardization that are essential to alliance strategy and to achieve the minimum level of interoperability required for operational effectiveness.[23] The study advises that new members should concentrate, in the first instance, on interoperability and accept NATO standardization doctrine and policies to help attain this goal. These standards will be based in part on conclusions reached through the PFP Planning and Review Process (PARP).[24]

The importance of these points is that they underscore both that the level of interoperability will be particularly relevant in demonstrating preparedness to join NATO and that the PARP will identify and effectively set the criteria in this regard. This is despite the fact that in all other areas the study resists defining fixed criteria. Thus, there is a fairly clear indication that interoperability will be an important first step in a country's advance preparations — at least on the military-technical level. The study does not speculate, however, on the extent to which some of these preparations can be undertaken before formal accession, or left until after such accession.[25]

Sixth, although it is important for NATO's force structure that other allies' forces can be deployed, when and if appropriate, on the territory of new members, the alliance has "no a priori requirement" for such stationing.[26] Similarly, as regards alliance nuclear posture, there is no a priori requirement for the stationing of nuclear weapons on the territory of new members.[27] Such statements stand in opposition to the concern of some observers that significant transfers of NATO infrastructure, matériel, and/or forces to the territories of new members would occur virtually automatically and that new members would be under obligation to accept such deployments without objection. In neither case — conventional or nuclear — does such a requirement exist. Nevertheless, the study does make it clear that a fundamental element of NATO membership is to share burdens associated with NATO defence and deterrence policies; changed circumstances in the security environment could, therefore, alter things.

Seventh, the costs of enlargement — both to the existing allies as well as to the new ones — remain difficult to estimate without knowing which countries will join and what will be their specific contributions to alliance collective forces and structures. Some effort has been made in the study in the area of common-funded programs, since a principle of proportionality in budget contributions can be assumed. For example, new members would be expected to contribute their share to the commonly funded programs and the Security Investment Program, with a contribution level based, in a general way, on "ability to pay." However, new members are warned that they face "considerable financial obligations when joining the Alliance."[28]

Eighth, and last, once decisions have been made to invite new members to join, negotiations will be undertaken on the content of the accession protocol. This would be followed by the ratification of the accession by all 16 allies, in accordance with their national constitutional procedures.[29] Too often overlooked is the fact that, while allied governments will issue the invitation to join, it will be their parliaments and congresses that will have the say in the actual ratification of accession to the Washington Treaty. There can be no way of knowing in advance what the disposition of the 16 parliaments will be on specific candidates for NATO membership, or even whether the advice of their governments to accept a given candidate will be followed.

Next Steps: The Agenda for 1996

The issue of how possible new members intend to contribute to NATO's collective defence is, according to the study, to be explored "through bilateral dialogue prior to accession negotiations."[30] The idea of a bilateral dialogue came to fruition at the NATO foreign ministers' meeting of 5 December 1995. According to the communiqué issued after that session, there would be three elements of the enlargement process unfolding during 1996:[31]

- intensive bilateral and multilateral consultations with interested partners, building on the foundation of the enlargement study and the earlier collective and bilateral briefings;
- further enhancement of the Partnership for Peace, not only to strengthen ties between the alliance and all partners but also to facilitate the ability of interested partners to prepare themselves for possible NATO membership; and
- consideration of what internal adaptations and other measures are necessary to ensure that enlargement preserves the effectiveness of the alliance — in particular, resource and staffing implications of enlargement.

In December 1996, NATO foreign ministers will assess the progress made and "consider the way forward."

The first objective above, namely intensified dialogue, is essentially two-fold. Through it, interested partners will learn more about the specific and practical details of alliance membership. NATO in turn will learn more about what individual partners might or might not contribute to the alliance and thus begin to identify areas for additional work. It should be underlined that participation in a program of intensified dialogue does not imply that interested partners will automatically be invited to begin accession talks with NATO.

To date, 14 countries have expressed an interest in taking part in the intensified bilateral dialogue on the enlargement process.[32] On the NATO side, a team composed of representatives of international staff and NATO military authorities are conducting bilateral (in a "16+1" format) and collective meetings on subjects of general application (e.g., minimum standards for interoperability; NATO administration, costs, budget matters, and procedures; the Security Investment Program; and intelligence-sharing and related issues).

Concerning substance, the dialogues, which take place in the framework defined by the NAC decision of 5 December 1995, address three matters: 1) questions raised in the earlier bilateral briefings held with interested partners on the study on enlargement; 2) individual discussion papers presented by partners, as a basis for the 16+1 meeting, summarizing their response to the various precepts and principles included in the study and specific questions of interest to them; and, 3) partners' responses to a range of questions (related *inter alia* to political, defence, and military concerns) to be identified by the alliance. The beginning of the individual dialogue starts with an expression of interest by a partner *and* submission of a discussion paper. The dialogues are now in progress.

As far as concerns the second element identified in the communiqué, some interested partners will clearly use the PFP to prepare themselves for the possibility of joining NATO. This is a perfectly legitimate aspiration that the alliance has fully encouraged, not only in the framework document of the Partnership for Peace but also in the enlargement study itself.[33] Indeed, the review and update of individual partnership programs is considered an important means of tailoring a partner's cooperation to assist in its national preparations for possible NATO membership, should it so wish.

The role of the Planning and Review Process (PARP) of the Partnership is of special interest. As set out in the PFP framework document, the PARP is to provide a basis for identifying and evaluating forces and capabilities that might be made available by partners for multilateral training, exercises, and operations in conjunction with alliance forces. The PARP will thus focus now on areas contributing to interoperability, such as communications, equipment standards, operating procedures, and linguistic skills. Other important PARP objectives pursued with increasing emphasis include promotion of democratic control of the armed forces in partner countries, and introducing partners to collective-defence planning consistent with NATO practices.

The third element highlighted in the December 1995 NAC communiqué tasked the Council in permanent session to examine, with the advice of the

NATO military authorities, alliance *internal adaptations* and other measures required to preserve its effectiveness as it enlarges. Pertinent areas for such examination would be several, and would likely include:

- *strategy and policies*: especially possible changes in the character of the risks to the alliance and the effects the extension of Article 5 guarantees to new members will have on NATO deployment and reinforcement concepts;
- *command structure*: especially whether new changes and new headquarters would be needed, and what effect accession of additional members would have on implementation of the Combined Joint Task Forces (CJTF) concept;
- *force structure*: particularly how accession of new members will affect the overall requirement for various categories of forces;
- *defence planning and procedures*: especially whether current procedures for alliance planning, including force, nuclear, logistics, civil emergency, armaments, and exercise planning can be adequately staffed;
- *crisis management*: especially in familiarizing new members with NATO crisis-management structures, procedures, measures, communications, and exercises; and
- *the accession process*: i.e., how to prepare the accession of new members to alliance structures.

The rest of 1996 will be devoted to continuing preparations in the three areas delineated in the December 1995 communiqué. There will be increasingly detailed 16+1 exchanges with interested partners, on the basis of their discussion papers as well as the specific questions that allies would wish to put to them. The Partnership for Peace will be utilized to the extent possible, either through individual partnership programs or participation in the PARP, to establish de facto standardization and interoperability criteria along the lines of those currently followed by NATO members. And examination will continue of the internal NATO adaptations required in order to ensure that new members do not jeopardize or impair the effectiveness of the alliance in fulfilling its core functions and carrying out the new tasks and missions of peace-support operations and crisis management.

But as these preparations continue, a question hangs in the air. Expressed in quintessential NATO parlance, it could be put something like this: Does a consensus exist, or is one emerging, among NATO governments on the "who" and the "when," taking into account the policy framework set out in the enlargement study and subsequent ministerial policy statements? A related, if perhaps even more important, question is: Is this extant or emerging consensus shared by the publics and parliamentarians of allied countries? For it is they who will have to support politically, economically and, above all, militarily, the new members. This applies especially to the parliamentarians, who in each allied country will have to ratify every single accession to the Washington Treaty.

Political winds can blow hard and change directions quickly. The combined pressure of the leading allies in favour of a decision could move things forward with quickening pace. But, as of this writing, it must be said that a consensus has yet to emerge on either the "who" or the "when." In fact, there has not been any specific, formal discussion of this by the North Atlantic Council. While there may be different national perspectives to take into account, particularly the election schedules of some allied governments, the central dilemma inheres not so much in the timing or modalities of accession per se. Instead, it resides in the lack of consensus over the fundamental strategic objectives of enlargement. In other words, the most germane question now may not be "who" or "when"; it may be "which." That is to say, which objective, if any, will be able to command the consensus needed to open the alliance's doors to new members?

Strategic Objectives of NATO Enlargement

At a minimum, accepting new members into NATO will result in a change in institutional membership. But this will occur within the context of a changing global structure, as the era of bipolar security politics has come to a close. It would be premature to suggest that a new security system or order has as yet replaced the bipolar one. Nevertheless, much rhetoric has been aired since the ending of the Cold War on the desirability of achieving — at least on the European continent — a "cooperative-security" order, one featuring mutual, cooperative relations between and among European security institutions.[34] As early as 1991, NATO endorsed this desire.[35] The decision in principle to enlarge NATO's membership constitutes another dynamic feature of an evolving European security order. As the enlargement study observes in its own understated way, the decision on new NATO members will have a "significant impact on the European security environment."

A cooperative-security order based on mutually reinforcing institutions and overlapping memberships is nevertheless one that can only emerge, if at all, from the policies and diplomacy of governments. It is thus entirely political. As such, the first order of political "business" must be the identification of the strategic objectives to be accomplished through and by such a security order. It is easy to imagine alternative security "orders." One such might be the imposition by a strong political power of a "hegemonic" security order. This does not appear likely. Instead, where consensus and agreement are the rule, as they are in NATO, then negotiations on regime evolution and reform become the effective equivalent of "policymaking." But for policy to be made in any meaningful way, the strategic objectives must be known and accepted by all.

There exist at least four main strategic objectives associated with NATO enlargement. Each offers different priorities and emphases concerning the goals of the enlargement process. These four can be summarized as follows:

- to *preserve the effectiveness of the alliance*, ranging from collective-defence commitments under Article 5 of the Washington Treaty to new roles and missions, including peace-support operations and crisis management;
- to *further the ongoing integrative process in Europe*, by extending membership in European institutions and building a European security architecture through a cooperative division of labour;
- to *prevent the redivision of Europe through new dividing lines* and stabilize areas of Europe by drawing them closer to the alliance through cooperative programs such as the Partnership for Peace; and
- to *consolidate democratic reform in former Warsaw Pact countries by extending the values of the western democracies*, particularly in the area of security and defence.

NATO allies may subscribe to each of these perspectives or emphases, however they may be labelled. But each holds different implications for the enlargement process. This is especially the case for the first item on the above list, to which we now turn.

Preserving NATO Effectiveness

Preservation of NATO's effectiveness as a collective-defence organization during a time of adaptation and change is particularly important. NATO must continue to function as a deliverer of specific "strategic goods," notably the maintenance of a collective-defence response to security threats and risks in a changed security environment.[36] Thus, the motivating strategic impulses for enlarging NATO arise from the need to defend vital shared interests and assure allied security against renewed hegemonic threats, as well as from the importance of long-term, institutionalized, transatlantic geopolitical cooperation.

The functions of an enlarged NATO would essentially be preservation of the capacity to defend the alliance against a range of possible threats. Threat analysis would be based on capabilities, not intentions, as a hedge against cooperative security giving way in future to adversarial politics in Europe. In terms of capabilities alone, the military forces of Russia — conventional and nuclear — are sufficient in size and quality to be considered, under extreme circumstances and if directed against allied states, a potential threat.

During the briefings on the enlargement study that were given in Moscow in January 1996 by NATO officials, Russian authorities raised a number of questions concerning the strategic objectives of enlargement.[37] They asked why the alliance was seeking to strengthen its collective-defence capability when the threat of military attack had essentially been removed. Did NATO enlargement mean the creation of special infrastructural facilities for accommodating and maintaining NATO armed forces, both conventional and nuclear? Would the holding of regular exercises on the territory of new members (as well as the transfer of forces) affect negatively the stability and level of trust between European states? And if NATO's strategic doctrine is based on defence and deterrence, exactly whom does the alliance intend to deter now that the Cold War is over and a new security environment prevails?

The reaction in Russia to NATO enlargement has also produced policy analyses of a more nuanced nature, with the focus on finding some modus vivendi between Russia and the alliance over this issue.[38] This trend is discernible in some of the policy statements issued by Russia's foreign ministry over the past few months.[39]

The principal Russian arguments against NATO enlargement can be summarized as follows. Enlargement will: 1) divide Europe, increasing thereby tension and the risks of confrontation with Russia; 2) marginalize Russia in European security spheres in which it has a legitimate great-power role; 3) bring NATO to Russia's borders, including stationed troops and nuclear weapons; 4) force Russia to take political and military countermeasures to reestablish a strategic balance in Europe (e.g., through greater reliance on nuclear weapons, strengthening CIS defence/security cooperation, and seeking other possible allies and partners); 5) undermine existing arms-control and disarmament regimes (e.g., the CFE Treaty and START); 6) prevent the development of a truly pan-European security order; 7) strengthen NATO as a military alliance, capable of large-scale military operations that can only be directed against Russia; and 8) severely damage Russia's arms exports and its defence industry, as countries preparing to join NATO begin to turn to western suppliers.

If the reaction of Russia to NATO's enlargement policy becomes the allies' prime consideration, then their efforts will be directed at reconciling Moscow to the "inevitable." However, to some, managing the reaction of Russia might counsel a slowing down or delay in deciding on the "who" and "when" of enlargement.

Preserving NATO's effectiveness involves more than simply the Russian factor, however important that may be. A second concern, from the strategic perspective, focuses on a new phenomenon, arising from the Persian Gulf War in 1990 and now evidenced in the Implementation Force (IFOR) in Bosnia. This concerns the need to develop coalitions of countries willing and able to contribute to combined military operations in the face of specific threats. This strategic issue is very much on the minds of a number of American policy analysts.[40]

From this perspective, NATO enlargement would be a congruent (though not necessarily simplifying) factor in the attempt to define new strategic goals for the alliance. Enlargement would, as it did in the past, inhibit the renationalization of European security and defence policies along lines witnessed in the 1930s and again, in a similar extremist and ethnically separatist fashion, today in the former Yugoslavia.

But enlargement would be about more than the desire to prevent renationalization. It would entail such classic state interests as halting the spread of weapons of mass destruction and missile systems, and preserving access to Persian Gulf oil in time of emergency. Needed, in the words of Ronald Asmus and his colleagues, is a "new transatlantic security bargain that would reharmonize U.S. and European perceptions of the vital national interests common to both sides of the Atlantic and the serious threats to them." They regard enlargement to be a "stepping stone" toward this goal, as well as being an indispensable means of stabilizing Central and Eastern Europe. Until and unless that part of Europe is stabilized, they argue, "it will be difficult if not impossible for our NATO Allies to broaden their strategic horizon to confront the serious challenges which lie further afield."[41]

Within this strategic perspective, a premium would be placed on attaining interoperability with prospective new members, in order to prepare for operational contingencies, possibly in Europe but also "out of area." Questions of standardization would come to the fore, as would the discussion of the major requirements for gaining and sustaining interoperability with NATO forces, organizational structures, and procedures. This discussion featured such considerations as communications and information systems (CIS); NATO doctrine; operational plans and procedures (including NATO's command organization); logistical plans and procedures; infrastructure; civil emergency planning; and intelligence and security.

Nevertheless, this strategic perspective, however much it might seem to suggest the need for rapid enlargement, could also lead to the opposite conclusion, and result in slowing down the decision on "who" and "when." The Partnership for Peace will be the main vehicle for orchestrating military cooperation among interested partners. But at some point a decision is going to have to be made. On the one hand, NATO could remain intact as a regional subgroup within the PFP, lending "its experience and, when appropriate, military capability to nurture and support other regional groupings that would gradually evolve in Central and Eastern Europe and the former Soviet Union."[42]

On the other hand, a demonstration of interoperability, perhaps similar to that currently evidenced by a number of partners contributing to the IFOR and the NATO-led "Operation Joint Endeavour," would constitute both the necessary and sufficient bases upon which to select the new members. In this latter instance, the technical-military achievement of interoperability would thus have triumphed over such political considerations as what to do about Russia, or about those countries that are not going to be invited to join NATO.

NATO and the Quest for an Inclusive Security Order

Overlapping but not identical memberships in European institutions may provide a certain synergy of effort, especially if strong and mutually reinforcing cooperative ties are established between them. But incongruent memberships create perceptions among those "excluded" that there are differing zones of security in Europe. Others worry about the loss of decisionmaking, influence, or operational effectiveness if memberships expand too far, too quickly.

Nevertheless, a prominent aim of NATO enlargement is to consolidate as well as continue the European integrative process that began in Western Europe after the Second World War and is now poised to embrace the countries of Central and Eastern Europe. NATO has contributed significantly to this process. By embedding Germany in the west, engaging the US in European security, and creating a common, multinational defence establishment, the alliance has been fundamental in the creation of a Europe united and at peace. Adding new members would therefore simply be a continuation of this integrative tradition.

This aspiration, however, comes into conflict with some other goals, and creates a problem similar to that faced by the European Union, the other great engine of European integration. That problem is whether first to "widen" or to "deepen" the organization. For example, NATO is in the process of adapting its internal structures and procedures so as to be able to conduct its missions more effectively. At the same time, making NATO's military structures more flexible will allow tangible support to be given to a European Security and Defence Identity (ESDI), which is a goal of the majority of allies that are EU members. This would strengthen NATO's so-called European pillar.

But should internal alliance adaptation be completed before new members are admitted? If so, then the decision on "who" and "when" will be affected. There is also the issue of the eventual broad congruence of European membership in NATO, the EU, and the WEU, as mentioned in the enlargement study. Will a "parallelism" first be required between the enlargement of the alliance and the prospective enlargements of the EU and WEU?[43] Or can NATO "widening" and "deepening" occur simultaneously?

Putting the integrative promise of NATO enlargement at or near the top of the strategic priorities means that extending institutional membership becomes an objective in and of itself. Gaining NATO membership thus becomes identified as the sine qua non for entry into the west. The concern, however, is that with no end of widening in sight, the military effectiveness of the alliance may become jeopardized. Continuous expansion and integration of new members will at some point undoubtedly affect NATO's efficacy and indeed reach perhaps to its fundamental nature as a defensive alliance. It is for this reason that the integrative objective of enlargement is viewed by some as a path leading eventually to the transformation of NATO into a collective-security organization.[44]

Others, however, put the emphasis not on collective security, but on cooperative security. As we saw above, one of the purposes of enlargement, according to the NATO study of September 1995, is to build a new cooperative-security order in Europe, based on the participation of all states in the Euro-Atlantic region as well as on mutually reinforcing ties between international organizations having a relevance to broad European security issues.

The Partnership for Peace is NATO's prime means for contributing to the building of co-operative security. Through it, NATO and non-NATO countries will be better able to address future crisis-management and peacekeeping challenges. But the Implementation Force in Bosnia has expedited the leap from theory to reality. In IFOR, allies have been joined by other countries, including countries from beyond Europe. It was the Partnership for Peace that laid the basis for assembling and deploying the IFOR, through its having fostered new habits of consultation and cooperation between partners and allies in respect of peace-support operations. Clearly, those partners currently under NATO's command in Bosnia will be encouraged to continue developing further their interoperability with NATO forces. Both the IFOR experience and the practical cooperation through Partnership for Peace will thus help them prepare for possible NATO membership.

Thus, IFOR has produced a dovetailing of cooperative-security objectives. The IFOR itself — the international "coalition for peace" in Bosnia[45] — is implementing the military tasks of the Dayton peace accords, on the basis of a UN Security Council mandate. In incorporating troop contributions from nearly 20 non-NATO countries and supporting closely and continuously the work of the various civilian agencies and organizations in Bosnia (including the UN, EU, the Council of Europe, and the OSCE), IFOR is an example of cooperative security in action. IFOR is also providing the opportunity for interested partners to move closer towards alliance interoperability and therefore improve their military-technical readiness to join NATO.

Can what has been said of PFP and IFOR also be said of NATO enlargement: Will it generate cooperative security? Or, to put it a different way, can cooperative security be achieved without NATO enlargement? It has been pointed out that the Partnership for Peace could become a "declining asset" once it is forced to shift from self-differentiation by partners to identification of enlargement candidates by the alliance.[46] Another potential difficulty is that NATO enlargement encourages the CEE emerging democracies to view membership as the answer to their security problems. The problem is, however, that stability in Central and Eastern Europe "depends primarily on building cooperation and trust among the new democracies themselves."[47] Ironically, the explicit statements from the alliance linking PFP to eventual full membership have encouraged Central and Eastern European states to eschew regional cooperation. Thus the "structure" of cooperative security being built through the policy initiatives of PFP and NATO enlargement resembles nothing so much as a wheel: NATO is the hub, and individual partners conduct their most intensive and committed security cooperation along the exclusive "spoke" formed by their relations with the hub.

Even IFOR has not been unambiguous on this question. A strong argument could be made that those interested partners who are IFOR troop contributors have, in Operation Joint Endeavour, cooperated and coordinated very closely and successfully with the alliance and its military structures in what is a complex and demanding peace-support operation. The inference drawn would be that having accomplished this level of interaction in such a short span of time, the next step should be a relatively simple one, to wit, the political decision to give these close IFOR collaborators NATO membership. However, the very same argumentation could lead to an opposite conclusion; for an important peace-support operation has been successfully mounted through IFOR without any ostensible need to extend NATO membership.

Consolidating Democratic Reform and Values

The preamble to the Washington Treaty expresses the determination of the signatories, *inter alia*, "to safeguard the freedom, common heritage and civilization of their peoples, founded in the principles of democracy, individual liberty and the rule of law."[48] This provides the basis for another strategic objective of NATO enlargement: to integrate the new democracies into a common security community of shared values.

There are therefore a number of normative issues impinging on the legitimation of NATO's enlargement policy. These would embrace the consolidation of democratic and market reform, including a firmly established, democratic parliament; a commitment to the principles of political and cultural pluralism; a functioning market economy; adherence to the principles of the Helsinki Final Act; civilian control of the military and paramilitary forces; and transparency of defence budgets and planning. As with most normative issues, there is sometimes difficulty in substantiating or verifying their existence. For example, how to assess the adequacy of civil and democratic control over the military? And how would the alliance judge the efforts of candidates for membership to solve territorial or other disputes with their neighbours peacefully?

The democratic-reform perspective nevertheless provides an argument for moving quickly on the "who" and particularly the "when" of NATO enlargement. It would cite the historic duty of western countries to consolidate and stabilize the new democracies in Central and Eastern Europe.[49] The "window of opportunity" is seen as now open for ensuring that democratic and market reforms in these countries are sustained for good. However, laying the emphasis on democratic development will make any further differentiation among possible new members even more difficult to sustain, for two reasons.

First, a community of values does not have natural boundaries that could suggest a political or geographical stopping point. Therefore there is no natural limit to enlargement. This invites the same comment as in the previous section — the larger the alliance, the more problematical it will likely be to retain decisionmaking coherence and military effectiveness. Second, focussing on democratic development as a primary objective of NATO enlargement risks disconnecting the alliance from its grounding in national-security interests and collective defence.

The result could be an increased pressure on individual allies in future to "slip out" somehow from the strict interpretation of the alliance's Article 5 security guarantee. The obligation to come to an ally's defence through military means and the commitment to a force posture of deterrence might be weakened. The result over time would be the evolution of the alliance into a collective-security organization embracing all or most of the new democracies in Europe. The distinction then between NATO and the OSCE would be small if not imperceptible.

Conclusion

Moving forward in the enlargement process requires alliance consensus across the board. This must involve both allied governments and their publics. While the former must agree first before the "who" and the "when" is decided, it is the latter who will have to support and pay for the common alliance costs associated with new memberships. Consensus will prove elusive unless the strategic objectives are first agreed, both as to their priority and emphasis, and then carefully presented and explained.

If the alliance is not to stumble into one of its most profound decisions, then a common, unifying vision must emerge to guide it through the next steps on enlargement. This vision seems as yet to be absent, even though allies share nearly all, if not all, of the strategic objectives I discussed in this chapter. The problem perhaps lies in the fact that allies are still unsure whether extending membership will over time weaken NATO, perhaps even endow it with new, ultimately irresoluble, conflicts and instabilities. It is not so much the fact that expectations concerning NATO membership are high on the part of interested partners that matters; rather, it is a question of what expectations these partners will carry with them concerning the alliance's ability to address all their security problems.

The final problem holding up the decision on "who" and "when" may also be attributable to the fear that NATO enlargement cannot help but drive a wedge between two security regions or communities — the European and the Eurasian.

At a minimum this would revive policies of power-balancing in European security affairs. It could also encourage the reconstitution of a Russian-dominated zone in territories once belonging to the Soviet Union. It would thus lead to a new, albeit familiar, division in Europe, something NATO governments have said they are seeking to avoid through their policy of enlargement. If so, then the history of power politics may become relevant once more. And the dominant theoretical approach to European security will again be infused with constructs such as the balance of power, and bipolarity.

Notes

1.   It is useful to recall the centrality of the containment objective and how other considerations of alliance membership flowed from this imperative. For example, the decision to invite Portugal to join the North Atlantic Treaty as one of the original members was taken not because of Portugal's subscription to the democratic principles set out in the Treaty's Preamble — at the time Portugal was under the Salazar dictatorship — but for *strategic* reasons. In 1949, US airlift operations to reinforce and resupply Europe in the event of war with the Soviet Union required refuelling stops at bases in the Azores. On this point, see Escott Reid, *Time of Fear and Hope: The Making of the North Atlantic Treaty, 1947-1949* (Toronto: McClelland and Stewart, 1977).

2.   While NATO — the North Atlantic Treaty *Organization* — was established in 1951 largely in response to Soviet actions at the time in Eastern Europe and occupied Germany, the North Atlantic Treaty, ratified in 1949, had been conceived by its architects as more than a means of collective defence against the armed forces of the Soviet Union. That the alliance would serve other purposes, particularly the goals and objectives of the United Nations Charter and the building of a new postwar international order, was clearly the intent of at least one of the principal negotiators of the Washington Treaty. See Escott Reid, *Radical Mandarin: The Memoirs of Escott Reid* (Toronto: University of Toronto Press, 1989), esp. chap. 15. See also the collection of essays in Nicholas Sherwen, ed., *NATO's Anxious Birth: The Prophetic Vision of the 1940s* (London: C. Hurst, 1985); and *"Fingerprints on History": The NATO Memoirs of Theodore C. Achilles*, ed. Lawrence S. Kaplan and Sidney R. Snyder, *Occasional Paper no. 1* (Kent, Ohio: Lyman L. Lemnitzer Center for NATO and European Community Studies, Kent State University, 1992).

3.   See, for example, Christoph Bertram, "NATO on Track for the 21st Century?" Address to the 40th General Assembly of the Atlantic Treaty Association, The Hague, 26 October 1994. Another version of this pessimism over NATO's continued existence calls for radical transformation of the alliance if its future is to be ensured. See Ronald D. Asmus, Robert D. Blackwill, and F. Stephen Larrabee, "Can NATO Survive?" *Washington Quarterly* 19 (Spring 1996): 79-101.

4 .   David G. Haglund, "Must NATO Fail? Theories, Myths, and Policy Dilemmas," *International Journal* 50 (Autumn 1995): 651-74. As Haglund puts it, "theory must have an indispensable role in any enquiry into the future of the Alliance."

5.   Ibid., p. 665.

6. See, for example, Karsten Voigt, rapporteur, "Special Report of the Working Group on NATO Enlargement," Defence and Security Committee (Brussels: North Atlantic Assembly, December 1994.)

7. The interrelatedness of this triad of questions is implicitly recognized in the study on enlargement, which showed that the "how" of enlargement could only be tackled in a generic sense. Further precision requires nomination of a specific country, that is, specifying the "who," before the "how" can be satisfactorily addressed — a reversal of the order conceived in the study.

8. The academic and editorial commentary on the pros and cons of NATO enlargement is burgeoning, almost becoming a bibliographic category in its own right. Key articles would include Ronald D. Asmus, Richard L. Kugler, and F. Stephen Larrabee, "NATO Expansion: The Next Steps," *Survival* 37 (Spring 1995): 7-33; Jonathan Dean, "Losing Russia or Keeping NATO: Must We Choose?" *Arms Control Today*, June 1995; Michael E. Brown, "The Flawed Logic of NATO Expansion," *Survival* 37 (Spring 1995): 34-52; Alexei Arbatov, "NATO and Russia," *Security Dialogue* 26, 2 (1995): 135-46; Strobe Talbott, "Why NATO Should Grow," *New York Review of Books*, 10 August 1995, pp. 27-30; Andrei Kozyrev, "Partnership or Cold Peace?" *Foreign Policy*, no. 99 (Summer 1995); and Sergei A. Karaganov et al., "Russia and NATO: Theses of the Council on Foreign and Defence Policy," *Nezavisimaya Gazeta*, 21 June 1995, trans. in *FBIS Daily Report*, 23 June 1995.

9. "Declaration of the Heads of State and Government Participating in the Meeting of the North Atlantic Council Held at NATO Headquarters, Brussels, on 10-11 January 1994," *NATO Handbook* (Brussels: NATO Office of Information and Press, 1995), pp. 271-72.

10. If NATO enlargement is to help overcome old divisions, not create new ones, and is not supposed to threaten anyone, but instead enhance stability and security for all of Europe, then logic would suggest that no enlargement would take place should these conditions seem impossible to achieve.

11. The study provides a succinct description of *why* NATO will enlarge. "NATO enlargement will contribute to enhanced stability and security for all countries in the Euro-Atlantic areas by: encouraging and supporting democratic reforms, including civilian and democratic control over the military; fostering patterns and habits of cooperation, consultation and consensus building which characterize relations among current Allies; promoting good-neighbourly relations in the whole Euro-Atlantic area; emphasising common defence and extending its benefits and increasing transparency in defence planning and military budgets; reinforcing the tendency toward integration and cooperation in Europe based on shared democratic values; strengthening the Alliance's ability to contribute to European and international security, including through peacekeeping under the UN or OSCE as well as other new missions; and by strengthening and broadening the Trans-Atlantic partnership." North Atlantic Treaty Organization, "Study on NATO Enlargement" (Brussels, September 1995), para. 3.

12. They could, for example, vary considerably in accordance with each specific country, depending on the current state of its armed forces, the contributions that NATO defence and military planners could expect from the country in fulfilling alliance collective-defence responsibilities, and so forth.

13. For a short overview of the study on enlargement by the NATO official who chaired the meetings that produced it, see Gebhardt von Moltke, "NATO Moves Towards Enlargement," *NATO Review* 44 (January 1996): 3-6.

14. "There must be no 'second tier' security guarantees or members within the Alliance and no modifications of the Washington Treaty for those who join." Para. 68.

15. Para. 6.

16. Para. 13.

17. Para. 13. "For countries that do not become members, NACC/PfP must constitute: a continuing vehicle for active cooperation with NATO; concrete evidence of NATO's continuing support and concern for their security; and their primary link to the Alliance, as a key Euro-Atlantic security institution." Para. 36.

18. Para. 20. It is also noted that the maintenance of the linkage between full members of the WEU and members of NATO is essential.

19. They are: Bulgaria, the Czech Republic, Estonia, Hungary, Latvia, Lithuania, Poland, Rumania, Slovakia, and Slovenia.

20. Para. 30.

21. Ibid. However, this may in itself not be enough. The parliament of the 17th member will also become involved in ratifying additional members and therefore could in theory withhold approval. Thus, a political commitment by the current government of the 17th (or a subsequent) member would not avoid this problem.

22. "A declaration at the time of the first invitation(s) being issued which clearly stated this would both reassure those countries that would not be among the first to be invited and reduce the likelihood of some of those countries submitting unsolicited applications to join the Alliance." Para. 80.

23. Para. 78.

24. Paras 74, 40. The study notes that current NATO standardization priorities include commonality of doctrines and procedures; interoperability of command, control, and communications and major weapons systems; and interchangeability of ammunition and primary combat supplies. Para. 76.

25. Para. 82.

26. Para. 45.

27. As the study notes: "In light of both the current international environment and the potential threats facing the Alliance, NATO's current nuclear posture will, for the foreseeable future, continue to meet the requirements of an enlarged Alliance. There is, therefore, no need now to change or modify any aspect of NATO's nuclear posture or policy, but the longer term implications of enlargement for both will continue to be evaluated." Para. 58.

28. Paras 65, 67.

29. Para. 81.

30. Para. 49.

31. "Communiqué of the North Atlantic Council in Ministerial Session, Brussels, 5 December 1995," para. 7.

32. They are: Albania, Bulgaria, the Czech Republic, Estonia, Finland, Hungary, Latvia, Lithuania, Poland, Rumania, Slovakia, Slovenia, the Former Yugoslav Republic of Macedonia, and Ukraine.

33. According to one of the basic PFP policy documents, "[a]ctive participation in the Partnership for Peace will play an important role in the evolutionary process of the enlargement of NATO." See "Partnership for Peace Invitation, Issued by the Heads of State and Government Participating in the Meeting of the North Atlantic Council held at NATO Headquarters, Brussels on 10-11 January 1994," *NATO Handbook*, pp. 265-68. The study also notes that active participation in NACC/PFP will help establish patterns of political and military cooperation with the alliance to facilitate a transition to membership. However, it will not of itself guarantee alliance membership. Para. 38.

34. A "cooperative-security" order would presumably have as its objectives: 1) to produce effective responses to regional tensions and instabilities; 2) to prevent conflicts by diplomatic means and possibly by operational deployment of military forces; 3) to manage conflicts, should they break out, through diplomatic efforts (e.g., negotiations, incentives to reach political settlement) and possibly through deployment of military forces; and 4) to provide through cooperative mechanisms resources, administrative direction, humanitarian assistance, and other forms of support for post-conflict rehabilitation.

35. "The challenges we will face in this new Europe cannot be comprehensively addressed by one institution alone, but only in a framework of interlocking institutions tying together the countries of Europe and North America. Consequently we are working towards a new European security architecture in which NATO, the CSCE, the European Community, the WEU and the Council of Europe complement each other." *Rome Declaration on Peace and Cooperation*, issued by Allied Heads of State and Government, 7-8 November 1991.

36. This argument would thus acknowledge the concerns of some Central European states that, following the Cold War, they face "grey area" security zones or indeed a security "vacuum" in the region.

37. These types of questions have been both echoed and amplified by numerous Russian commentators, parliamentarians, and academics. A typical version of the Russian critical reaction to NATO's enlargement policy is Alexander Konovalov, Sergei Oznobishchev, and Sergei Kortunov, "The Poverty of NATO-Mania," *Nezavisimaya Gazeta*, 20 March 1996, pp. 1-2. "By virtue of its structure and mechanisms, [NATO] can most effectively carry out only one task — actively respond to an attack from the east." See also Martin Butcher, Tasos Kokkinides, and Daniel Plesch, *Study on Enlargement: Destabilising Europe* (London: Joint Report of the British American Security Information Council [BASIC] and the Centre for European Security and Disarmament [CESD], 1996).

38. One of the more thoughtful pieces is Karaganov et al., "Russia and NATO: Theses of the Council on Foreign and Defence Policy."

39. The best summary of Foreign Minister Primakov's policy can be found in his interview with *Izvestiya*, 6 March 1996, trans. in *Summary of World Broadcasts*, 7 March 1996, SU/2554. See also "New Foreign Minister Primakov Outlines Four Main Foreign Policy Priorities," *ITAR-TASS Agency*, Moscow, 12 January 1996.

40. See, for example, Stanley R. Sloan, *NATO's Future: Beyond Collective Defense* (Washington: CRS Report for Congress, 15 September 1995); and Idem, "Negotiating a New Transatlantic Bargain," *NATO Review* 44 (March 1996): 19-23.

41. Asmus, Blackwill, and Larrabee, "Can NATO Survive?" pp. 92, 94-95.

42. Charles A. Kupchan, "Strategic Visions," *World Policy Journal* 11 (Fall 1994): 120.

43. The Treaty of Maastricht (1991) gives to EU members the right to become full members of the WEU. If new EU members take up that right, then a link becomes established de facto with NATO, because today full members of the WEU are also members of NATO. Thus, as the enlargement study points out, due to the cumulative effect of the security safeguards of Article 5 of the modified WEU Brussels Treaty and of Article 5 of the Washington Treaty, the current linkage in membership should be maintained. Para. 20.

44. See, for example, Kupchan, "Strategic Visions," p. 120.

45. See Javier Solana, "NATO's Role in Bosnia: Charting a New Course for the Alliance," *NATO Review* 44 (March 1996): 3-5.

46. See, for this claim, Nicholas Williams, "Partnership for Peace: Permanent Fixture or Declining Asset?" *Survival* 38 (Spring 1996): 98-110.

47. Kupchan, "Strategic Visions," p. 117.

48. "The North Atlantic Treaty, Washington DC, 4 April 1949," reproduced as Appendix VIII, *NATO Handbook*, p. 231.

49. As Asmus et al. point out, the "creation of the Atlantic [a]lliance was not only a response to a Soviet threat, but also part of a larger effort and vision to build a new and stable European order. Western leaders understood that a security framework was needed to stabilise democracy in post-totalitarian Germany and to thwart the return of nationalism and destructive geopolitics in Europe as a whole....It is a vital U.S. and Western interest that the gains of the end of the Cold War are not squandered and that democracy in East-Central Europe is not allowed to fail or be crushed." Asmus, Kugler, and Larrabee, "NATO Expansion: The Next Steps," pp. 27-28.

PART II

SELECTED CASE STUDIES

CHAPTER SIX

Symbol and (Very Little) Substance in the US Debate Over NATO Enlargement

Douglas T. Stuart

"The expansion of the NATO Alliance should be preceded by a new formulation of its raison d'être, its mission and its identity..."

Czech President Vaclav Havel[1]

Introduction

The evolving debate over NATO enlargement has temporarily obscured a more fundamental question within the American foreign policy community: whether the United States should attempt to preserve a protectorate relationship with the countries of Western Europe now that the Cold War is over. It can be argued that this has been a positive development, since it has given NATO governments an opportunity for cooperation in an otherwise tense period in transatlantic relations. Before long, however, the larger question, "Why are we still there, and what are we getting for it?," is likely to resurface within the United States foreign policy community. When it does, unresolved issues relating to NATO enlargement are likely to make it harder for the proponents of a continued US military presence in Europe to argue convincingly their case.

This chapter will survey the brief history of the NATO enlargement debate in the US and highlight some of the questions that need to be addressed before the alliance is extended eastward. It will also consider the problems that both the United States and Europe will confront if NATO enlargement comes to be seen as an "American show" with a West European supporting cast.

Background

Even before the formal collapse of the Soviet Union, commentators on both sides of the Atlantic began to make dire predictions about NATO's future. As early as 1990 the Stockholm Peace Research Institute published an influential volume entitled *Europe After an American Withdrawal: Economic and Military Issues*. Jane Sharp summarized the findings of the American and European contributors as follows:

> Although maintaining the status quo might be the preferred option of most, there was general recognition that the US presence in Europe may not be sustainable for much longer if the perception of a Soviet military threat continues to fade and Congress continues to cut US defence spending.[2]

Over the next three years, this theme began to be developed by influential experts on US foreign policy. George Kennan observed in 1993 that

> the time for the stationing of American forces on European soil has passed, and ... the ones now stationed there should be withdrawn...as soon as this is conveniently possible.

Kennan argued that such action "would not mean the end of NATO," although his long-term hope was for the development of a "new European security structure ... of which the United States was *not* a member."[3]

Ronald Steel went even further in the same year, in a speech at the Library of Congress:

> The problem with NATO is that changes in world politics have outrun the organization's logic. When we were defending Western Europe against the Soviet Union, the alliance cost more than $100 billion a year. It still costs us nearly that much, even though we can no longer identify an enemy....
>
> Trying to maintain an outdated dependency — either from a reluctance to relinquish control, or from a belief that the Europeans are incapable of dealing with their problems — is neither in Europe's interests nor in ours. The Europeans will not behave responsibly until they are obliged to exercise responsibility. They have the means to do so. What Europeans have lacked is the will. And that is because they have had little need to develop it.[4]

America's European allies did not make it any easier for those individuals within the US policy community who disagreed with the arguments put forth by Kennan and Steel. The importance that Western Europeans accorded to the economic and social aspects of the Maastricht Treaty reinforced the arguments of policymakers and experts on both sides of the Atlantic who saw NATO as an anachronism. By contrast, the articles of the Maastricht Treaty dealing with Common Foreign and Security Policy (CFSP) were among the most vague and conditional portions of that document. They nonetheless made it clear that in the future European security would be the purview of the Western European Union (WEU) as the defence component of the European Union and the "means to strengthen the European pillar of the Atlantic Alliance."[5]

The underdeveloped nature of the WEU was treated by many defenders of Maastricht as an institutional challenge rather than a serious security problem, since post-Cold War European security was undergirded by the principles of the Helsinki Final Act (1975) and the Charter of Paris (1990) and bolstered by the evolving institutional identity of the Conference on Security and Cooperation in Europe (CSCE).[6] Some of these themes were also put forward by the Canadian government to justify its decision in 1992 to withdraw all of its military forces from Germany by 1994.[7]

The implosion of Yugoslavia injected cynicism and recrimination into the evolving intra-NATO debate. American commentators missed no opportunity to bludgeon Western European governments with EU negotiator Jacques Poos' assertion that "this is the hour of Europe." The Europeans retaliated with pointed references to America's willingness to fight to the last French, British, or Canadian soldier to bring peace to the former Yugoslavia.

Under these circumstances, it is not surprising that various US Congressmen began to ask, "What's in it for us?" Les Aspin, then-chairman of the House Armed Services Committee, summarized the Congressional mood in 1992: "The heartburn on our side is that we should have to pay to keep US troops in Germany, and for what?"[8] Since that time, the House has voted each year to support amendments to the Department of Defense authorization bill that would require America's NATO allies to move toward a target of providing 75 percent of the support costs for its troops stationed in Europe, based upon the precedent of the US-Japan Host Nation Support agreement. To date, the legislation has been blocked each year in the Senate, but no one who follows such issues can fail to appreciate the breadth and depth of support — both within the Congress and the electorate — for such proposals.[9]

"Out of Area or Out of Business"

The debate about NATO enlargement should be understood against this background of transatlantic misunderstandings and mutual recriminations. To its credit, the Clinton administration has been consistent in its commitment to the preservation of NATO. But it has also been acutely sensitive to domestic and international criticisms of its leadership, resolve, and coherence in foreign affairs.[10] Following an initial period of caution and reticence, the Clinton team became enamoured of NATO enlargement as an issue that could help to preserve the alliance while concurrently enhancing President Clinton's image as a statesman.

Prior to the summer of 1994 the enlargement issue was one of several topics that NATO was confronting in a measured and incremental way. In response to pressures from Central and Eastern European (CEE) governments, the alliance created the North Atlantic Cooperation Council (NACC) in November 1991 and the Partnership for Peace (PFP) in January 1994. These innovative and potentially valuable initiatives were criticized by various CEE governments as instruments for delaying a decision on full NATO membership. This accusation was at least partly correct. The NACC and PFP initiatives nonetheless made perfect sense in view of the still-transitional nature of the post-Cold War situation and in light of the costs and risks of a more comprehensive and ambitious NATO commitment.

If the Clinton administration had chosen to do so, it could have taken the lead in a dialogue with the CEE governments regarding the potential benefits of NACC and PFP as instruments of NATO outreach. It could have argued, for example, that the Article 4 commitments associated with PFP membership are more than a pretext for disregarding security challenges in Central and Eastern Europe. To make this case, it could have referred to the more than 30 instances in NATO history in which the alliance has been used as a forum for discussing, and in some cases resolving, problems that fall under Article 4 of the NATO Treaty.[11] Instead, the Clinton team permitted the NACC and the PFP to be marginalized in the evolving security debate and chose instead to throw their support to the proponents of full NATO membership for CEE countries.

Tables 1 and 2 in the Appendix provide a snapshot of the debate that ensued within the United States security community in the months spanning the autumns of 1994 and 1995. Appendix Table 3 summarizes two pieces of US legislation that have contributed to the debate within the American government on the topic of NATO enlargement.

America Embraces Enlargement

Rather than discuss specific arguments for and against NATO enlargement, I will offer two summary comments about the nature of the American debate itself. I will then discuss four reasons for concern about a too-rapid NATO extension and make some very modest recommendations for slowing this process.

First, it is interesting to note both the rapidity of the policy changes within the American government on the issue of NATO enlargement and the speed at which this issue has become a central focus of debates among defence experts and think tanks in the United States. The fact that America's NATO allies were caught by surprise by the US campaign for expeditious enlargement illustrates the extent to which the American decision was driven by domestic considerations. One important consideration was the 1996 presidential election. By the fall of 1994, both Democrats and Republicans had begun to develop strategies for the 1996 presidential race. The leadership in each party appreciated that of the 14 states with the largest East European ethnic populations, Clinton had carried 12 in 1992. Since these states accounted for more than half of the electoral votes that Clinton received in that year, they were recognized as indispensable for a victory in 1996.[12] These considerations helped to convince the Republican leadership to become involved in the debate about NATO expansion during the spring of 1994, coming out publicly in its "Contract with America" in support of rapid and full NATO membership for Central and East European governments.

These partisan political considerations provided a backdrop for the debates that took place within the executive branch during the first half of 1994 on the issue of full NATO enlargement. Key members of the Clinton administration were sensitive to the kinds of arguments put forward by Poland's foreign minister, Andrzez Olechowski, who described PFP as "too small a step in the right direction." Intense, and at times acrimonious, internal debates took place within the Clinton team during the first half of 1994 on the relative merits of PFP and full NATO enlargement. By July 1994, when President Clinton visited Warsaw, it was clear that the momentum within the executive branch had shifted in favour of rapid accession of CEE states to the Washington Treaty. The president assured the Polish parliament that NATO expansion was "no longer a question of whether, but when and how."[13] Two months later, Richard Holbrooke was appointed assistant secretary of state, with a mandate to press the case within the US government for rapid and full NATO enlargement. This is the point at which the issue of enlargement became the focus of attention in the prestige media and within the community of professional defence experts.

This leads to a second general observation about the NATO enlargement debate within the US government and the foreign policy community — the relative lack of attention to specific questions of cost and risk and the marginalization of the US military community in the discussions about NATO enlargement. Within the executive branch, there was an apparent interest by the fall of 1994 in not letting such messy and confusing issues derail the decisionmaking process in favour of enlargement. Indeed, at one point during this period Assistant Secretary Holbrooke reportedly accused General Wesley Clark of the Joint Chiefs of Staff of "insubordination" because of the latter's expressed concern about "some issues we need to discuss" regarding inclusion of the CEE states in NATO.[14]

A comparable desire to avoid cognitive dissonance has been evident in Congress, where support for the principle of rapid and full NATO enlargement has been identified as a low-cost and high-reward political move. The two pieces of legislation summarized in Table 3 are the result of these calculations. These initiatives have done more than reinforce the Clinton administration's position on NATO enlargement. They have put additional domestic political pressure on the executive branch to be more visible and more ambitious in their support for this policy. Senator Sam Nunn and Representative Lee Hamilton have been two of the small number of legislators who have expressed concern about the dangers of this kind of blank-cheque lawmaking. Senator Nunn's incisive arguments are summarized in Table 2. Representative Hamilton has been similarly critical, arguing that "[i]t seems to me that we have not really grasped the significance of sending young men and women from my home state of Indiana to defend the Hungarian border from a Romanian attack."[15]

Debate within the professional foreign policy community has also suffered from a "disconnect" between abstract principles and operational realities. Neither the geopolitical analysis of Henry Kissinger and Peter Rodman nor the neoliberal rhetoric of Zbigniew Brzezinski and William Odom has been conducive to nuts-and-bolts discussion of the modalities of enlargement. The problem is illustrated by Brzezinski's assertion that

> a distinction should be made between political criteria ... and operational and logistical standards for effective military integration....The former need to be satisfied before admission; the latter can be pursued over a number of years both before and after admission.[16]

Missing from much of this debate, and from most of the discussions within the executive and legislative branches, is an in-depth analysis of the implications of NATO enlargement for the defence budgets of current NATO members. Such an analysis would need to begin with a consideration of the pattern of defence cuts since the end of the Cold War, which led former NATO Secretary General Manfred Wörner in 1993 to warn about the risk of "free-fall structural disarmament" within the alliance.[17] This situation is not likely to improve anytime soon, in light of the commitments to deficit-cutting by the leading European allies and in view of the recent agreement between the White House and Congress to balance the federal budget in seven years.[18]

Reasons for Concern About Rapid NATO Enlargement

Under pressure from Washington, NATO completed its study on enlargement on 28 September 1995. The document reiterated the alliance's commitment to eastward expansion and specified the preconditions for accession to the Washington Treaty.[19] Aside from the general problem created by this document — that it makes it harder for NATO governments to resist the demands of domestic constituencies and CEE governments for rapid progress toward full alliance membership for CEE states — the document raises four more specific problems.

The first and most well-known problem is the exacerbation of Russian fears, which could undermine the forces of democratization and international co-operation in that country. Since so much has already been written about this problem, I will contribute only two observations. First, the relative lack of concern that some US commentators have expressed about the risk of Russian overreaction may be informed (either consciously or unconsciously) by the events of 1989-90, when the then-Soviet leadership communicated its intense concern about the prospect of German unification but subsequently accepted the *fait accompli*. According to this logic, Moscow can be expected to swallow the bitter pill of NATO expansion just as it swallowed the pill of German unification, as long as the west is united and strong in its messages to Russia. This may be correct, but it seems to be at least as likely that, having convinced the Russian people to accept a unified Germany in Central Europe, the Russian government will be either unwilling or unable to ask for more forbearance from its citizens on the issue of NATO enlargement.[20]

This leads to my second observation about the risks of Russian overreaction to NATO enlargement. Based upon the US government's own assessment of America's post-Cold War national security interests, Washington should be in the forefront of the countries warning against a too-rapid NATO enlargement, rather than serving as the cheerleader for the pro-enlargement group. For example, if one considers the four threats to US national security identified in the Clinton administration's Bottom-Up Review (regional conflicts, proliferation of weapons of mass destruction, threats to US economic security, and the failure of democracy in the former Soviet bloc), US-Russian cooperation is indispensable for the protection of three of the four.[21] By contrast, Western European governments have a more direct and immediate interest in the stability of Central Europe and should be in the forefront of the campaign to find ways to enhance that stability.

The second problem raised by the draft report on NATO expansion has to do with the explicit offer of a *nuclear guarantee* to any CEE governments that join the alliance. This offer may be attractive to some proponents of NATO enlargement because it makes it easier for them to claim that there is no need for the alliance to preoccupy itself with military details, since the core of NATO security is still the American nuclear commitment. At a time when the whole logic of America's extended nuclear deterrent strategy is in need of reconsideration, it would be a grave mistake to make this argument. Furthermore, there are both practical and moral issues raised by the draft study's requirement that "[n]ew members will be expected to support the concept of deterrence and the essential role nuclear weapons play in the Alliance's strategy of war prevention as set forth in the Strategic Concept."[22] Finally, at a time when the United States is engaged in substantive arms-control negotiations with the Russian government, such a policy seems not only counterproductive but gratuitously threatening.

The third problem with the American policy of support for NATO expansion is that it may backfire at home. President Clinton's campaign for the eastward extension of the alliance is an important part of a larger effort to steer the American foreign policy debate away from isolationism. As such, NATO enlargement is linked to the evolving policy of US military involvement in Bosnia, and will be seen as such by the American people. The prospect of 20,000 Americans in Bosnia will wonderfully concentrate the minds of American legislators and commentators over the next several months. Ideally, this will mean that the comfortable situation that the proponents of NATO enlargement have enjoyed thus far will come to an end. Abstract rhetoric will no longer be a substitute for specific information about the costs and risks of NATO enlargement. Within Congress, the focus of the NATO enlargement debate will shift from "when" to "how and why." If this more substantive debate does not take place, however, and the process of NATO enlargement moves forward while the Bosnia mission is ongoing, there is a real danger that the entire structure of assumptions and expectations that are currently being imposed upon NATO may collapse in the face of military problems in the Balkans.

The fourth and final reason for concern about the draft study on NATO enlargement is its implications for the "new security architecture" of Europe. [23] The American-sponsored campaign in support of NATO expansion has occurred at a time when key decisions about the future of the European Union and the Western European Union should have been taken. If NATO marches eastward too quickly under an American banner it could make it easier for Western European governments to defer decisions on the enlargement of the EU and tip the scales in favour of the proponents of a three-speed (three-class?) integration process. More importantly, it could bolster the position of those factions within Western Europe who wish to establish the EU as an exclusive (and exclusively) "civilian club" that leaves the messy issues of regional and global security to Washington.

Conclusion

Any discussion of the risks and problems associated with NATO enlargement must confront the fact that the allies have already committed themselves to this undertaking. To paraphrase Senator Sam Nunn, the ox is already in the ditch. Fortunately, NATO governments appear to have recognized that they were moving much too quickly on the issue of enlargement and that the enlargement campaign was gaining too much momentum. The official statements at the conclusion of the December 1995 NATO ministerial conference indicate that the alliance will continue to study the issue of enlargement, and discuss the prospects for membership with interested CEE governments, but there will be no substantive action on enlargement during 1996. This is good news, in particular because it will permit the members of the European Union to address the inter-related subjects of EU enlargement and the European Security and Defence Identity (ESDI) during the 1996 Intergovernmental Conference (IGC), without preemption by NATO. In the interim, Washington would be well advised to lend its diplomatic support to those factions within the EU that wish to use the IGC process to accelerate the eastward expansion of the European Union.[24] The Clinton administration should also encourage those European experts and policy makers who have been pressing the EU to take greater responsibility for the stability and security of Western Europe and of the EU's neighbours to the east and south.

Ideally, EU membership can still be established as an intermediary stage in the process of NATO enlargement. But even if this goal cannot be accomplished, Washington will be able to use the time between now and the end of the IGC to continue to work with Moscow to make NATO enlargement as palatable as possible to the Russian people.

Notes

The author would like to thank Jason Ashline for his indispensable assistance in the construction of the tables in this chapter.

1. Quoted by Rafael Estrella, General Rapporteur for the North Atlantic Assembly, "Structure and Functions: European Security and Defence Identity (ESDI) and Combined Joint Task Force," Draft General Report, International Secretariat, October 1995 (internet edition), p. 4.

2. Jane Sharp, ed., *Europe After an American Withdrawal: Economic and Military Issues* (Oxford: Oxford University Press/SIPRI, 1990), p. 48.

3. George Kennan, *Around the Cragged Hill* (New York: Norton, 1993), pp. 223-24.

4. Ronald Steel, *Temptations of a Superpower* (Cambridge: Harvard University Press, 1995), pp. 78-79.

5. CFSP is discussed by the author in "Can Europe Survive Maastricht?" *Research Monograph* (Carlisle Barracks, PA: US Army War College, Strategic Studies Institute, 4 February 1994), pp. 4-5.

6. The best articulation of the neoliberal institutionalist vision of Europe's future is by Kalevi Holsti, "The Post-War 'Settlement' in Comparative Perspective," in *Discord and Collaboration in a New Europe: Essays in Honor of Arnold Wolfers,* ed. Douglas Stuart and Stephen Szabo (Washington: Johns Hopkins Foreign Policy Institute, 1994), pp. 37-70.

7. For background, see Roy Rempel, "Canada's Troop Deployments in Germany: Twilight of a Forty-Year Presence?" in *Homeward Bound? Allied Forces in the New Germany,* ed. David G. Haglund and Olaf Mager (Boulder: Westview, 1992), pp. 213-48.

8. Les Aspin, speaking on "*Congressional Connection*," hosted by Representative Joan Kelly Horn, 1 July 1992, quoted in Joseph Lepgold, "Does Europe Still Have a Place in U.S. Foreign Policy?" in *Discord and Collaboration*, p. 186.

9. According to the Fiscal Year (FY) 96 DOD Authorization Act (H.R. 1530), which passed the House on 20 June 1995, the president would be "urged" to press the European allies to move toward a goal of contributing 75 percent of the nonpersonnel costs for US troops based in Europe by 1999. Failure to fulfill the 75-percent target would result in progressive annual cuts in US troop strength in Europe (based upon a formula of 1,000 troops cut for each 1 percent below the target figure) down to a floor figure of 25,000 troops.

10. Without gainsaying the Clinton administration's humanitarian and strategic motivations, it was no coincidence that the president referred to leadership 19 times in his speech to the American people in support of a US troop commitment to Bosnia.

11. For a history of NATO discussions during the Cold War about Article 4 type challenges, see Douglas Stuart and William Tow, *The Limits of Alliance: NATO Out-of-Area Problems Since 1949* (Baltimore: Johns Hopkins University Press, 1990); and Douglas Stuart, "Can NATO Transcend Its European Borders?" *Research Monograph* (Carlisle Barracks,PA: US Army War College, Strategic Studies Institute, 21 February 1991).

12. For an insightful analysis, see Dick Kirtschten, "Ethnics Resurging," *National Journal*, 25 February 1995, pp. 484-87. Kirtschten also points out that George Bush lost considerable support within this community in 1992 because he was judged to be too slow in recognizing the breakaway states of the former Soviet Union.

13. Quotes and chronology are from Jeffrey Simon, "Central European Civil-Military Relations and NATO Expansion," Institute for National Strategic Studies, *Working Paper no. 39* (Washington: National Defense University, April 1995), pp. 10-11.

14. See Michael Dobbs, "Securing the New Europe," *Washington Post*, 5 July 1995, p. 3.

15. Quoted by Michael Dobbs, "U.S. Lawmakers Have Stood on Both Sides," *Washington Post*, 7 July 1995, p. A24.

16. Zbigniew Brzezinski, "A Plan for Europe," *Foreign Affairs* 74 (January/February 1995): 32-33.

17. Quoted in *Strategic Survey: 1993-1994* (London: Brassey's/International Institute for Strategic Studies, May 1994), p. 115.

18. See Richard Stevenson, "Deficit-Cutting Has Now Gone International," *New York Times*, 9 November 1995, pp. 1, 4.

19. See North Atlantic Treaty Organization, "Study on NATO Enlargement" (Brussels, September 1995).

20. For a discussion of the problem from the perspective of the Russian foreign policy community, see "Russia and NATO: Theses of the Council on Foreign and Defense Policy," unpublished summary of a working group headed by S. A. Karaganov, 25 May 1995.

21. See US Secretary of Defense Les Aspin, "Report on the Bottom-Up Review" (Washington: USGPO, October 1993), p. 20.

22. "Study on NATO Enlargement," chap. 4, sec. D.

23. Ibid., chap.1, sec. A.

24. EU governments have agreed to begin formal negotiations with 10 CEE governments interested in full EU membership by the end of 1997. EU officials predict that once these negotiations begin it will take from two and a half to five years before the first CEE countries are admitted to the European Union. See Nathaniel Nash, "European Union Offers Timetable for Talks with Applicants," *New York Times*, 17 December 1995, p. 17.

APPENDIX

TABLE 1: PROPONENTS OF ENLARGEMENT

Henry Kissinger	Table 1: For Enlargement
Rationale:	If NATO does not expand, Russian opposition is likely to grow as its economy gains strength; the nations of Central Europe may drift out of their association with Europe. A vacuum between Germany and Russia could develop. Germany will sooner or later seek to achieve its security by national efforts, encountering on the way a Russia pursuing the same policy from its own side.
Who:	The Visegrad four initially.
When:	Now.
Criteria:	No specific information available but Kissinger argues that the Visegrad countries need both membership in the EU and NATO. Kissinger states "in truth, membership in one institution implies membership in the other. Since most members of the EU are members of NATO and since it is inconceivable that they would ignore attacks on one of their members after European integration has reached a certain point, membership in the EU will, by one device or another, lead to at least de facto extension of the NATO guarantee" (p. 824).
Policy toward Russia and Ukraine:	NATO should not extend membership to Russia. Russian membership would dissolve the Atlantic alliance into a vague system, would weaken the internal structure of the alliance, and extend NATO territory commitments to China. NATO enlargement should also reject a Russian veto. A security treaty between NATO and Russia should be established so that a truly cooperative relationship can be established. Such a treaty would provide that no foreign troops be stationed on the territory of new NATO members. The CSCE (now OSCE) could be given expanded functions to anchor Russia to the Atlantic nations (p. 825).
Military/Defence posture:	No information available.

Sources: Henry Kissinger, "Expand NATO Now," *Washington Post,* 19 December 1994, p. A27; Idem, *Diplomacy* (New York: Simon and Schuster, 1994), pp. 823-25.

Peter Rodman	Table 1: For Enlargement
Rationale:	Argues that NATO expansion is "inescapable" and "necessary" in order to prevent a reimposition of Russian dominance in Central Europe. "Our geopolitical interests are clear...The West's vital stake does not depend on the progress of internal economic or political reforms of these countries. Our stake is their independence." "Russia is already getting back on its feet geopolitically, even before it gets back on its feet economically. The only potential great-power security problem in Central Europe is the lengthening shadow of Russian strength, and NATO has the job of counterbalancing it."
Who:	Initially the Visegrad four.
When:	As soon as possible.
Criteria:	No specific information but "the administration's delay in order to work out criteria for new membership is an evasion."
Policy toward Russia and Ukraine:	There will not be a Russian veto over expansion. Russia must accept that "geopolitical revisionism" and a sphere of influence over Central and Eastern Europe will not be tolerated. "For Russia, acceptance of this new status quo in Central Europe must be the sine qua non of any relationship with us." "If the four are admitted to NATO, there will be a brief period of tension and some fallout: Russia may opt out of PFP but the relationship between Russia and NATO will be determined by other long-term factors..." (Not specified).
Military/Defence Posture:	No information available.

Source: Peter Rodman, "4 More for NATO," *Washington Post,* 13 December 1994, p. A29.

Zbigniew Brzezinski	Table 1: For Enlargement
Rationale:	"...[NATO enlargement] should be pursued not as a hostile initiative but as a part of a larger architectural effort designed eventually to span Eurasia" (41). The author does not see any immediate Russian threat to the security of Europe, but if the Euro-Atlantic alliance is going to endure, then NATO will have to expand. According to Brzezinski, "as the EU reaches out for new members, so will Europe's security organ, the WEU....With most of the EU's members also participating in NATO, neutrality by the alliance in the face of an attack on a WEU member will become inconceivable. As a practical matter, the issue of formally widening the alliance can thus no longer be avoided" (27).
Who:	Would depend on the criteria but the Visegrad four would be considered initially. However, the criteria, theoretically, "would leave open the possibility for others, including Russia itself" (33). Additionally, during this process of deciding who, differentiation may become necessary; instead of the Visegrad four considered all at the same time, "the first cut might include only Poland and the Czech Republic. Slovakia, for internal reasons, may qualify later, and that could have the effect (for geographical reasons) of somewhat complicating Hungary's admission, unless NATO is willing to leapfrog spatially" (33).
When:	"Even the initially limited expansion of NATO would take several years" (33). "Nonetheless, it is certainly possible, given effective and focused leadership, to complete the political phase of the admissions process by the years 1996-1998...and in any case for all four [Visegrad] by the end of the decade" (34).
Criteria:	"...a distinction should be made between political criteria that qualify a state for admission into an allied community and operational and logistical standards for effective military integration once within the community. The former need to be satisfied before admission; the latter can be pursued over a number of years both before and after admission. Basic criteria should include: a stable democratic system based on a functioning market economy; the absence of entangling territorial or ethnic disputes; an evident respect for the rights of national minorities; preferably, geographical continuity to the alliance; constitutionally grounded civilian control over the military; and transparency in defense budgets and policy. As a practical matter, interoperability in logistics, communications, command and control, and weaponry would be desirable, but these could be pursued after formal admission" (32-33).

... continued

| Zbigniew Brzezinski | *(continued)* |

| Policy toward Russia and Ukraine: | *Russia*
The expansion of NATO should, therefore, not be driven by "whipping up anti-Russian hysteria that could eventually become a self-fulfilling prophecy." "The Kremlin must be made to understand that bluster and threats will be neither productive nor effective and may even accelerate the process of expansion. Russia has the right neither to veto NATO expansion nor to impose limited sovereignty on the Central European states" (35).
Russia should be approached on a two-track basis.
1. the independent decision of the alliance to enlarge its membership
2. the simultaneous invitation to Russia to help create a new transcontinental system of collective security, one that goes beyond the expansion of NATO proper.
This proposal would have two components:
1. A NATO-Russian Federation treaty of cooperation
2. A new mechanism for special security consultations within the OSCE (35), "perhaps through a special consultative mechanism involving the major players: the U.S., Russia, UK, France, Germany, Italy, Poland, and Ukraine" (36).

Ukraine
"The overarching NATO-Russian treaty should include a special annex containing a joint, formal, and very explicit commitment by both parties to Ukraine's independence and security. At this stage, such a commitment should neither foreclose nor promise any future relationship between Ukraine and NATO, nor any special and truly voluntary cooperation between Russia and Ukraine. It would provide assurance to Ukraine that its political status is respected, enduring, and in the interest of both NATO and the Russian Federation — irrespective of the innermost fantasies of the Russian signatories" (38).

Baltics
"The Baltic reaction to NATO expansion is quite predictable: the Balts will step up their efforts to become the next members. Their eventual membership will have to be addressed in the wider Scandinavian context" (37). |
| Military/Defence Posture: | "Since any foreseeable expansion of the alliance is likely to be pacific, the specific military dispositions arising from enlarged membership need not involve the forward deployment of NATO troops — especially American and German forces — on the territory of the new Central European members" (34). |

Source: Zbigniew Brzezinski, "A Plan for Europe," *Foreign Affairs* 74 (January /February 1995): 26-42.

William Odom	Table 1: For Enlargement
Rationale:	The best argument for NATO's expansion is found in its reason for its inception: "The concern of its proponents with internal political and economic affairs in Western Europe." The primary purpose of NATO expansion must be the internal transformation of new member states. External military security is also a reason but the military threat is not imminent. The military threat could reappear in the long run if NATO is not expanded (45).
Who:	Poland, the Czech Republic, and Hungary — initially. Slovakia can not be disregarded because it would provide a contiguous border between the present NATO boundary and Hungary. Rumania and Bulgaria are too problematic in their internal developments. Same is true for the Baltics, Ukraine, and Belarus. NATO may bite off more than it can chew (45).
When:	Delay is not the answer (47).
Criteria:	"By advocating criteria that include significant reform and upgrading of potential members' militaries so that they are near the level of NATO's, the day of expansion is delayed" (47). As for political and economic criteria, matter of judgement about the "prospects for members to stay on the reform track" (47).
Policy toward Russia and Ukraine:	Essentially the same as Kissinger and Brzezinski towards Russian membership. Russian membership in NATO would destroy the character of the alliance and weaken its internal structure. Also, Russia shows no interest in joining. The task of accommodating Russia is global — not just relegated to Europe (46). On a global level, Russia could be brought into the G-7. On a European level, a so-called security committee within the OSCE could be created. It would be composed of Russia, Germany, France, Britain, and the US. A consensus among these states to act would be necessary. In such circumstances, NATO would be the fall-back for military action. This OSCE type grouping would provide Russia with the opening to participate as cooperatively as desired and to block OSCE action it opposed. All of these proposals for Russia would improve the climate for Ukraine, Belarus, and the Baltic states because it would force Russia to play by the rules (46).
Military/Defence Posture:	No information available.

Source: William E. Odom, "NATO's Expansion: Why the Critics are Wrong," *National Interest* (Spring 1995): 38-49.

James Morrison	Table 1: For Enlargement
Rationale:	Advocates "a vibrant and growing NATO that continues the NACC and PFP outreach programs that extends member-ship to selected states in Central and Eastern Europe. NATO would be a leading participant in an active, broader web of European Security Institutions (OSCE, NACC, PFP, EU, WEU). NATO would not, at least in the near future, extend membership to states in the CIS, but would work to develop effective relations, especially with Ukraine and Russia" (126).
Who:	The Czech Republic (128), as a first step.
When:	Invite at least one country to join NATO soon. This would emphasize NATO's vitality and strength (128).
Policy toward Russia and Ukraine:	Develop a unique relationship with Russia and Ukraine. A treaty between NATO and each state might be considered. The treaty should not have as its focus an official Russia-NATO security guarantee. The treaty, also, should not deny deployment of forces of other NATO members (129).

Source: James W. Morrison, *NATO Expansion and Alternative Future Security Alignments* (Washington: National Defense University, 1995) .

Ronald D. Asmus, Richard L. Kugler, and F. Stephen Larrabee	Table 1: For Enlargement

Rationale:

In light of the failed policy concerning Bosnia, NATO should expand rapidly. The authors coin this policy, *Promote Stability.* They argue that the political situation in Eastern and Central Europe is fragile. There is a security vacuum between Russia and Germany. This vacuum may undercut the progress that the fragile democracies are making because of the possible threat of nationalism and geopolitical competition between Russia and Germany (9). This policy provides the countries of CEE with the political and security anchor they want. It also allows the US and NATO to determine the pace and scope of criteria for expansion. NATO will also be in better position to respond militarily (11). This option is the most difficult politically because it requires integrated security and economic stability. NATO and EU should expand and integrate. NATO must drive the process.

Who:

Initially the Visegrad four (28).

When:

By the end of the decade (earlier if possible). Simultaneous EU and NATO integration will increase support on Capitol Hill because it may show that the Europeans are picking up more of the burden, while at the same time not isolating Russia (29).

Criteria:

They do not state outright their own ideas on criteria. Allude to using the original criteria contained in the Washington Treaty of 1949 (12).

Policy toward Russia and Ukraine:

Enlargement cannot destabilize Russia and Ukraine. Three factors must be addressed concerning Russia and Ukraine: the modalities of enlargement, the timetable, the status of special relationships between NATO and Russia and Ukraine (29). "The policy challenge is to include Russia as an active participant in all European processes while not giving it a veto over either NATO or the EU's future, minimize the negative impact on Russian politics of NATO expansion, and guard against any Russian counter measures that could damage important Western Interests" (22).

... continued

Ronald D. Asmus, Richard L. *(continued)*
Kugler, and F. Stephen Larrabee

The following policies should be pursued towards Russia:

Political and Economic
– Intensify G-7 (make it G-8)
– Expand economic cooperation and trade
– Increase technical assistance
– Strengthen parliamentary ties (Duma and west)

Security Related
– NATO-Russian treaty
– OSCE Security Council
– Regular meetings between Russia and NATO
– Amend the CFE treaty
– Expand the PFP
– Bilateral military contacts between US and Russia

Towards Ukraine:
– Independence from Russia is the key. "Further economic development and like Russia, a special partnership or treaty could be necessary" (p. 27).

Source: Ronald D. Asmus, Richard L. Kugler, and F. Stephen Larrabee, "NATO Expansion: The Next Steps," *Survival* 37 (Spring 1995): 7-31.

Richard Holbrooke	Table 1: For Enlargement
Rationale:	"The goal remains the defense of the alliance's vital interests and the promotion of European stability...The goal is to promote security in Central Europe by integrating countries that qualify into the stabilizing framework of NATO" (45). NATO expansion must be part of a new security architecture which should involve not only NATO but the EU and the OSCE among others. EU expansion is vital also. EU and NATO are mutually supportive and their expansions will not proceed on the same pace. The WEU should serve as a strong European pillar but should not dilute NATO (46-47). OSCE must be strengthened. It must provide an avenue for addressing potential conflicts earlier, and continue to support the spread of democratic values and the legitimization of human rights. OSCE, however, cannot be a substitute for NATO or the EU (48).
Who:	There is no list of nations. Each nation will be considered individually, not as part of some grouping (45).
When:	There is no timetable (the "how" and "why" questions will be answered by the end of the year when NATO completes its year-long study) (45).
Criteria:	Decisions will be made exclusively by NATO. No outside nation will exercise a veto. No criteria have been determined, certain precepts are non-negotiable (as contained in the 1949 Washington Treaty). New members must be democratic, have market economies, be committed to responsible security policies, and be able to contribute to the alliance (45).
Policy toward Russia and Ukraine:	The US supports deeper Russian participation in the G-7, and is sponsoring Russian membership in the World Trade Organization (WTO) (50). A NATO-Russian Treaty might be helpful. Any such arrangement must consider Ukraine. Its independence and integrity are crucial (51).
Military/Defence Posture:	No information available.

Source: Richard Holbrooke, *"America,* A European Power," *Foreign Affairs* 74 (March/April 1995): 38-51.

TABLE 2: OPPONENTS OF ENLARGEMENT

Sam Nunn	Table 2: Against Expansion
Rationale:	There has not been a clear and convincing rationale of why NATO should expand. "Somebody had better be able to explain to the American people why, or at least why now." Furthermore, rapid NATO enlargement will be widely misunderstood in Russia and will have a serious negative impact on political and economic reform in that country for several reasons: 1. It further promotes Russian nationalism. 2. The Russian people may resist NATO enlargement.
NATO Expansion Is Flawed:	"NATO is fundamentally a military alliance. If you denigrate the military side of it, then it becomes a political and psychological alliance, which is something very different." "The last thing we need is a repeat of what happened before World War II, when commitments were made that were not backed up by military capabilities and intentions."
Alternative Policies:	*A two-track approach should be pursued:* 1. Advocates the evolutionary enlargement of NATO. Enlargement would depend on the political and economic developments within the European countries who aspire to full NATO membership. When a country becomes eligible for EU membership, it will also be eligible to join the WEU and then be prepared for NATO membership. The advantage of this method is a natural process connecting economic and security interests. It is not aimed at Russian insecurities. 2. Advocates enlargement which will depend largely on Russian behaviour. The following types of Russian behaviour will prompt enlargement: 1. aggressive moves against other sovereign states. 2. significant violations of arms control and other legally binding obligations pertinent to the security of Europe. 3. emergence of a nondemocratic Russian government.

Source: Sam Nunn. Speech delivered to the SACLANT Seminar 95, NATO Public Data Service, June 1995.

Michael Brown	Table 2: Against Expansion
Rationale:	There is no strategic or political rationale for NATO expansion at the present time. NATO expansion should be tied to strategic circumstances: If Russia takes steps to threaten Central Europe, militarily, NATO should offer membership to as many states in the region as possible. Some of the steps that would trigger NATO expansion include: Russia withdrawal from the CFE treaty, a buildup of Russian conventional forces near neighbouring states in the west, the use of military threats against any neighbouring state, discontinuation of the denuclearization process, violation of Moscow's pledges to respect Ukraine's sovereignty, absorption of Ukraine or Belarus into the Russian Federation, or transformation of the CIS into a federal entity. Otherwise, NATO expansion could spark a backlash in Russia (A29).
NATO Expansion Is Flawed:	Four reasons: 1. Russian aggression in Europe is highly unlikely. 2. If the states of Central Europe "feel threatened" as Henry Kissinger contends, then why are Poland and Hungary, in particular, reducing military conscription and the Czech Army reducing its mechanized and infantry forces? 3. If Germany was worried about a "security vacuum" in CEE, it would be urging the US to move faster — not slower — on NATO expansion. 4. There would be a Russian response. "No matter how NATO expansion is packaged, it would involve American nuclear guarantees to states in Central Europe" (A29).
Policy toward Russia and Central Europe:	*In the meantime, there are two interrelated security problems that need to be addressed and in which NATO and the EU have vital roles:* 1. How to discourage Russian aggression in Central Europe. 2. How to keep instability in Central Europe to a minimum (p. 44). *In order to address both questions, western strategy towards Russia should be:* 1. Strengthen PFP ties with Russia and Central Europe (45). 2. A NATO-Russian formal treaty (46). 3. Closer political and economic ties between Russia and the EU(46). *As far as western strategy towards the countries of Central Europe:* 1. Continue through bilateral and multilateral approaches to develop closer links and to make the military forces of NATO and non-NATO Europe more interoperable (46). 2. The EU can help to dampen intrastate and interregional conflicts (46-47). 3. The EU can stimulate economic development as it should expand as quickly as it can (47).

Sources: Michael E. Brown, "NATO Expansion: Wait and See," *Washington Post,* 26 December 1994, p. A29; Idem, "The Flawed Logic of NATO Expansion," *Survival* 37 (Spring 1995): 34-48.

Michael Mandelbaum	Table 2: Against Expansion
Rationale:	"NATO expansion, under present circumstances and as currently envisioned, is at best premature, at worst counter-productive, and in any case largely irrelevant to the problems confronting the countries situated between Germany and Russia." There is no security vacuum, NATO is not capable of promoting democracy, and there is already a "new security architecture" in place. This does not mean, however, that NATO should be abandoned. NATO is vital for strong and active American participation in Europe. Also, NATO expansion, under certain threatening circumstances cannot be ruled out.
	Expansionists fall into two camps. Those who want to expand the alliance because they claim that there is a real military threat from Russia and those who believe that the alliance can promote and foster democracy and free markets. However, both rationales for expansion are flawed.
	First, if the promotion of democracy is the key to NATO expansion, as declared by Richard Holbrooke ("America, a European Power" *Foreign Affairs*, March/April 1995) then expansion, as currently envisioned does not reach far enough to the east. "For the countries under active consideration (Visegrad) are precisely those best placed to make a success-ful transition to democracy and free markets without NATO membership." It is Russia, Ukraine, the Baltics, and other countries of Eurasia that would benefit the most concerning democracy. However, NATO is not and was never capable of promoting democracy (p. 9). NATO is a military alliance. The EU should be the cornerstone of any democratic promotion (10).
	Second, if the expansion of the alliance has to do with a military threat from Russia, then the current rationale for expansion (known as "neo-containment") under these terms is also flawed because, once again, expansion does not go far enough to include Ukraine. (10). However, Ukraine has expressed no desire to join NATO. "Ukrainians, at least, do not seem to believe that expanding the Atlantic alliance will benefit them. On the contrary, they appear to feel that the extension of NATO membership to Central Europe would relegate Ukraine to the dangerous side of a new dividing line" (11). Also, there is no security vacuum as some claim. Additionally, this latter rationale for expansion will inevitably hamper Russian democrats, and "Russia would regard the new configuration of European security that an expanded NATO would produce as illegitimate because it had been imposed over Russian opposition — instead of with its cooperation" (12).

... continued

Michael Mandelbaum	*(continued)*

| | There is already a "new security architecture" in place. The post-Cold War settlement rested not on the age-old balance of power, but rather on consensus and cooperation. It has three main features: First, it is the product of negotiations. Second, "Europe's military forces have been reshaped so that they are more suitable for defense than attack" (CFE treaty) (12). Third, "as a result of the verification provisions of the arms treaties... military forces are transparent: each country can see not only what forces all the others have but also what the others are doing with their forces" (13). This does not mean that NATO should be dissolved. NATO can expand under three developments: First, Russian violation of the political or territorial integrity of its western neighbours. Second, serious violation of arms control treaties. Third, the advent of an aggressive or hypernationalist Russia (13). |
| **Alternative Policy:** | No information available. |

Source: Michael Mandelbaum, "Preserving the New Peace: The Case Against NATO Expansion," *Foreign Affairs,* 74 (May/June 1995): 9-13.

Fred C. Iklé	Table 2: Against Expansion
Rationale:	Argues that expanding NATO now would fatally weaken the alliance. "The Atlantic alliance must not become a chain letter — some Ponzi scheme that escapes bankruptcy by signing up new members." Although Iklé does not rule out NATO expansion in the event that the alliance faced a "threat of external aggression," he states that "Inviting new members into a consensus-based alliance is always risky. It is foolhardy if the new members have not worked together in a collective endeavor to overcome a common danger" (referring to NATO establishment after the end of World War II among the allies in the war). Furthermore, expansion of NATO would weaken the alliance because "a revived K.G.B. would find collaborators among its former colleagues in Eastern Europe" (who could pass on military secrets to the Russians). Iklé further rebuts expansionists by stating that if NATO is to fill the security vacuum in Eastern Europe, then why is there talk of offering membership to one county and not another? "But, if, say, Slovakia, is a vacuum, why not Slovenia; if Slovenia, why not Macedonia, Moldova or Belarus? By expanding eastward NATO would merely shove the vacuum ahead of itself." Also, expansionists argue that NATO membership helps further to consolidate democracy. However, Iklé states: "In fact, NATO membership neither guarantees nor requires democracy. Greece had been a member of the alliance for 15 years when a 1967 coup led to seven years of military rule. Yet it remained a member the entire time the colonels were in power."
Alternative Policy:	No information given.

Source: Fred C. Iklé, "How to Ruin NATO" *New York Times,* 11 January 1995, p. A21.

Ted Galen Carpenter	Table 2: Against Expansion
Rationale:	"The premise that originally underlay the alliance was the fundamental compatibility of interests between the United States and its European allies. Although that premise seemed convincing during the Cold War, when the Western democracies faced a powerful common adversary, the validity of assumptions abut transatlantic solidarity is far more questionable in the post-Cold War era....The pertinent question for U.S. policy makers is whether it makes sense from the standpoint of American interests to preserve a transatlantic alliance that was designed in a vastly different era to deal with a mutual threat that no longer exists. That point is important, not only because America's continued leadership of NATO involves significant financial costs — some $90 billion a year — but because new missions being contemplated for the alliance would entail grave risks....American leaders should not only resist suggestions to enlarge NATO's security jurisdiction, they should seriously consider a policy that moves in precisely the opposite direction — toward giving the venerable alliance a well-earned retirement....Although European and American security interests may overlap, they are, nevertheless, distinct and sometimes may even be in conflict. Rather than strive to preserve an outdated transatlantic alliance, Washington would be wise to encourage the European states to form new security structures or to strengthen such existing bodies as the Western European Union and the France-German Eurocorps for NATO" (8).
Alternative Policy:	The OSCE and the WEU, especially, should be strengthened. The WEU should replace NATO as the military arm of European defence. The United States should "establish a more limited and flexible security relationship with the nations of Western Europe. Such a relationship need not — in fact, should not — be enshrined in elaborate treaties that attempt to codify cooperation on a wide range of diverse issues. A worthwhile step would be to replace NATO with a security coordination council. In a relatively low-threat environment, the council would serve primarily as a forum for discussing political and military issues of mutual concern. That forum could quickly become a mechanism for consultation if a significant security problem began to emerge" (146). "In addition to establishing a more limited and focused security relationship with Western Europe, the United States should

... continued

Ted Galen Carpenter   *(continued)*

seek ways to expand its economic ties with the entire Continent. The latter objective needs to include not only a more effective relationship with the EU — as well as upgraded bilateral links to the key member states of that association — but also more coherent policies toward the nations of Eastern Europe and the former Soviet Union" (147). "Instead of trying to preserve NATO, it would be more useful for U.S. leaders to propose the creation of a transatlantic economic council that would focus on preventing or resolving U.S.-West European economic disputes. The mandate for the council should be to promote and protect the most open commercial system possible" (148).

Source: Ted Galen Carpenter, *Beyond NATO: Staying Out of Europe's Wars* (Washington: CATO Institute, 1994).

Owen Harries	Table 2: Against Expansion

Rationale:

Argues that "the west" as we know it was not a permanent political and military entity but a highly artificial one that existed only to protect the "west" from a life-threatening "east." Alliances, however, rarely outlive their purpose. Europe is now in a new time and place (41-42).

Thus, NATO should not expand for six main reasons:

1. The proposal takes no account at all of Russian suscepti-bilities and interests and envisages no role for Russia in Eastern Europe (42).

2. The proposal suffers from a massive credibility problem given the pathetic performance of the western countries in the Bosnian crisis. "Why should anyone in Eastern Europe take such a guarantee seriously?" (43).

3. If a NATO guarantee were to be honoured, then such a commitment would likely tax the overall military capabilities of member countries to the point of distorting the force structures away from those best designed to meet their core security needs (44).

4. A policy of blanket guarantees would most likely lead to intramural disputes in NATO over distribution of blame, as well as the most appropriate acts to take in specific cases (44).

5. The proposal jettisons the concept of American-European action and fails to consider whether a division of labour might be preferable (45).

6. In the event of a military intervention, there would be the high likelihood of numerous casualties and domestic divisions (46).

Alternative Policy:

US should focus more on its domestic interests and avoid being placed in the role of Europe's permanent protector.

Source: Owen Harries, "The Collapse of 'The West'," *Foreign Affairs* 72 (September/October 1993): 41-53.

TABLE 3: KEY DOCUMENTS RELATING TO ENLARGEMENT

"NATO Participation Act of 1994." US Public Law 103-447, 103rd Congress, 2nd Session, Title II, enacted into law 2 November 1994.	Table 3: For Enlargement
Rationale:	The legislation states that NATO leaders are to be commended for reaffirming that NATO membership remains open to PFP countries and encourages NATO membership for the Visegrad states and any others that meet six criteria.
Who:	Visegrad states but could include others.
When:	No timetable.
Criteria:	Six specific criteria: maintaining their progress toward establishing democratic institutions; free-market economies; civilian control of armed forces; rule of law; remain committed to protecting the rights of all of their citizens; respect the territorial integrity of their neighbours (Morrison 149-50).
Policy Toward Russia and Ukraine:	No information available.
Military/Defence Posture:	The legislation authorizes the president to designate PFP countries to receive US assistance in the effort to facilitate transition to NATO membership if they meet six criteria: democratic institutions; free-market economies; civilian control of armed forces; rule of law; able to further the principles of the North Atlantic Treaty; able to contribute to the security of the North Atlantic area; not selling or transferring defence articles to a state that conducts known terrorist acts (Morrison 151-52).
	US assistance could support joint planning, training, and military exercises with NATO forces; greater interoperability of military equipment, air-defence systems, and command, control and communications systems; conformity of military doctrine. Furthermore, the legislation authorizes the president to provide assistance in the form of the transfer of defence articles, education and training, and foreign military financing. Finally, designated countries should be included in activities related to increased standardization and enhanced interoperability through coordinated training and procurement activities (69).

Source: James W. Morrison, *NATO Expansion and Alternative Future Security Alignments* (Washington: National Defense University, 1995): 69-71; 149-53.

H.R. #7 National Security Restoration Act. Title VI "NATO Revitalization and Expansion Act" 1995	Table 3: For Enlargement
Rationale:	The bill would amend the NATO Participation Act of 1994.
Who:	The Visegrad four and others not yet determined.
When:	The Visegrad four should be invited to become full NATO members no later than 10 January 1999.
Criteria:	Shared values and interests, democratic governments, free-market economies, civilian control of the military and of the police and intelligence services, adherence to values, principles, and political commitments embodied in the Helsinki Final Act of the CSCE, commitment to further the principles of NATO and to contribute to the security of the North Atlantic area, commitment to accept the obligations, responsibilities, and costs of NATO membership, commitment to implement infrastructure development activities that will facilitate participation in and support for NATO military activities, remain committed to protecting the rights of all their citizens and respecting the territorial integrity of their neighbours (Morrison 161).
Policy toward Russia and Ukraine:	No information available.
Military/Defence Posture (Amendments from the Previous bill):	The bill would amend the NATO Participation Act of 1994 in the following ways: – The bill would mandate the president to establish a program to assist designated states in the transition to full NATO membership (instead of leaving it to the president's discretion). – Authorizes "other European countries" instead of other "PFP countries" to receive assistance. – Congress designates the Visegrad four instead of stating that the president "may designate countries emerging from communism and participation in PFP." – With respect to countries other than the four Visegrad states, the president would be given discretion to designate other states, but, again the countries would have to be "European countries." – The bill would add "Economic Support Fund" and "nonproliferation and Disarmament Fund" to types of assistance. – The bill modifies the language prohibiting assistance to states that have cooperated with states supporting international terrorism. – The bill requires an annual report from the president (the latter is taken from Morrison 71).

Source: James W. Morrison, *NATO Expansion and Alternative Future Security Alignments* (Washington: National Defense University, 1995): 69-71; 155-67.

CHAPTER SEVEN

Canada and the Expansion of NATO: A Study in Élite Attitudes and Public Opinion

Paul Buteux, Michel Fortmann, and Pierre Martin

Introduction

The starting point for any discussion of Canada's policy on the future of NATO must be the question of whether, for Canadian decisionmakers and foreign-policy élites, as well as for the Canadian public, NATO remains what it used to be, namely the lodestar of the country's defence and security policy. No longer does the alliance appear to be the centrepiece of Canadian policy either in declaratory terms or as gauged by military commitments. On the other hand, NATO is still the only multilateral alliance of which Canada is a member and it remains relevant to the country's overall strategic position.[1] Moreover, NATO continues to influence Canada's military posture in important ways, and membership in the alliance twice in recent years has been an important influence on the country's decision to deploy military units in a combat or near-combat role overseas (Desert Storm and the former Yugoslavia). Thus there is at present something of a contradiction in Canadian policy between the downplaying of NATO at the political level and the fact that NATO remains an important determinant of Canada's security policy and commitments.

The Contradictions of Policy

There are precedents, or at least analogies, for the current contradictions in Canadian policy to be found in the defence and foreign-policy reviews conducted in the late 1960s by the Liberal government of Pierre Trudeau. Then, as now, Canadian security policy was being framed on the basis of benign assumptions and appreciations of Canada's security environment; then, as now, there was pressure to cut the defence budget; and then, as now, there existed a belief that Canada's freedom of action with respect to its international security had increased.

Echoes of the 1960s are to be found in two recent expressions of alternative opinion on Canadian security policy after the Cold War.[2] Interestingly, with respect to NATO and its enlargement, the "Citizens' Inquiry" called for the alliance to expand into a pan-European security organization, while the *Canada 21* report made support for NATO contingent on the evolution of a future European defence identity into an inclusive collective-security organization. Both reject the continuation of NATO as a collective-defence alliance.

It is unlikely that Canada's security environment is as benign as some would assert, but it is true that with the ending of the Cold War Canada no longer faces any direct external threat to its physical security. It is also true that in principle the new situation does allow Ottawa a wider range of options as to its involvement in issues of international security. The key problem facing Canada in this respect is that internationalist choices make demands on resources, and current Canadian policy is driven greatly by restrictive fiscal considerations.

Budgetary constraints are but one factor impelling a political agenda in which defence and security policy are accorded far less salience and priority than once was the case. The government's policy choices with respect to the deficit are of course bound up with fundamental constitutional issues that also have the effect of directing the government's political energies inward. These factors reinforce the more general and well-documented phenomenon in advanced industrial societies of a breakdown of the operational distinction between foreign and domestic policy.

In Canada this "domestication" of foreign and defence policy has in recent years been accompanied by the breakdown of the bipartisan consensus on the fundamentals of the policy that existed in the postwar period. The overall result has been to politicize many aspects of security policy that in the past would have been treated as routine and relatively uncontroversial. Good examples are provided by the politicization of recent defence procurement decisions such as the EH-101 helicopter and various proposals concerning the submarine fleet.

In these circumstances governments have had strong incentives to tread warily before making defence-policy choices and in undertaking new security commitments. In Canada at present the rhetoric associated with internationalism and functionalism, the twin pillars of the post-1945 foreign-policy consensus, still has resonance, but the ability to provide such military and other resources as may be necessary to give substance to these principles is in many ways lacking. One result is that the "commitment-capability gap" is still with us, but in a different form.

Canada's NATO "Problem"

It is within this domestic political context that NATO can now be understood as a problem for Canada. A recent "insider" analysis of Canadian policy towards security in the transatlantic region suggests that Canada remains committed to do the "things that matter in European security."[3] The question that arises, however, is whether Canada will have the wherewithal if called upon to do the things that matter. Directly or indirectly, Canada comes under pressure as a member of NATO to undertake substantive operational commitments in support of western interests. This was true in the case of the Gulf War, was true of Canadian UN peacekeeping commitments in Croatia and Bosnia, and is true of Canada's current participation in the enforcement of the Yugoslavian peace accords. The political value of merely token responses must be in doubt if Canadian policy is still to be based on the presumption that Canada should remain an international actor of consequence.

It is worth remembering that Canada's policy towards security in the Euro-Atlantic region was developed in the 1940s in response to an élite perception that the country's interests were best served by active engagement in areas of central strategic concern, and by ensuring that Ottawa had a voice in the counsels of the North Atlantic area that reflected Canadian resources and status in the international community. In short, it was believed to be in the Canadian interest for the country to "punch its weight" internationally, and this included a recognition, albeit a reluctant one, that this required military as well as political and economic commitments.

In the present climate of Canadian security discourse it is doubtful that government officials regard regional security problems in Europe as of central strategic or political concern. (Whether this view is also held by the public we discuss later in this chapter.) Intimations of a return to the mentality of the "fire-proof" house are to be found in some public-opinion data as well as in governmental and élite statements. The political and strategic rationale for continued Canadian engagement with European security issues simply does not carry the conviction that it did even less than a decade ago, and this notwithstanding that in general terms, as we argue below, support for Canadian membership in NATO remains high. Canada's international security environment might change for the worse, and undoubtedly this would have a major impact on Canadian opinion, but for the present Canadian policy towards an extension of its international security commitments will be governed by a low-risk and low-cost calculus. (Parenthetically, it is possible to argue that this is more characteristic of the historical Canadian foreign-policy tradition than were the internationalist policies pursued during the Cold War period.)

Nonetheless, short of a major upheaval in Canada's domestic circumstances, the policy of the government toward NATO will remain that of seeking to preserve membership in good standing, if for no other reason than that the long-term determinants of Canada's strategic situation do not change suddenly or rapidly. The central problem for Ottawa becomes, then, balancing a low-risk, low-cost policy against the exigent demands of its allies that it do more in support of the alliance — possibly even in the context of an expansion of the latter.

The calls that have been made in a variety of Canadian fora that NATO, through expansion and in conjunction with the OSCE, should be transformed into a pan-European "security regime" do not resolve Ottawa's policy dilemma. First, there is the fact that Canada, as a consequence of its existing commitments to NATO and the OSCE, and along with the United States, would be a guarantor of any new, pan-European security architecture. Rather than diluting Canadian obligations and commitments to European security, such a development would reinforce them. Secondly, as the September 1995 NATO study on enlargement makes clear, the evolution of alliance policy on expansion eastward does not envisage the abandonment of its central function of collective defence. In other words, an enlarged NATO would be an element (it is asserted that it would be a stabilizing one), in an overlapping and complementary set of institutional arrangements in Europe, but it would not be subsumed under a wider European security arrangement, nor would it be a substitute for existing institutions that possess a security mandate.[4] Thirdly, Canada has already signed on to enlargement in principle and, arguably, on whatever terms the alliance can agree upon. To back away now would be politically and diplomatically damaging.

Ottawa and the Enlargement Issue

The latter point begs the question of what position Canada is taking and might take on enlargement. There is no evidence that Ottawa is departing from its traditional practice of seeking consensus and of supporting any consensus that might emerge. At the same time, it is taking a low key approach and the issue has not been accorded a high profile in government policy statements. Not too much should be made of the fact that in its response to the recommendation of the Special Joint Parliamentary Committee Reviewing Canadian Foreign Policy the government did not subscribe to the Committee's advice *against* enlarging NATO.[5] By the time the Joint Committee reported, Canada had committed itself to the principle of enlargement, at the Brussels summit of January 1994. Given the caution with which the allies have approached enlargement, the government had no incentive to reverse its position. For now, the issue of enlargement remains one of low-cost and low-risk.

This, however, could change quite rapidly. As recent events in Central and Eastern Europe (CEE) have demonstrated, the political situation in the region remains a volatile one, and, in particular, the moment for consolidating CEE ties to the west might not be as long as is currently envisaged. Of course, for the most likely candidates for NATO membership, their strategy of integration with the west involves more than joining the alliance. Parallel to their search for security guarantees from NATO is their desire for membership in the European Union. The danger for democratic development in Central Europe and for the western desire to extend the European "zone of stability" eastward is that without definite western commitments, domestic developments in the aspirant countries might no longer sustain their eligibility for membership. A time horizon of five to ten years, which is seemingly being considered as appropriate both for NATO and EU membership, quite possibly could be overtaken by events in Central and Eastern Europe that would make enlargement impossible. There are strong arguments for enlarging NATO sooner rather than later.

The downside of the speedy accession to membership of the CEE front runners is, as the chapter by David Law and Neil MacFarlane explains, that it would likely create new dividing lines in Europe. In particular, the alliance would have to confront the hostility of Russia to such a development. The study on enlargement valiantly tries to square the circle on this point by emphasizing NATO's commitment to dialogue with all interested parties and by stressing that an enlarged alliance would be but one element in a broader architecture that "transcends and renders obsolete" dividing lines in Europe.[6] This could occur, however, only if Europe from the "Atlantic to the Urals" did in fact evolve into a classic "pluralistic security community" in which relations between the parties were governed by expectations of peaceful change. Were this to happen then the problem of NATO for Canada would simply disappear, and the aspirations of those who would make Canadian involvement in European security conditional on its evolution in the direction of common or cooperative security would be fulfilled.

Undoubtedly, NATO policy statements commit the alliance to this aspiration and the allies would not wish to foreclose the evolution of European politics in this direction, but the problem is that the desired outcome does not lie within any feasible policy deadline. Having ostensibly settled the question of the "why and how" of enlargement, the alliance now faces the much more difficult issues of "who and when." If enlargement eastward does take place, then this will result in a major change in the politics of the alliance and usher in the biggest transformation in the structure of European security since the end of the Cold War. The implications of such a development for Canadian policy are substantial.

These implications may be presented in summary form as follows.[7] Enlargement will involve the extension of Article 5 security guarantees eastward. For all the allies this will thus represent an expansion of their security perimeter. The credibility of these new arrangements will require new military arrangements and almost certainly will imply the full participation of the new members in the integrated military structures of the alliance. This, in turn, raises the question of how and to what extent Canada will fit into the new arrangements.

The unilateral decision by Ottawa to cut its contribution to the NATO infrastructure program by half might have to be reconsidered. In short, enlargement will reinforce the impact of NATO membership on the shaping of Canadian defence policy. Enlargement will set minimum limits to the size and capabilities of the Canadian armed forces if Ottawa intends to play an active role in shaping the evolving politics of the alliance. Doing the "things that matter" in an enlarged alliance will not be less demanding than current commitments. A widened commitment-capability gap could develop, and be politically embarrassing.

An enlarged alliance will reinforce what appears to be an emerging contradiction in Canada's policies towards international security. On the one hand, recent government statements can be interpreted as enlarging the country's security interests to include not only Europe, but Latin America and the Asia-Pacific region as well; on the other hand, in straitened budgetary circumstances there is a desire to restrict any security commitments that make substantial demands on Canadian resources. The Canadian government's support for NATO enlargement only reinforces this contradiction because it reinforces Canada's security obligations in Europe.

Of course, *faute de mieux*, Ottawa might well make only token commitments to the alliance as the resources to do anything else become simply unavailable. In this case the realities of Canadian security policy will match the trends towards "continentalism" to be found in many other aspects of the country's external relations. In this event, the role of NATO as a counterweight to the US would finally be abandoned. At present, there is no significant public support for such a development, and it is unclear, as the analysis offered in the following parts of this chapter suggests, whether there would be public acceptance of it. Suffice it to note at this juncture that the evolution of the alliance with respect to enlargement and the priority that the Canadian government gives to bringing it about are potentially of great significance for the future of Canada's place in the Euro-Atlantic relationship, and indeed for the postwar tradition of Canadian atlanticism, to which we now turn our attention.

The Question of Canadian Atlanticism

The editor of this volume has written, in a different context, that "NATO's success will continue to depend upon policy élites in important countries."[8] So far, we have been couching our argument almost exclusively in the context of policy élites and their view of Canada's alliance interests. Now we change tack, and ask what (and how) the Canadian public thinks about NATO in particular and atlanticism in general. We note, *pace* the above-quoted claim of David Haglund, that an increasing number of scholars maintain that states do not conduct their foreign policy only for "strategic" reasons or according to grand designs developed by foreign-policy élites. The roots of foreign and security policies, rather, lie in the social and economic structure of states.[9] Without going as far as those who define *Innenpolitik* as the only source of foreign policy, we see no point in denying that domestic politics has become a crucial dimension of foreign policymaking especially at a time when domestic and foreign economic policies are increasingly perceived as being linked and mutually supportive, and when demands for a greater "democratization of the foreign policy process" are heard from all quarters.[10]

It may be inferred that any policy, to be effective, has to be based on an understanding of what the public thinks; stated otherwise, any national policy has to reflect the values and perceptions of the community from which it emanates. These values and perceptions, in turn, are interwoven in the social, historical, and economic fabric of a society and they evolve with it. In short, "public opinion" is not an amorphous (reactive) set of shifting moods to be managed by political marketing experts[11] but rather is an echo of an "embedded political culture."[12] The latter has to be carefully analyzed in order to ensure that foreign policy is in tune with the domestic community it is supposed to represent.

In this regard, our objective in the remaining part of this chapter is to probe NATO's standing in Canada in order to assess, in a preliminary fashion, the depth of political support for NATO's transformation in the post-Cold War environment and, more specifically, for its opening to the east. More generally, the issue of NATO enlargement offers an appropriate opportunity to evaluate the state of Canada's "atlanticism." The key question we are asking is: To what extent are Canadians, in 1996, ready to make a significant political investment in the alliance?

Our argument is divided in three parts. In the first section the roots of Canada's atlanticism — according to conventional wisdom — are briefly recalled. The second section revisits the claim we made earlier in the chapter, namely that the underlying elements of Canada's traditional attachment to Europe seem progressively to be disappearing. In the third section, we assess the more relevant aspects of current public-opinion surveys presenting the views of Canadians about Europe and NATO.

Canada as a European Nation

From the point of view of public perceptions, the Canadian "privileged relation"[13] with Europe has traditionally rested on three pillars: a common social, political, and cultural heritage; membership in a transatlantic commonwealth built on mutually profitable trade relations and investments; and a vivid perception of common security interests.

The first of these components hardly needs belabouring. As Kim Nossal has noted: "The idea of Canada as a European nation did not suddenly originate with the acceleration of Anglo-American cooperation after the fall of Western Europe in May 1940; it had been deeply rooted in Canadian self-perception and political practice from the country's initial settlement and the defining decision of the 1770's not to follow the US into independence. The vast majority of those living in the northern half of North America had always felt the transatlantic ties of birth, family, national origin, politico-cultural inspiration, commercial intercourse, and even, it has been argued, psychological dependence."[14]

From its inception, NATO was thus a natural expression of the transatlantic bond that had existed before 1949, and it simply recognized a fact of life for 89 percent of Canadians whose European origins tied them to their ancestral homeland (Table 1A). Desmond Morton aptly reflects this perception when he writes, apropos himself, that "[f]or a Canadian born in 1937, the North Atlantic Treaty Organization is an old and familiar element in my cosmogony. It would be hard to imagine the world without it."[15] By the same token, the Atlantic vision, articulated in 1948 by Lester B. Pearson, of a "commonwealth of nations which share the same democratic and cultural traditions,"[16] was certainly more than an abstract political slogan. It was a deeply felt reality.

Similarly, the fact that the United States and Britain were Canada's main trading partners in the 1950s and 1960s underlined the extent to which the economic well-being of the country depended on harmonious relations with the countries of the Atlantic area. Although the economic significance of Canada-US trade relations dwarfed during those decades (as it does today) the significance of Canadian-European trade, it is nonetheless remarkable that more than 35 percent of Canadian exports were going to Europe as late as 1960.[17]

Finally, if during the interwar period Canada could still be described in Senator Raoul Dandurand's memorable words as a "fireproof house" far from Europe's recurring geopolitical conflagrations, the experience of World War II showed very clearly to Canadians that their country's security could be tightly bound to Europe's. To defend its interests and those of its allies, Canada had put a million and a half men in uniform for the two world wars. More than a hundred thousand died, a very high price for such a small country to pay. After the second of the global conflicts, it became an article of faith that Canadian security depended on collective-defence arrangements binding Europe to North America. NATO therefore would find a natural place in the Canadian collective psyche. To quote Desmond Morton again: "The Free World stood four square against a Stalinist tyranny comparable, we were regularly reminded, with the Hitlerian horror my late father had helped to vanquish. His generation had been trapped by unpreparedness into appeasement. History, we were told, would not let us repeat that error."[18]

For these reasons, NATO came to have a special significance for Canadians, and it is hardly surprising that in 1949 a vast majority of them would support their government in its decision to join the new alliance. A year earlier, indicative of a growing sense of internationalism, surveys had already shown that

90 percent of Canadians thought their country should join the UN, and 78 percent were supportive of sending Canadian soldiers abroad in order to maintain world peace.[19]

In sum, Pearsonian liberal internationalism — with its emphasis upon collective security, atlanticism, arms control, and peacekeeping — found fertile soil in these perceptions. It could even be argued that the durable public appeal of a foreign policy characterized by multilateralism, diplomatic pragmatism, and the search for compromise owes much to this linkage between doctrine and "political culture" — even if it is true that the latter variable can be notoriously imprecise.

It is thus not unusual that Canadians should have, during the postwar years, consistently supported policies promoting transatlantic cooperation and/or European peace and stability. This held true even as late as 1983, when 90 percent of Canadians endorsed the country's ongoing participation in NATO (see Table 1A). Significantly, Canadian public opinion has been sensitive to issues involving European stability even when these have transcended the strict NATO framework. In this regard, it can be stressed that Canada has been, since the beginning, an active supporter of pan-European security in the framework of the Conference on Security and Cooperation in Europe (CSCE), reflecting among other things the fact that a portion of the population had roots in Central and Eastern Europe.

The End of Atlanticism in Canada?

Although Canada's atlanticism has arguably been firmly embedded in the country's foreign-policy culture, it has become fashionable for foreign-policy experts since 1989 to descry a fundamental shift in public attitudes.[20]

First and foremost, this shift is said to have been fostered by Canada's evolving demography. As Geoffrey Pearson expresses it, "[t]here is a growing sense of multiple identities, based not only on a three oceans environment, with the Pacific assuming more importance as East Asia develops strong commercial attraction, but also the impact of immigrants and refugees from around the world who retain close ties with their countries of origins."[21]

It is true that Canada has long been a haven of choice for the world's emigrants and refugees. But since the 1970s, this inflow of population, coupled with falling domestic birth rates, has drastically changed the country's ethnic composition. In 1971, 82 percent of Canadians were of Western European stock (44 percent British, 29 percent French, 6 percent German, 3 percent Italian, 2 percent Dutch). In 1991, by contrast, only 49 percent of Canadians came from these above-mentioned traditional sources of immigration. Indeed, the influx of European immigrants to Canada had fallen from 46 percent of all arrivals in 1974 to a mere 15 percent in 1994. Asians were providing 68 percent of the 250,000 newcomers in that latter year, and it is no surprise that Chinese has become the fourth main language in Canada, after English, French, and Italian.[22]

It is now being said that Canada, like the United States, is fast turning into a "non-European" country. But even were it not for this ethno-demographic mutation many observers would highlight the significance of demography, in noting that more than 70 percent of Canadians have been born after 1945, or some 20 million people.[23] This generational shift, it is said, is capable in and of itself of erasing the collective memory that once legitimized and sustained Canada's atlanticism.

A second claim relates to economics not demographics. It is said that economic regionalization is weakening Canada's transatlantic ties. Experts note that while, in absolute terms, the value of Canada's exchanges with Europe has actually increased (albeit slightly) over time, the reality of regionalism in the framework of NAFTA has dispelled the 1970s' hope of an increasing diversification of Canadian external trade, in the event through a "third option" directed toward Europe. These experts also note that at the moment, Canadian exports of goods and services to the United States are 13-times greater than exports of goods and services to the European countries. Perhaps even more to the point, since few expect Europe to be a greater trading partner for Canada than is the US, the fast-growing trade between Canada and the Asia/Pacific region is eclipsing the volume of commercial transactions between the former and Europe.[24] Canada may be more dependent than ever on its American trading partner (in 1993, 80 percent of its exports went south compared with only 10 percent going to Europe)[25]; it is also clear, however, that Canadian businesses see the fastest-expanding markets and investment opportunities not lying across the Atlantic but rather the Pacific.

A third set of causes that ostensibly helps account for the transformation of Canada's foreign-policy culture is more directly related to security. During the Cold War there was general agreement — in Canada as in Europe — that the most pressing issue in international relations was the risk of a nuclear exchange between the United States and the Soviet Union. There was also general agreement that the west deserved support because the adversary was the symbol of totalitarianism, whose object of attack was the very way of life in the west. NATO, in this perspective, was one of the essential elements of the west's deterrence strategy. As one analyst put it, the "stakes rising from a potential conflict were high, and so the commitment to collective security [sic] was broad and deep."[26]

Paradoxically, although Europe today is riddled with conflicts and disputes, the risks they entail for North America appear almost insignificant in comparison with those of the Cold War period. In the words of the Economist, these conflicts are "wars of conscience," not "wars of interest."[27] They concern small powers or weak subnational groupings in pursuit of limited goals. The weapons they involve are unimpressive in comparison with nuclear arms, and the risk of spill-over from these disputes is minimal. The actual threat they represent for distant countries like Canada is difficult to explain to anyone, especially the public.

In other words, military threats to NATO are perceived increasingly as being local or regional rather than global. In addition, the diversification of security risks in Europe is progressively creating a new agenda in which Canada, as a North American country, has no obvious part. If terrorists plant bombs in Paris it may well sound alarms in Bonn and London, but it will not directly concern Ottawa. Similarly, if waves of Albanian refugees land on the coast of Italy or if another small conflict erupts in the Balkans, this will not mean much for Montrealers or Albertans. Accordingly, if NATO in the coming years gets increasingly involved in the complex business of brushfire fighting across Europe, this may well be perceived by Canadians as another demand on their already strained resources, rather than as an essential contribution to their own security.[28]

Is the Public Ready for the European Challenges of NATO?

As NATO grapples with major political challenges in the near future, Canadian political leaders will be torn between their responsibilities to the alliance and their belief that public support for active Canadian participation in NATO is inexorably waning. But is the latter in fact the case? Can it be said that there has been genuine public disaffection with Canada's atlanticist tradition? If not, how resistant would public opinion be to a major *new* political investment in the Atlantic alliance, such as that entailed by NATO's expansion? These questions should be the topics of important debates among students of Canadian foreign policy. As a first step toward an informed answer, we analyze in this section opinion surveys with a view to assessing the extent of public support for (or, to the contrary, disaffection with) any Canadian participation in the challenges likely to confront NATO in the future, including that of expansion.

Two basic questions must be addressed before one can speculate meaningfully on the future degree of public support for NATO in Canada: What is the current level of support for Canada's alliance commitments?, and How has that support evolved in recent years? Here we look at three dimensions of Canada's commitments: support for Canadian membership in NATO; support for active involvement in European security, notably the ongoing peacekeeping operation in Bosnia (only now under NATO not UN auspices); and the relative significance accorded to Atlantic security issues in light of competing domestic and foreign policy priorities of the public.

Before we turn to these questions, a few words about public opinion and foreign affairs are in order. Among international relations specialists, the assumption that public opinion is volatile, incoherent, and irrelevant is widely shared.[29] In recent years, however, a substantial body of research has questioned this assumption, noting that aggregate public opinion on foreign affairs tends to be stable and to change in reasonable ways in response to events.[30] This does not mean that the public is perfectly informed about international events; it generally is not. What it does mean is that, with the little information they do get from the media and from their leaders, most members of the public can rely on a core set of beliefs to form a reasonable opinion about international events. In short, the randomness inherent in the formation and measurement of public opinion does not alter the fact that collective opinion is generally stable and coherent.

As we argued above, the end of the Cold War has led several commentators to doubt that the public would much longer support Canada's involvement in the Atlantic alliance. Public opinion surveys do not fully confirm such pessimism. As the data in Table 1 show, the Canadian public is generally supportive of Canada's active participation in the alliance. It is clear, however, that support for NATO did erode throughout the 1980s, as the waning of the Cold War called into question what had been the raison d'être of the alliance (Table 1A). Still, in recent polls, support for Canada's either withdrawing from NATO or declaring its neutrality has not reached beyond 27 percent (Tables 1B, 1D, 1G). In sum, the end of the Cold War would seem to have caused a decline of about 15 percentage points in approval of NATO participation, but the alliance is still favoured by a comfortable majority.

Table 2A also shows that a majority of Canadians approve the recent NATO decision to participate actively in the conflict over Bosnia. In September 1995, 58 percent endorsed NATO's decision to launch a military offensive against the Bosnian Serbs. The Canadian public, however, is much more divided about the involvement of Canadian troops in the midst of a conflict that has long seemed intractable. In 1994 and 1995, as Table 2B shows, approval for the level of Canadian involvement in the former Yugoslavia oscillated between 43 and 46 percent, while calls for a reduction or an elimination of the efforts varied between 43 and 48 percent. Throughout this difficult period, however, support for overall Canadian participation in peacekeeping missions around the world remained at a relatively high level (between 59 and 62 percent approving), in spite of the difficulties in the former Yugoslavia (Table 2C).[31]

Table 2D shows that the Canadian public rejects (albeit not by much, 47 to 35 percent) the notion that the conflict in the former Yugoslavia is a strictly European problem. When it comes to intervention, however, the public is very sensitive to the risks incurred by Canadian troops, but tends to be willing to participate in military actions if they are conducted jointly with allies. In short, the experience of Canadian involvement in the seemingly impossible mission of keeping the peace in Bosnia has met with mixed reactions from the Canadian public. Nevertheless, this difficult episode has not completely eroded the traditional public support for Canada's internationalism, as exemplified by its participation in peacekeeping missions.

Assessing Demographic Obstacles to Atlanticism

How can we explain the variation in public support for NATO? As we indicated earlier, the most commonly encountered hypothesis is that the decline in support for NATO and atlanticism in Canadian foreign policy is attributable to demographic factors, from which stem two major assertions, namely that generations born after World War II will be less willing to accept active participation in NATO, and that the influx of "new" immigrants will inevitably weaken traditional ties to Europe.

It is intuitively attractive to believe that younger generations, born after World War II, might be less sensitive to the horrors of war and to the historic role played by their elders on the battlefields of Europe. As is sometimes the case, however, the conventional wisdom does not stand up to a simple empirical test. Indeed, none of the measures of support for Canada's foreign involvement presented in Table 3 supports this hypothesis. The young are, in fact, less likely to oppose Canada's membership in NATO (Table 3A), notably more likely to support Canada's peacekeeping efforts in Bosnia (3B), less likely to see the conflict in the former Yugoslavia as a strictly European problem (3C), and more likely to see Eastern Europe as a foreign policy priority (3E).

The hypothesis that immigration is changing the outlook of the Canadian public on Europe as a focus of foreign policy may also be intuitively attractive, but it does not seem to stand up under closer scrutiny. Although country of birth and ancestral origins are not commonly included in surveys, we found two that also had references to NATO. Tables 4A and 4B show that these two factors have little effect on demands for withdrawal from, or dismantlement of, NATO. Even Asian immigrants do not seem to differ notably from people of other origins on measures of support for an alliance that has little to do with Asia. In sum, analysts who rely on demogaphic trends to project the decline of Canada's commitment to atlanticism should perhaps consider other hypotheses.

Although the Canadian public has traditionally been disposed both to internationalism and the maintenance of alliance commitments in Europe, analysts have noted that this support may be compromised by three kinds of competing priorities: the rise of other geographic areas as centres of policy attention; the relative decline of security concerns as the main focus of foreign policy; and budgetary concerns.

Tables 5A and 5B show the relative importance that the public thinks should be accorded to other countries or regions in Canadian foreign policy. Not surprisingly, the United States tops both lists. What is interesting is that, with the exception of the rise of Japan and the slight decline of Britain, the pattern of relative importance of Europe remains relatively stable. When Western Europe as a whole is mentioned rather than individual countries, it ranks equally with Japan in the priority list (Table 5B). Although these data indicate that new regions might have risen in importance in the eyes of the public during the last 15 years, it is hard to conclude that Europe has sharply declined as a priority of Canadian foreign policy.

As far as international issues go, the top concern of the Canadian public in recent years has tended to be the environment. In the absence of a clear threat to Canada's physical security and in light of the frequent discussions in the media about the ozone layer and depleted fish stocks, this level of concern for the environment is hardly surprising. Table 6A shows that there is a great deal of variety in individuals' principal foreign policy concerns, but protecting the environment tends to top the list.[32] One might infer from this situation that individuals who do not assign peace and security issues the highest priority would be less inclined to support Canada's role in NATO. As Table 6B shows, however, support for NATO is not related to preferred foreign policy priorities.

Concerns about costs may be a source of public disaffection with foreign policy activism and might pose an obstacle to increased NATO commitments in the coming years, as foreign policy competes with domestic priorities for access to a shrinking public purse. Table 7A suggests that a plurality of Canadians believe that their government spends too much time and money trying to solve problems abroad at the expense of domestic problems. The same respondents, however, confessed to being concerned about world instability, and claimed that Canada had a "moral responsibility to take an active leadership role on important international issues." This suggests that while citizens appreciate the necessity of international leadership, taxpayers are becoming increasingly unwilling to pay the diplomats' or soldiers' travel accounts.

As a result, one might expect to observe less support for NATO and a lower priority for Europe among people who express concern about the costs of foreign commitments. Tables 7B, 7C, and 7D, however, show only small differences based on perceptions that too much is spent on foreign policy.

Conclusions

What explains variations in public support for atlanticism? Table 1 suggests that the gradual decline in support for NATO is consistent with the decrease in world tensions associated with changes in the Soviet Union in the mid-1980s, and then with the end of the Cold War. Is approval of NATO linked to perceptions of world instability? Although the decrease in overall support is a reasonable reaction to the end of the Cold War, this hypothesis does not seem to explain variations across individuals (Table 8A). Table 8B suggests a different way of looking at support for atlanticism. Indeed, support for Canadian participation in the alliance might be related in good measure to perceptions of the relationship with the United States. Thus, inevitably, any major political initiative taken within the framework of NATO will possibly be interpreted by the Canadian public as a function of Canada-US relations rather than as a signal of the waning of "traditional ties" with the old continent.

Despite appearances to the contrary, public support for NATO and the Atlantic connection in Canada still seems relatively solid, and this notwithstanding the end of the Cold War. Much remains to be learned, however, about the structure of opinion on NATO, especially as concerns the vital question of the alliance's enlargement, a topic that has engendered the same kind of debate in Canada as it has in other alliance countries surveyed in this volume — which is to say, a debate redolent of the "sounds of silence."

This chapter began by suggesting that NATO had lost place as an organizing device for Canadian defence priorities in recent years. Nevertheless, and irrespective of the merit of that contention, it is hard to detect much in the way of a public demand that NATO be deemphasized. We suggested, more by way of inference than anything else, that a careful reading of the public's views and preferences might (or perhaps should) be an essential element of defence and security policymaking. In the end, however, we are left with the unavoidable impression that our inference is no more than half the story. Indeed, any snapshot of the public mood cannot provide a ready-made set of preferences or political guidelines, but must rather constitute simply a broad outline of what is likely to be acceptable to, and supported by, that public. In the Canadian case, our findings show an indisputable reservoir of good will regarding the alliance. At the same time, it is obvious that this reservoir has to be tapped wisely by policy shapers, and this implies that there be reasonably clear and coherent policy choices if the latter hope to rally the support of a majority of Canadians.

In other words, the political signals from Ottawa regarding Canada's alliance policies have to appear less ambiguous than they do at the moment. No less a figure than the minister of national defence, David Collenette, has recently explained to Europeans that "[t]raditionally, we have been Eurocentric in our outlook, but trading patterns and the movement of peoples have really made us more aware of the Pacific Rim."[33] Although this may be the case, such a statement can sow some confusion when other Canadian officials state at the same time that "nous n'avons pas l'intention de nous détourner de l'Atlantique. Nous avons des liens atlantiques forts, et nous demeurerons un pays atlantique."[34] Of course, the opening toward Asia and the Pacific is a necessity for Canada but this should not be an obstacle to the mobilization of opinion behind a renewed commitment to Atlantic security issues. If the Canadian government wants public opinion to remain on board when it commits itself, as it appears to have, to the enlargement of the Atlantic alliance, it will be essential to maintain a greater degree of coherence in the messages it sends out.

In conclusion, David Haglund may be right after all: even in matters of public opinion, the success of alliance policies will ultimately depend on élites who know how to read public preferences and can demonstrate an ability to act upon them.

Notes

The authors wish to thank Anne-Marie Boissonnault for her research assistance, and David Haglund for his careful editing. Financial assistance from the Canadian Department of National Defence's Security and Defence Forum is warmly acknowledged. As well, Michel Fortmann and Pierre Martin are grateful to NATO for having awarded them an institutional research fellowship.

1. Paul Buteux, "Sutherland Revisited: Canada's Long-Term Strategic Situation," *Canadian Defence Quarterly* 24 (September 1994): 5-9.

2. "Transformation Moment: A Canadian Vision of Common Security," Report of the Citizens' Inquiry into Peace and Security (March 1992); and *Canada 21: Canada and Common Security in the Twenty-First Century* (Toronto: Centre for International Studies, University of Toronto, 1994).

3. Kenneth J. Calder, "Doing the Things that Matter: Canada and Euro-Atlantic Security," *International Journal* 50 (Autumn 1995): 701-20.

4. North Atlantic Treaty Organization, "Study on NATO Enlargement" (Brussels, September 1995).

5. *Government Response to the Recommendations of the Special Joint Parliamentary Committee Reviewing Canadian Foreign Policy* (Ottawa, 7 February 1995). The Joint Committee's report, *Canada's Foreign Policy: Principles and Priorities for the Future* (Ottawa, November 1995), took the view that the alliance should be encouraged to "continue moving to a collective security role for the whole of Europe, in cooperation with the Partnership for Peace participants." Needless to say, the alliance is not moving in the direction of a collective-security arrangement; rather, it is a cooperative-security approach that is being fostered.

6. "Study on NATO Enlargement," p. 5.

7. See, for these implications, Allen S. Sens, "Saying Yes to Expansion: The Future of NATO and Canadian Interests," *International Journal* 50 (Autumn 1995): 675-700.

8. David Haglund, "Must NATO Fail? Theories, Myths, and Policy Dilemmas," *International Journal* 50 (Autumn 1995): 674.

9. For an excellent summary of the *Aussenpolitik-Innenpolitik* debate, see Fareed Zakaria, "Realism and Domestic Politics: A Review Essay," *International Security* 17 (Summer 1992): 179-81.

10. *Canada in the World* (Ottawa: Department of Foreign Affairs and International Trade, 1995), p. 4.

11. This view of the public as an object to be acted upon was clearly reflected by a recent NATO pamphlet stating that it "is one thing for an institution to have a clear set of policies and quite another to insure that these messages are clearly understood by its public. The fact that institutional policy is developed by the best thinkers in government, industry and the aca-

demic world, is no guarantee that today's 'information society' will translate these messages accurately to the publics whose opinions influence the institution's future and policies." Information Brief, NATO Public Opinion Seminar, Brussels, April 1995.

12. For a good definition of the concept of political culture, see Laurence McFalls, *Communism's Collapse, Democracy's Demise: The Cultural Context and Consequences of the East German Revolution* (New York: New York University Press, 1995), pp. 76-84. The notion of "embedded political culture" is taken from John Kirton, "Une ouverture sur le monde: La nouvelle politique étrangère canadienne du gouvernement Chrétien," paper presented to the conference "La politique extérieure du Canada: 1995," Montréal, 24 November 1995, p. 13.

13. Panayotis Soldatos, "La relation privilégiée Canada-Communautés européennes: un test de diversification," in *Le Canada à l'ère de l'après-guerre froide et des blocs régionaux*, ed. Panayotis Soldatos et al. (North York, ONT: Captus, 1993), p. 17.

14. Kim Richard Nossal, "A European Nation? The Life and Times of Atlanticism in Canada," in *Making a Difference? Canada's Foreign Policy in a Changing World Order*, ed. John English and Norman Hilmer (Toronto: Lester, 1991), p. 81.

15. Desmond Morton, "The NATO Alliance: Do North Americans Care?" *National Network News* 3 (April 1995): 4.

16. John Holmes, *The Shaping of Peace: Canada and the Search for World Order, 1943-1957* (Toronto: University of Toronto Press, 1982), 2: 111.

17. *Canada's Foreign Policy: Position Papers*, Report of the Special Joint Committee Reviewing Canadian Foreign Policy (Ottawa: November 1994), p. 49.

18. Morton, "NATO Alliance," p. 5.

19. Quoted in Jack Granatstein, "Canada: Peacekeeper," in *Peacekeeping: International Challenge, Canadian Response*, ed. Alistair Taylor et al. (Toronto: Canadian Institute of International Affairs, 1968), p. 96.

20. For a sampling of this trend, see Nossal, "European Nation?"; Kirton, "Ouverture sur le monde"; *Canada's Foreign Policy*; and in general what may be dubbed the "Toronto school of Canadian IR."

21. Geoffrey Pearson, "Canada, NATO and the Public Mood," in *Canada and NATO: Uneasy Past, Uncertain Future*, ed. Margaret O. MacMillan and David Sorensen (Waterloo: University of Waterloo Press, 1990), p. 125.

22. These figures are taken from the *Time* special issue on Canada, 20 November 1995, p. 22.

23. Ibid.

24. Jens U. Hettmann, "La politique extérieure canadienne vue de l'Europe: Fin de siècle pour les rapports canado-européens," paper presented to the conference "La politique étrangère du Canada: 1995," Montréal, 24 November 1995, pp. 11-12.

25. *Canada's Foreign Policy*, p. 52.

26. William Thorsell, "Indifference is Bliss: NATO and Canada in Uncertain Times", *Globe and Mail* (Toronto), 21 October, 1995, p. D6.

27. "A Survey of Defence in the 21st Century," *Economist*, September 1992, p. 4.

28. It is not surprising, in this framework, to find the notion of Canada as a "fireproof house" back in fashion. See Joel J. Sokolsky and Joseph Jockel, "Dandurand Revisited: Rethinking Canada's Defence Policy in an Unstable World," *International Journal* 48 (Spring 1993): 401.

29. This view, which borrows largely from Tocqueville, has been branded the Almond-Lippmann consensus, given its articulation in Walter Lippmann's *Public Opinion* (New York: Macmillan, 1922), and *The Phantom Public* (New York: Harcourt, Brace, 1925); as well as in Gabriel A. Almond, *The American People and Foreign Policy* (New York: Praeger, 1950).

30. For a survey of research on this topic, see Ole R. Holsti, "Public Opinion and Foreign Policy: Challenges to the Almond-Lippmann Consensus," *International Studies Quarterly* 36 (December 1992): 439-66. On the stability of public opinion, see Benjamin I. Page and Robert Y. Shapiro, *The Rational Public: Fifty Years of Trends in Americans' Policy Preferences* (Chicago: University of Chicago Press, 1992).

31. Note that Tables 2B and 2C provide a very clear illustration of the general stability of public opinion on foreign policy. If public opinion were as volatile as is commonly alleged, one would expect much wider variations across these two years. For a more thorough analysis of how Canadian public opinion perceives the country's involvement in peacekeeping, see Pierre Martin and Michel Fortmann, "Canadian Public Opinion and Peacekeeping in a Turbulent World," *International Journal* 50 (Spring 1995): 370-400.

32. More recent polls, conducted in 1994 by Goldfarb and in April 1995 by Insight Canada, confirm this pattern.

33. Quoted in *Jane's Defence Weekly*, 10 June 1995, p. 120.

34. The chair of the standing committee on external affairs and national defence, on the occasion of a visit of an Atlantic Council delegation in May 1995.

APPENDIX

TABLE 1: EVOLUTION OF SUPPORT FOR NATO IN CANADA, 1983-95

1A) Decima Quarterly, 1983-90, Question R 761: *"As you may know, Canada is a member of NATO. NATO is an alliance of nations designed to provide its members with protection against attack. As members of NATO, Canada and other nations contribute money, troops, equipment, and weapons to create a combined defence force. Do you strongly approve, approve, disapprove, or strongly disapprove of Canada's participation in NATO?"*

Response Options	Winter 1983-84 %	Fall 1987 %	Summer 1990 %
Strongly approve	30	21	20
Approve	59	59	54
Disapprove	8	15	17
Strongly disapprove	3	4	6
No opinion	1	1	2

1B) Decima, Autumn 1987, Question R 1516: *"Some people have been saying that, by participating in NATO, Canada's defence capability is divided. They say that the best way for Canada to protect itself is to withdraw from NATO and concentrate on increasing our defence capability in Canada. Other people say that, although it is important for Canada to have its own defence capability, because of our geography and size, the best way we can protect ourselves is by participating in NATO and other defence alliances. Thinking of these two points of view, which one best represents your own?"*

Response Options	Percent
Withdraw from NATO	16
Stay in NATO	83
No opinion	2

... continued

1C) CIIPS, 1989, Question 25b: *"In your opinion, how important is Canada's participation in the North Atlantic Treaty Organization?"*

Response Options	Percent
Very important	52
Somewhat important	34
Not very important	14

1D) Environics, 1989, vol. 3, Question 86: *"Do you think that Canada should remain an ally of fhe United States and Western Europe or should Canada become a neutral country?"*

Response Options	Percent
Should remain an ally	67
Should become neutral	27
DK/NA	6

1E) Environics, 1989, vol. 3, Question 87: *"With the changes taking place in the Soviet Union, there is little left for NATO to do in defending Western Europe. (Do you agree?)"* *"Question 87d: "It is important to keep NATO strong over the next few years in case the reforms in the Soviet Union do not continue. (Do you agree?)"*

Response Options	Little Left for NATO %	Important to Keep NATO Strong %
Strongly agree	6	41
Somewhat agree	25	31
Somewhat disagree	28	9
Strongly disagree	21	3
DK/NA	20	16

... continued

1F) Decima, Summer 1990, Question R 2172: *"Canada has been a member of NATO since it was created in 1949. Since that time, NATO has been the basis of the West's defence against the Soviet Union and Eastern Europe. Some people say that with all the changes in Eastern Europe over the last year, there is no longer a need for NATO. Other people say that there are still threats to security and stability in Europe and NATO still has an important role to play. Which view is closest to your own?*

Response Options	Percent
NATO no longer a need	20
NATO still has a role	77
No opinion	3

1G) Decima, November 1991, Question 38: *"There is no longer any need for Canada to belong to military alliances like NATO. (Do you agree?)"*

	Percent
Disagree	59
Ambivalent '	18
Agree	23

TABLE 2: SUPPORT FOR CANADA'S PARTICIPATION IN RECENT MILITARY OPERATIONS IN EUROPE AND ELSEWHERE

2A) Gallup, September 1995: *"Do you agree with the decision taken by NATO and approved by the United Nations to launch a military offensive against the Bosnian Serbs?"* (exact wording not available)

	Percent
Agree	58
Disagree	25
No opinion	18

2B) Gallup, 1994-1995: *"Do you believe Canada's presence in the former Yugoslavia as part of the United Nations peacekeeping forces should increase, remain the same, decrease, or be eliminated altogether?"*

	Jan. 1994 %	Dec. 1994 %	June 1995 %	Sep. 1995 %
Increase	11	12	9	12
Remain the same	32	33	34	34
Decrease	17	16	15	15
Be eliminated	26	27	33	29
No opinion	14	12	10	10

2C) Gallup, 1994-1995: *"Do you believe that Canada's role in United Nations peacekeeping efforts around the world should increase, remain the same, decrease or be eliminated altogether?"*

	Jan. 1994 %	Dec. 1994 %	June 1995 %	Sep. 1995 %
Increase	16	17	14	15
Remain the same	43	45	45	47
Decrease	20	16	19	18
Be eliminated	12	13	16	13
No opinion	9	8	7	7

... continued

2D) Decima, May 1993, Question 14: *"The war in Yugoslavia is a European problem and should be solved by Europeans themselves."* Question 15: *"If future efforts efforts to end the war in Bosnia increase the risk to Canadian troops, we should just pull them out."* Question 20: *"In the event that the international community decides to take more more forceful action, I think Canadian troops should participate, even if that means Canadian lives may be lost."*

	European Problem %	Pull Out if More Risk %	Participate With Others %
Totally disagree	21	11	18
Somewhat disagree	26	22	19
Neutral	18	20	18
Somewhat agree	21	24	31
Totally agree	14	22	13

TABLE 3: SUPPORT FOR ELEMENTS OF ATLANTICISM IN CANADIAN FOREIGN POLICY, BY AGE GROUP

3A) Decima, November 1991, Question 38: *"There is no longer any need for Canada to belong to military alliances like NATO".*

	No Need for NATO		
	Disagree (for NATO) (%)	Depends (%)	Agree (against NATO) (%)
Age			
18-29	68	20	12
30-49	67	24	9
50+	67	16	17
TOTAL N=1500	67	21	12

3B) Gallup, 29 June 1995, Question 2: *"Do you believe that Canada's presence in the former Yugoslavia as part of the United Nations peacekeeping forces should increase, remain the same, decrease or be eliminated altogether?"*

	Canadian Troops in Former Yugoslavia				
	Increase (%)	Remain Same (%)	Decrease (%)	Eliminated (%)	No Opinion (%)
Age					
18-29	11	39	16	28	6
30-49	9	38	15	27	10
50+	6	27	14	43	11
TOTAL N=1005	9	34	15	33	10

... continued

3C) Decima, May 1993, Question 14: *"The war in Yugoslavia is a European problem and should be solved by Europeans themselves."*

	War in Yugoslavia Only a European Problem		
	Disagree (%)	Depends (%)	Agree (%)
Age			
18-29	45	33	22
30-49	43	29	28
50+	27	35	37
TOTAL N=1000	39	32	29

3D) Decima, November 1991, Question 15: *"I'm going to read you a list of countries and regions in the world. For each one, I would like you to tell me how high or low a priority you feel Canada should put on its relationship with each. '1' means that you feel this relationship with that country or region should be of the lowest priority and '7' means you feel it should be of the highest priority (...). On a scale of 1 to 7, what priority should Canada place on its relationship with...Western Europe?"*

	Western Europe as Priority for Foreign Policy		
	Lowest Priority (1 or 2) (%)	Medium Priority (3,4,5) (%)	Highest Priority (6 or 7) (%)
Age			
18-29	6	58	36
30-49	6	53	40
50+	8	52	40
TOTAL N=1500	7	54	39

... continued

3E) Decima, November 1991, Question 16: *"On a scale of 1 to 7, what priority **should** Canada place on its relationship with ... Eastern Europe and the Soviet Union?"*

	Eastern Europe and USSR as Priority for Foreign Policy		
	Lowest Priority (1 or 2) (%)	Medium Priority (3,4,5) (%)	Highest Priority (6 or 7) (%)
Age			
18-29	7	51	42
30-49	8	59	33
50+	12	60	28
TOTAL N=1500	9	58	34

TABLE 4: SUPPORT FOR NATO BY PLACE OF BIRTH OR ANCESTRAL ORIGIN

4A) Canadian Election Study, September 1988, Question L3: *"Should Canada stay in NATO or get out?"*

	Stay in NATO or Get Out		
	Stay (%)	Get Out (%)	DK/NA (%)
Country of Birth (N)			
Canada (3100)	75	11	14
W. Europe (208)	83	12	5
E. Europe (45)	89	7	4
Asia (65)	80	8	12
Americas (39)	87	5	8
Other (11)	91	9	0
TOTAL N=3609	76	11	13

4B) Decima, September 1992, Question 19: *"As you may know, Canada is a member of the North Atlantic Treaty Organization, or NATO. NATO is an alliance of nàtions designed to provide its members with protection against attack. There has been some discussions lately about what NATO's role should be in light of the major changes in the former Soviet Union and in Eastern Europe. Which of the following statements best expresses what you believe?"*

	Future Status of NATO		
	Military Alliance (%)	Political Organization (%)	Should Be Dismantled (%)
Ancestral Origin (N)			
British (352)	67	17	15
French (200)	58	28	14
Other Western Europe (285)	68	19	13
E. Europe (91)	59	16	24
Asia/Oceania/Middle East (46)	63	17	20
Other (37)	57	22	22
TOTAL N=1200	64	20	16

TABLE 5: PUBLIC OPINION ON GEOGRAPHIC FOREIGN POLICY PRIORITIES

5A) Environics, Focus Canada Report, 1980-1995: *"In your opinion, is it very impor-tant, somewhat important, not very important, or not at all important for Canada to have overall good relations with the following countries?"*

| | Percent Answering "Very Important" | | | | |
	1980	1983	1989	1993	1995
United States	82	85	76	82	82
Japan	57	57	55	61	64
P.R. of China	48	43	33	39	46
Great Britain	64	65	54	56	—
Germany	47	44	36	45	—
France	43	42	37	42	—
USSR/Former USSR	46	46	49	43	38

5B) Decima, November 1991: *"I'm going to read you a list of countries and regions in the world. For each one, I would like you to tell me how high or low a priority you feel Canada **should** put on its relationship with each. '1' means that you feel this relation-ship with that country or region should be of the lowest priority and '7' means you feel it should be of the highest priority (...). On a scale of 1 to 7, what priority **should** Canada place on its relationship with ... Western Europe?"*

	Mean score
The United States	5.62
Western Europe	5.02
Japan	5.01
Eastern Europe and the Soviet Union	4.81
China	4.38
The Middle East	4.06
Africa	4.03
Southeast Asia, excl. China & Japan	4.00
Latin America	3.95

TABLE 6: DESIRED PRIORITIES OF FOREIGN POLICY

6A) Decima, November 1991 and September 1992, Question 3:*"Through its foreign policy, Canada can try to do a number of things. I'd like to read you a number of possible objectives and ask you to tell me which one you feel should be given the highest priority. Is it...?"*

	1991 (%)	1992 (%)
Promoting Trade Opportunities	15	12
Protecting the World's Environment	36	33
Promoting Human Rights	12	14
Working for Peace and Arms Control	24	21
Helping Poorer Countries Develop	12	20

6B) Decima, November 1991, Question 38: *"There is no longer any need for Canada to belong to military alliances like NATO"* by desired priority of foreign policy (Question 3, same as above).

	No Need for NATO		
	Disagree (%)	Depends (%)	Agree (%)
First Priority of Foreign Policy			
Promote Trade	74	17	10
Environment	68	20	12
Human Rights	63	22	15
Peace/Arms Control	63	23	14
Aid to Development	65	23	11
TOTAL N=1500	67	21	12

TABLE 7: OPPOSITION TO FOREIGN POLICY SPENDING AND ITS IMPACT ON SUPPORT FOR ELEMENTS OF ATLANTICISM

7A) Decima, November 1991: *"I'm going to read you a list of statements various people have made at one time or another. Please tell me how you **personally** feel about each statement by giving me a number between -5 and +5, where '-5' means you **totally disagree** with the statement and '+5' means you **totally agree** with the statement."*

	Mean Score
"As a country, we spend too much time and money on the world's problems and not enough time and money on problems here at home"	+2.30
"I'm concerned about the instability of the world with so many changes taking place."	+2.28
"Canada has a moral responsibility to take an active leadership role on important international issues."	+2.97

7B) Decima, November 1991, Question 38: *"There is no longer any need for Canada to belong to military alliances like NATO"* by "too much time and money" (7A; -5/-2=Disagree; -1/+1=Depends; +2/+5=Agree).

	No Need for NATO		
	Disagree (%)	Depends (%)	Agree (%)
Too Much Spending			
Disagree (16%)	69	20	11
Depends (16%)	63	27	10
Agree (68%)	67	20	13
TOTAL N=1500	67	21	12

... continued

7C) Decima, November 1991, Question 15: *"On a scale of 1 to 7, what priority should Canada place on its relationship with ... Western Europe?"* by "too much time and money" (see 7A).

	Western Europe as Priority for Foreign Policy		
	Lowest Priority (%)	Medium Priority (%)	Highest Priority (%)
Too Much Spending			
Disagree (16%)	5	53	42
Depends (16%)	6	48	46
Agree (39%)	7	56	37
TOTAL N=1500	7	54	39

7D) Decima, November 1991, Question 16: *"On a scale of 1 to 7, what priority should Canada place on its relationship with ... Eastern Europe and the Soviet Union?"* by "too much time and money" (7A).

	Eastern Europe and USSR as Priority for Foreign Policy		
	Lowest Priority (%)	Medium Priority (%)	Highest Priority (%)
Too Much Spending			
Disagree (15%)	8	55	37
Depends (16%)	5	62	33
Agree (69%)	10	57	33
TOTAL N=1500	9	58	34

TABLE 8: SUPPORT FOR NATO BY CONCERN FOR WORLD INSTABILITY AND PERCEPTIONS OF RELATIONSHIP WITH THE UNITED STATES

8A) Decima, November 1991, Question 38: *"There is no longer any need for Canada to belong to military alliances like NATO"* by Question 35: *"I'm concerned about the instability of the world with so many major changes taking place."*

	No Need for NATO		
	Disagree (%)	Depends (%)	Agree (%)
Concern about World Instability			
Disagree (13%)	70	18	12
Depends (18%)	67	25	8
Agree (70%)	66	20	13
TOTAL N=1500	67	21	12

8B) Decima, November 1991, Question 38: *"There is no longer any need for Canada to belong to military alliances like NATO"* by Question 37: *"I think Canada is becoming too much like the United States."*

	No Need for NATO		
	Disagree (%)	Depends (%)	Agree (%)
Canada Too Much Like US			
Disagree (28%)	78	13	9
Depends (20%)	63	29	8
Agree (52%)	62	22	16
TOTAL N=1500	67	21	12

Sources of Survey Data

Canadian Election Study. 1988 (Computerized data set; interviews conducted in August 1988).

Canadian Institute for International Peace and Security. 1989. *Security, Arms Control and Defence: Public Attitudes in Canada.* (December, Interviews conducted in September and October 1989).

Canadian Institute for International Peace and Security. 1990. *Changing Conceptions of Security: Public Attitudes in Canada.* (December, Interviews conducted in September and October 1990).

Decima Research. 1983-1993. *Decima Quarterly* (Various Issues).

Decima Research. 1987. *Report to the Department of National Defence: Nationwide Survey* (#2672; November, Interviews conducted on 20 and 21 November 1987).

Decima Research. 1991. *Perspectives of a Changing World: What Canadians Think and Feel About International Affairs* (Interviews conducted between 4 November and 28 November 1991).

Decima Research. 1992. *Perspectives of a Changing World: What Canadians Think and Feel About International Relations* (Interviews conducted between 4 September and 9 September 1992).

Decima Research. 1993. *A Decima Research Report to the Department of External Affairs and International Trade: Public Opinion on Peacekeeping; Update 1993* (Interviews conducted on 1 May 1993).

Environics. 1980-1995. *Focus Canada Report.* Various Issues.

Gallup. 1994-1995. *The Gallup Report: One-Third Want Canada Out of Former Yugoslavia* (29 June 1995; Interviews conducted between 10-17 January 1994; 5-11 December 1994; 12-16 June 1995). September results were obtained from "Sondage Gallup: 58% des Canadiens d'accord avec l'offensive de l'OTAN en Bosnie," *La Presse* (Montréal), 18 September 1995, p. A7.

CHAPTER EIGHT

NATO's Enlargement, France's Dilemma

Pascal Boniface

Introduction

On the topic of the enlargement of NATO, can France even have an opinion, let alone express one? The question might seem provocative. Paris, after all, is renowned for having views on everything, and for expressing them as energetically as it can, and in this regard it resembles the United States, for like its transatlantic partner France sees itself to be both purveying a worldwide message and incarnating universal values. This stance often irritates other countries, which might be willing to tolerate a certain amount of pretence on the part of their distant protector, but are loath to accept it when it comes from a country they have held to be more of a troublemaker than a faithful ally.

In NATO circles, France is often considered to be something of an outsider. Not belonging to the full gamut of the alliance's integrated military councils, and never having hesitated to make known its differences with its allies, France triggers among the latter a yearning for it to adopt a low profile and to learn to stay in its place, which is to say somewhere outside the inner sanctum, where its voice, if raised at all, will be adequately muffled. Whenever France behaves in a manner at odds with that yearning, it gets accused of seeking to enjoy representation without the inconveniences of taxation.

As interesting as the above observations might be in their own right, they become even more interesting when placed in the context of the current debate over enlarging the alliance. This, of course, is a very topical, and sensitive, issue, both inside and outside NATO. Nor can it be expected to grow any less sensitive over time, given that important deadlines regarding new admissions will be drawing closer (or possibly the reverse!). NATO's enlargement will be a determinative issue for the future of European security, and will bear directly on the post-Cold War European order, the integration of the Central and Eastern

European (CEE) states into the western camp, and the role of both Russia and the US in Europe.

All of this appears to be so self-evident that it has been deemed desirable to change the very vocabulary of the current debate: instead of the earlier usage, which had NATO "expanding" or "extending" itself — both terms suggestive of territorial gains if not outright conquest — today the talk is of "enlargement," a kinder, gentler term, linked to the notion of a peaceful integration of new members.[1] This change in terminology has not really altered the policy, although it surely constitutes the first instance of "political correctness" being elevated to the level of grand strategy. Still, this would hardly be the first time in history when, because problems had become too difficult to resolve, a change of wording was proposed as the next best thing. Accordingly, in what follows I will adhere to the more "correct" usage, and refer to the alliance's enlargement, and not its expansion.

France versus Enlargement, or France versus NATO?

There has been in France a marked coolness toward the enlargement of the alliance — a sentiment that attained its maximum currency just prior to NATO's Brussels summit of January 1994, where enlargement was accepted by all 16 heads of state and government. This opposition continues to exist, but no one dares express it officially in France, for three reasons.

In the first place, the logic underlying France's position on both the alliance and its enlargement is not what it once was, prior to 1994. By this I mean simply that the relationship between NATO and the emerging European Security and Defence Identity (ESDI) is no longer seen to be one marked by fierce competition, but instead today bears the hallmarks of complementarity.

Secondly, it is thought in Paris that enthusiasm for enlargement is waning in other alliance capitals, now that the implications of enlargement are becoming more obvious. Thus, it is asked, why should France bear the costs of having to be the villain of the piece, barring the door to the CEE states' entry into the western camp all by itself? Thirdly, and from the direct opposite perspective, France knows that *if* enlargement were going to occur, it could not be derailed by the solitary opposition of Paris.

Thus, in respect of France's stance on enlargement, one could do worse than to paraphrase Cocteau to the effect that "if we cannot prevent disorder from occurring, we can at least pretend to be one of its creators." In sum, if enlargement is going to take place, France has no reason to oppose it, because it cannot prevent it. And if it does not take place, or at least take place too quickly, what point is there in France serving as the object of wrath for the CEE states? In either case, staking out a position firmly cannot help but sow discord between France and the countries that are candidates for NATO membership, without in the slightest way being able to modify the course of events.

Nor is it only in France that NATO's enlargement causes concern. Reticence seems to reign in the majority of alliance states, including even those who once ranked as the most enthusiastic promoters of enlargement, such as Germany and possibly even the United States.[2] In the end, we may well discover that the only supporters of enlargement turn out to be the candidate countries themselves, with the current allies showing themselves to be much cooler to the idea.[3]

For its part, France engenders suspicion right off the bat: if it is against enlargement, then it is thought to be against NATO. In refusing to sanction a new role for NATO and to task it with unprecedented missions, France is held to be working out a cunning strategy aimed ultimately at unseating the alliance and getting the Americans to leave Europe. It is almost as if we are confronted with having constantly to combat the same old rumourmongering. A rumour, let it be recalled, is a falsehood intended to damage someone's reputation. Yet at the core of every rumour, despite the "inexact" (indeed, outright false) quality of the information imparted, there is a kernel of reality that serves to endow it with a semblance of credibility.

The "rumour" about French intentions vis-à-vis NATO has a dual origin. One source, the oldest, dates back to 1966. General de Gaulle, having then so loudly slammed the door on NATO, guaranteed by his act that France's relations with the alliance could henceforth be perceived, only with the greatest difficulty, to be "normal." That France, up to the very end of the Cold War, would always show itself whenever it truly mattered to be an indispensable, loyal, and steadfast ally never seemed to register. The rumour's second source goes back only a few years, to the beginning of the 1990s, when the quest to make NATO more relevant in Central and Eastern Europe appeared to French leaders to be a deliberate attempt to frustrate the creation of the ESDI.

Nevertheless, by the time enlargement, or something like it, first started to be bruited at the start of this decade, the French-NATO relationship had already had much of the venom drawn from it, including in France itself — or, more precisely, especially in France. Antiamericanism, which had always been the leading "carrier" of antiatlanticism, was practically a spent force in France by the early 1980s. Both during the Euromissile deployments and the Gulf War there had been total convergence of the French and American positions, and this without stirring up any polemics in France.[4] Today, no one in any of the major political parties can be found to object in principle either to France's adherence to NATO or to the need to maintain a strong and solid NATO in Europe.[5] The only genuine debate now takes place not over the principle — accepted now by everyone — but rather over the breadth and pace of the current rapprochement between France and NATO.[6]

This new consensus prevails as well among the experts. Thus, Gabriel Robin, former French ambassador to the alliance and reputed to be one of its sternest critics, has written recently that Europe's neighbours, whether to the east or to the south, hardly have the means to menace it. To upset the regnant balance, according to Robin, the weight of Russia would have to be added. In that event, "Europe would be powerless, it would need America, and it would have to seek recourse in the alliance. The 'Europe of defence' can be an element of Atlantic defence. In no case should it seek to become its substitute."[7] Robin's predecessor, François de Rose, considered to be a steadfast supporter of the alliance, can only ratify this sentiment: "Whatever the nature of the problems that will confront the west, the Atlantic alliance will continue to be, for all its members, their best guarantee of a peaceful future."[8]

France's policy of small steps towards NATO, begun in 1991, would pick up speed gradually before experiencing a burst of acceleration on 5 December 1995, when the minister of foreign affairs, Hervé de Charette, announced that the country would play more of a role in a range of alliance governing bodies, without, however, returning France to the pre-1966 status quo in its NATO relations. Specifically, the defence chief of staff (or his representative in Brussels) would participate fully on the Military Committee.

The Perception of a NATO-ESDI Rivalry

Initially, France had been enthusiastic about creating a dialogue with the CEE states. At the London summit of July 1990, France had given full support to the initiatives intended to enhance NATO's relationships with the members of the Warsaw Treaty Organization (WTO), notably the invitation extended to Soviet leader Mikhail Gorbachev and his WTO counterparts to come and address the North Atlantic Council and establish regular diplomatic liaison with the alliance. At the Rome summit of 7 and 8 November 1991, France agreed to a broadening of contacts with the CEE states, at the same time cautioning against the alliance attempting to interfere in the domestic affairs of those states, especially the Soviet Union.

Broadening contacts with the CEE states represented a continuation of traditional French diplomacy toward the east, whether that diplomacy took the form of de Gaulle's celebrated vision of a "Europe from the Atlantic to the Urals," or of François Mitterrand's invocation of the aspiration to transcend the "Yalta order." But French enthusiasm for — or to put it more accurately, good will toward — this eastern outreach began to wane markedly once it was determined that reinforcing NATO by giving it an eastward vocation would prove incompatible with the affirmation of a "European identity," above all in the sphere of defence. To be sure, the Rome summit had reaffirmed in principle the need for a European identity, but from France's perspective, the euphoria that followed the US-led coalition's triumph in the Gulf War rekindled the hegemonic spark in Washington's diplomacy.

The failure of the European "confederation" idea (which had been conceived as such by Mitterrand but was in fact a traditional French theme that could as easily have been associated with de Gaulle) threw into stark relief the misunderstandings between the French, the Americans, and the Central and Eastern Europeans. The notion of a confederation was interesting, but the least that can be said about it is that it was poorly presented by the French. It was resented by the CEE states, who took it to be a diversion aimed at preventing them from establishing tight links with the United States. In France, its failure was held to have torpedoed the pan-European project.[9]

French reactions to the creation of the North Atlantic Cooperation Council (NACC) were, to say the least, unenthusiastic. To be sure, the defence minister, Pierre Joxe, would complain about not being allowed to participate in the new entity. President Mitterrand refused, time and again, to accede to his requests.[10] At that moment, he regarded NACC to be an American effort to expand US influence in Central and Eastern Europe, at little cost to it but to the detriment of the countries of Western Europe, who would be called upon to supply the bulk of any economic aid given to the CEE states.

Moreover, in France it was thought that when it came to building bridges to the former adversaries in the WTO, the alliance was the least appropriate institution one could imagine. It had certainly played a prominent role in the defence of Western Europe, and it would doubtless continue to have an essential place in its members' security, but times had changed. It was precisely its role in the realm of defence that rendered NATO such an institutional misfit for the new situation. Either the rapprochement with the CEE states was really only intended for a select few among them, in which case the others would feel themselves excluded, not to say regarded as potential adversaries, or it was to be intended for *all* the CEE states, in which case there would hardly be any further purpose in a defensive alliance such as NATO.

In sum, to the extent that a new phase in relations with the CEE states was about to begin, it was held necessary to establish a new institutional mechanism. NATO was a defensive alliance, but it was not primarily military problems that were determining the agenda of cooperation between Western Europe and the CEE states. As well, French leaders in this period were attempting to accelerate the construction of a European pillar of defence. Doing so would fulfill a longstanding French desire to develop European institutions. It was not an issue of replacing NATO — as might have been dreamed of in the Paris of the 1960s — but rather of erecting a structure that was at one and the same time complementary and autonomous. France's démarche reflected several considerations:

- Had not the Americans from the very outset of the alliance demanded that the Europeans organize themselves? Subsequently, they would lament that the defence burden was not resting heavily enough upon European shoulders. Logically, then, it would hardly do for Washington to try to frustrate the building of a European pillar.
- The Euromissile crisis had demonstrated the fragility of public opinion with regard to defence policy. French leaders thought that, in part, this fragility stemmed from a feeling of dependence vis-à-vis the United States.
- Paris was on guard against further shocks and brusque reversals in American diplomacy. The collapse of the Berlin Wall, it felt, could not help but reinforce isolationist sentiment in the US. It was altogether proper, therefore, to lay the foundation for the European pillar of defence, which could serve to complement the American presence in Europe, or in the event the latter were to disappear, to serve even more important purposes.
- There might exist situations where Europeans and Americans did not share identical views on security problems. In those situations, it would be all the more necessary for Europe to have at its disposal some autonomous capability.
- Last, but certainly not least, the construction of a Europe of defence seemed to be dictated by the logic of the construction of Europe.

On 6 December 1990, Chancellor Helmut Kohl and President Mitterrand addressed a common letter to the president of the European Community — at that time Giulio Andreotti — in which they argued that "political union needed to include a genuine common security policy, which would lead ultimately to a common defence." On 4 February 1991, the Dumas-Genscher proposal revived the idea. In response to this, Britain's foreign secretary, Douglas Hurd, remarked on 15 February that Europe already possessed a common defence, one that was lodged in the midst of NATO. But the Franco-German initiative presupposed an eventual integration of the Western European Union (WEU) into the EC, with the former becoming the latter's military arm. To London, however, the WEU could be nothing other than the European pillar of NATO, and not an autonomous structure.

On 14 October 1991, Kohl and Mitterrand proposed the creation of a joint Franco-German corps, which would develop into the Eurocorps. London immediately demanded that the status of this new unit vis-à-vis NATO be clarified. In this context, France would interpret the desire to endow NATO with new missions (whether in the form of an opening to the east or of out-of-area operations) to be nothing other than a ploy of the United States, supported by the British and the Dutch, to preempt the emergence of a European defence identity and at the same time to pressure Germany into restricting its relations with France. The fact that the creation of NACC was proposed in a joint declaration by James Baker and Hans-Dietrich Genscher could not help but reinforce this perception.

France was convinced that the United States was determined, at any price, to confer new missions on the alliance — even if those did not correspond with its traditional, and natural, vocation — so as to thwart the emergence of the WEU and the Conference on Security and Cooperation in Europe (CSCE). The WEU, whose revitalization Paris had been promoting since 1984, seemed to it to be the European pillar of defence in waiting. For its part the CSCE, in the aftermath of the 1990 summit and the adoption of the Charter of Paris for a new Europe, seemed to present itself as the means through which a new collective-security architecture could emerge in Europe.

The United States played, by definition, no role in the WEU, and only a modest one in the CSCE, the procedures of which tended, in any case, to minimize the influence of the great powers. Washington therefore resumed the offensive so that NATO — within which America's might was neither masked nor contested — would not be seen simply as an organization resting on its laurels, fit only for a strategic environment that had become obsolete, and thus deserving to be relegated to the shadows of the WEU and CSCE, dynamic entities appropriate to the task of meeting the new strategic challenges, the former in the sphere of defence, the latter in that of collective security.

Optimism then was the order of the day, when it came to the prospects of the CSCE. On 27 November 1990 the Charter of Paris was signed, giving rise to expectations of a "new Europe." The Cold War was officially declared over. The members of the Cold War's rival alliances proclaimed that they had ceased to be adversaries, and all acknowledged that the era of Europe's division had drawn to a close. Even if France did not succeed in getting included some mechanism by which solutions might be found for intrastate conflict, its foreign minister, Roland Dumas, could still laud the Paris summit as being the "most important development since 1945."

The CSCE's conflict prevention centre was set up on 18 March 1991. But the hopes that had been placed in this institution were soon to be dashed against the walls of conflict that were thrown up in the former Yugoslavia and the former Soviet Union. Within a short period of time, analysts could write of a "race being run," pitting partisans of extending the role of European institutions in the realms of security and conflict management against champions of maintaining and enlarging the NATO system for crisis management inside and, indeed, outside Europe.[11] Other writers also found utility in the metaphor, noting that it was a very unequal race, "between an existing organization that had already shown its mettle and an entity (the WEU) still in the stages of development."[12]

This would all become apparent with the opening to the CEE states. In parallel with the goal of James Baker to put in place a security architecture extending from "Vancouver to Vladivostock" there would be a French initiative to organize periodic meetings between the foreign affairs ministers of the WEU members and their counterparts in eight countries of Central and Eastern Europe. The first of these was held on 19 June 1992. A half-year later, in January

1993, the NACC set up an ad hoc group on cooperation in the area of peace-keeping. On 29 March, following a meeting of defence ministers, the group produced a draft common statement on peacekeeping, with reference both to its theoretical and operational aspects.

This simply reinforced France's fear of seeing NACC become the de facto military arm of the CSCE. This fear was magnified by the similarity in member-ship of the two organizations. What was the point of enlarging NACC's composition to the level of the CSCE if not to drain the latter of any substance? NATO's central role, it therefore followed, was going to be reaffirmed to the detriment of both the CSCE and WEU.

France expressed its reservations about NATO's new role. Henceforth, the alliance's opening to the east would be subjected to increasingly critical scru-tiny. As well, Paris demonstrated strong resistance to the prospect of NATO assuming missions outside the geographical limits of the North Atlantic Treaty (that is to say, "out of area"). But Paris would find itself on shaky ground both with its Western European partners and with the CEE states.

The Western Europeans could only think that despite its new, and on some points slightly more conciliatory, discourse on NATO, France continued to dem-onstrate an ill-disguised hostility toward the alliance. Could France really claim that it welcomed a continued American presence in Europe while at the same it was rejecting reforms needed to render that presence more legitimate in the court of American public opinion? Could one declare oneself in favour of NATO but refuse to let it adapt to new realities? And as for the Central and Eastern Europeans, they had to think that notwithstanding France's longstanding avowal of a need to transcend Yalta, the country lacked a basic understanding of their interests, demonstrated by its refusal to open the doors either to NATO or the European Union.

Thus it was that Alain Juppé, after first having broached the subject with his German and Polish counterparts, proposed to the parliamentary assembly of the WEU on 1 December 1993 that it develop closer relations with the coun-tries to the east by creating the status of association within the organization. Given that Russia had little prospect, in the short to medium term, of joining either the EU or the WEU, this would provide associated countries with the advantage of being involved with an institution from which the principal source of their insecurity would be absent, without at the same time triggering an iso-lationist reaction from the Russians.

The Clinton administration objected that such an accession of the CEE states to the WEU ran the risk of creating "undesirable back-door security guar-antees from the United States."[13] The fear was of the US becoming engaged against its will in a conflict resulting from intemperate actions on the part of a CEE state. But such a risk would equally exist as a result of the enlargement of NATO. Therefore, why oppose WEU expansion? The latter at least had the al-lure, from the perspective of the CEE states, of offering both a security guarantee and a politico-economic association, it being understood that the WEU served as an antechamber for the EU.[14]

There was more to come. In April 1993, France's prime minister, Edouard Balladur, proposed a "stability pact" whose object was to erect a framework of preventive diplomacy that might serve to resolve minority and boundary problems within and among the Central and Eastern European states.[15]

Skirmish before the Enlargement Summit

Even before the Brussels summit of January 1994, it was clear that the principle of enlargement would likely be officially accepted, notwithstanding the frequently expressed doubts of various French officials that enlargement would confer few advantages upon the alliance. France was at this time experiencing another period of constitutional cohabitation, with a socialist president and a centre-right government sharing power. Even so, the country's divers political actors were expressing similar concerns, which they hoped might weigh in the summit deliberations.

Sifting through various official declarations, one sees two particular worries highlighted: one concern was about the dilution of the alliance, and the other about the hardening of antiwestern tendencies in Moscow. Interestingly, the eclipsing of the European pillar of defence was never evoked officially; still, one could say of this apprehension what used to be said of an earlier policy aspiration, the restoration of Alsace and Lorraine to France — namely that the French should never speak of it, but always think of it. Foreign observers believed that it was the European-pillar argument that accounted for the bulk of the French opposition to enlargement.[16]

As the Brussels summit approached, and with it the moment of decision, various French policymakers hunkered down for a barrage of arguments and counterarguments. To be sure, they declared themselves ready to take into consideration the aspirations of the CEE states that, in an increasingly unstable environment, were trying to bring themselves within the embrace of European and Atlantic institutions.[17] But the obstacles remained too large.

On 10 October 1993, the French foreign minister declared before the United Nations that the "fundamental mission of the alliance, which is to serve as a system of collective defence for its members against eventual aggression — as expressed through Article 5 — cannot simply be relegated to the closet. Consequently, the immediate adherence of a large number of new members to the alliance appears premature." Ten days later, on the occasion of an official visit by the Russian foreign minister, Juppé stated that everyone would have to strive to bring about stability everywhere on the European continent, without in the process recreating in a different way antagonistic camps, each with its own bloc and artificial boundaries.

On 28 October, during a debate on financing for his department, Juppé pronounced himself to be "reserved on the question of the rapid adhesion of a certain number of countries to the alliance."[18] He invoked the danger that a rapid expansion of NATO might lead to the reconstruction of blocs in Europe, and signalled again his concern about the dilution of the alliance.

Prime Minister Balladur was also busy. On 23 October he gave an interview to journalists from four major European newspapers, at which he emphasized France's desire to contribute to the security and stability of the entire European continent, without creating new barriers or blocs.[19] But the labouring oar was wielded mainly by Juppé, who went before the parliamentary assembly of the WEU on 1 December to repeat the government's two chief objections to a rapid enlargement of NATO. A precipitous enlargement, he said, ran the risk of so watering down the alliance that it would render Article 5 useless; as well, it would also resurrect a bipolar system in Europe.

On 2 December, during a press conference held at the close of the NAC ministerial meetings, Juppé returned to the same arguments, invoking the need for NATO not to furnish any pretext for Russia's transforming the Commonwealth of Independent States (CIS) into a competitive organization. Should that happen, the result of enlargement would simply to have been the shifting eastward of the "frontiers of a bloc system that we thought had disappeared four years ago." It was not time to enlarge the alliance, he continued. For the moment, the Partnership for Peace (PFP) was a good step. "It can give rise to such concrete forms of cooperation as joint maneuvers, and even joint planning exercises."[20]

The minister of defence, François Léotard, was blunter: "To knock at NATO's door is to knock at America's, to demand an American guarantee. That may be understandable, but it is not how we see things. We want the demand for security to come to Europe, hence our proposal of association with the WEU."[21]

Appeasement after the Enlargement Summit

Things would change after the January 1994 NATO summit in Brussels. All of a sudden, as one analyst observed, the "question of relations between the Atlantic alliance, in the central role, and the other European institutions (the WEU and CSCE) has become less conflictive."[22] In the first place, since the principle of enlargement had become enshrined in the declarations of the assembled heads of state and government, what was the point of carrying on the struggle against it? Furthermore, since the deadline for new members' joining had been set sufficiently far into the future, and since there was every reason to expect that PFP could serve as a waiting room (if not a sidetrack) for aspirants to membership, French officials perceived that the hitherto gathering momentum for enlargement had been exhausted. Finally, and most importantly, the complementarity of approach of both NATO and the "Europe of defence" had been vigorously reaffirmed at the summit, when the heads of state and government announced at the 11 January closing session that "our alliance reflects the existence of a European security and defence identity progressively affirming itself as the expression of a greater Europe."

After the summit, François Mitterrand was moved to remark on the altered thinking within the alliance regarding the European pillar. "Between Rome and Brussels," he noted, "there has been a considerable shift in tone. What had literally to be dragged out of the Americans at Rome, namely the recognition of a European defence identity, seemed at Brussels to flow perfectly naturally." The president went on to affirm that it was now necessary to act upon that recognition. For him, it was a matter of balancing the desire of the CEE states to move closer to NATO with Russia's worries about becoming encircled. Faced with this dilemma, Mitterrand concluded that PFP was a "reasonable" response, and he reasoned that this alliance program signified the reality that any conflict occurring in Central and Eastern Europe was bound to become a matter of great concern to the members of NATO. And that, he believed, meant that the CEE states did have a "real guarantee" of their security, even if they lacked the formal guarantee constituted by Article 5 of the NATO Treaty. Mitterrand also recalled that France had proposed associate status for the CEE states within the WEU.

After Brussels, Mitterrand acknowledged the legitimacy of the CEE states' quest for security. He agreed that they had the right to join a defensive organization, "whether it be NATO or the WEU," but he also stressed that the exercise of this right would imply obligations and responsibilities. Moreover, he continued, the defensive organization itself must not become a factor exacerbating the security dilemma of third parties. Mitterrand pointed out the most immediate threats to the security of the CEE states resided above all in the problems of borders and minorities, menaces that might be resolved through the stability pact proposed by his prime minister.[23] He brought up the same point a few days later, speaking on Bulgarian television.[24]

François Léotard had, in early 1995, expressed the wish not to "brutalize NATO," and declared that the first priority should be reinforcing PFP. He raised anew the need for the CEE states initially to draw nearer to the EU before they could move toward NATO.[25] Later that January, on the occasion of the tenth anniversary celebration of a centre dedicated to policy analysis and forecasting (le Centre d'analyse et de prévision), Léotard's cabinet colleague, the minister of foreign affairs, declared that the debate over the enlargement of NATO needed neither to be dramatized nor ignored, but rather to be situated within the larger context of European integration. He admitted that enlargement was an inevitability. So as not to offend Russia, however, Juppé asked, "Why not envisage a treaty between the alliance and Moscow?"[26]

Several months later, Juppé's successor, Hervé de Charette, announced that France "looked favourably upon the enlargement of the alliance to the countries of Central and Eastern Europe. The process is already underway. It will be completed in coming months and I can assure you that France supports this endeavour."[27] President Jacques Chirac would declare at year's end, in an interview in *Time*, that it was "evident that the Atlantic Alliance must expand eastward. But, I say simply that we must be careful to reach an agreement with the Russians that will permit this enlargement without threatening or humiliating them."[28]

France's period in outspoken opposition to enlargement had clearly drawn to an end. How can we explain its new, conciliatory attitude? To start with the obvious: the January 1994 NATO summit had been regarded in Paris as a success. The launching of PFP was accompanied by the recognition of a European defence identity. No longer would an ESDI and NATO have to be regarded as competitive; instead, they could be taken as two sides of the same coin, something President Bill Clinton confirmed in his address to the National Assembly in June 1994. France was finally able to satisfy itself that the alliance could work in harmony with the Europe of defence, and it responded by rejoining some of NATO's military entities.

By the same token, France understood that the emergence of the European pillar would prove to be a longer process than previously imagined. The European countries were simply unprepared, politically and economically, to provide themselves with genuine strategic autnomy. Even France itself, which up until 1993 had continued to safeguard its defence budget against cuts, would follow the European trend to reduce military spending, as Chirac undertook to slash the procurement budget for the armed forces by between 15 and 20 percent. It was patently becoming more difficult for the Europeans to endow themselves with what autonomy would require, especially in the areas of intelligence and force projection. If anyone needed proof of this contention, there was the spectacle of the former Yugoslavia to furnish it.

Moreover, French worries about enlargement triggering a Russian "encirclement complex" are, in fact, shared by the country's alliance partners, whether European or North American. It is true that in an objective sense, the security context of the CEE states has never been so favourably configured as it is today.[29] For the first time in their history, they no longer have an enemy to the west, and as for their big eastern neighbour, it is hardly in shape to menace them with military conquest. Furthermore, these states are cutting their defence expenditures even as their economies are expanding, notwithstanding that their doing so contributes to the creation of a security vacuum. If the Russian bear may be said to have a hearty appetite in respect of the "near abroad," that latter category is widely held to consist solely in territories once part of the

USSR, and not former WTO members elsewhere in Europe. The west may be culpable in letting Russia have a free hand in both the near abroad and in regions even closer to home (viz., Chechnya); but it is acting responsibly when it adopts a prudential attitude vis-à-vis Moscow's (so far) restrained behaviour toward its former allies in Central and Eastern Europe.

Paris' cautions regarding enlargement remain, but paradoxically they testify to a French attachment to the alliance, rather than to any antipathy toward it. Curiously, the worry of the moment, insofar as concerns NATO's moving eastward, is that it might have a boomerang effect on the *American* commitment to European security. The debate on enlargement began uniquely in the United States. Up until now, it has appeared to have positive connotations only to many Americans. Enlargement would consecrate the west's great victory in the Cold War; it would give greater say to a group of countries about whom the west still feels a sense of guilt for having left them so long under the Soviet yoke; and — from a domestic electoral standpoint — it would send the right signal to sizeable ethnic minorities with roots in Central and Eastern Europe. Being wooed, as Washington is, by a group of states in whose eyes the principal advantage of NATO membership is the American guarantee that accompanies it, cannot help but go over well in America, creating a comfortable feeling that displaces the more traditional mood of wrangling in the transatlantic household.

But with the deadline for enlargement approaching, the feeling could change to discomfort. Enlargement is not going simply to have platonic effects. It will come with a price tag — between $10 and $40 billion over a decade merely for the countries of the Visegrad triangle — and it will mean the undertaking of a set of important security obligations, because as NATO's enlargement study of September 1995 made clear, there will be no differentiated participation.[30]

Enlargement cannot help but lose its current romantic aura. It cannot occur without the necessary ratifying procedures coming into play nationally, and one can only with great difficulty foresee the American Senate mustering the required two-thirds majority to make it possible. (For that matter, one can only with great difficulty imagine the Senate generating a two-thirds majority on anything!) The regnant soft consensus on enlargement in the US is probably doomed to dissipate once action is required to implement it. In that event, the disillusionment felt in the CEE states is likely to be great. Even worse, once the debates over enlargement get started in Washington, they can be expected to open up another debate, on the relevance of the alliance itself. Since it will be claimed by proponents of enlargement that it would be immoral to refuse to Poland and the Czech Republic that which is accorded to Germany and Italy, there is a risk of the discussion backfiring, with the opponents questioning the wisdom of America continuing to guarantee the security of the latter.

Conclusion

Conceived as a means of renewing NATO, enlargement could result in its demise instead. The dangers of "strategic overstretch," so well-illuminated by Paul Kennedy nearly a decade ago, can apply equally to alliances as to great powers.[31] Bolstered by the experience with European Union, France has come to have an instinctive distrust of rapid enlargements, especially those that are touted with a minimum of critical reflection, and whose negative consequences only appear late in the day. NATO's enlargement study released in September 1995 cannot but be pleasing to France. Presenting the problems clearly, and stressing *obligations* as well as rights of members, the study serves as a "reality check," minimizing thereby the danger of today's aspirants to membership, so boundless in their support for the alliance, becoming tomorrow's new members, so unreasonable in the demands they put upon it.

In this respect, Paris' reluctance to see NATO enlarge too rapidly — a reluctance that may increasingly go unexpressed but is for all that shared by a large number of current allies — should ironically be taken as the proof of France's attachment, rather than hostility, to the alliance.

Notes

1.   François Heisbourg has drawn attention to this terminological distinction, in noting that in most languages, "expansion" conjures up images of territorial acquisition, and asking how Americans might feel were Russia to seek to "expand" its security perimeter. See his "NATO: A Cautious Path to Enlargement," *International Herald Tribune*, 5 April 1995.

2.   See, for example, Michael Brown, "The Flawed Logic of NATO Expansion," *Survival* 37 (Spring 1995): 34-52; and Michael Mandelbaum, "Preserving the New Peace: The Case Against NATO Expansion," *Foreign Affairs* 74 (May/June 1995): 9-13. As well, see the chapters by Douglas Stuart and Reinhard Wolf, in this volume.

3.   This, at least, was the impression I received while listening to a series of interventions made by delegates from CEE states attending the 41st General Assembly of the Atlantic Treaty Association, held in Toronto from 4 through 7 October 1995.

4.   With the notable exception, during the Gulf War, of Jean-Pierre Chevènement, the defence minister who tendered his resignation to express his opposition to France's participation. Chevènement explains this action at some length in his *Une certaine idée de la République m'amène à ...* (Paris: Albin Michel, 1992).

5.   Nevertheless, Philippe Séguin (RPR), president of the National Assembly, could declare as late as 20 January 1994 that the alliance was "from now on increasingly unstable, incapable of responding to the needs of the new European environment. We must put something else in its place." Quoted in *Revue défense nationale* (April 1994): 12. That would be the last time he would issue such a stern judgement on NATO.

6. For an analysis of the French debate over relations with NATO, the reader might wish to consult the chapters on France in the last five annual editions of *L'Année Stratégique*, ed. Pascal Boniface (Paris: Éditions Dunod, 1991-95).

7. Gabriel Robin, *Un monde sans maître* (Paris: Éditions Odile Jacob, 1995), p. 245.

8. François de Rose, *L'Alliance Atlantique et la Paix* (Paris: Desclee de Brouwer, 1995), pp. 151-52.

9. A conference on European confederation was held in Prague in June 1991, under the joint invitation of Mitterrand and the Czechoslovakian president, Vaclav Havel. Mitterrand's initial proposal called for a series of concrete cooperative initiatives in such spheres as energy, transportation, telecommunications, the environment, and culture. But errors in the way the French presented this proposal touched off opposition from the CEE states. The confederation came to be perceived as a device to retard their integration into the European Community. When Mitterrand declared, realistically enough, that total integration into the EC would likely take 10 to 15 years to occur, the effect was simply to reinforce the CEE states' distrust of the French proposal. Moreover, the French had originally proposed to convene a truly "pan-European" conference, one including the Soviet Union but excluding the US. Because the CEE states would not accept the latter's exclusion, an invitation was sent to Washington as well.

10. Joxe deplored the fact that while defence ministers from the former Warsaw Pact, to say nothing about those from the former Soviet Union, could participate in NACC meetings, he could not. He was echoing the views of the general staff and of defence ministry officials traditionally in favour of a rapprochement with NATO; for its part, the foreign affairs bureaucracy has been more reserved on the merits of such a rapprochement.

11. Yves Boyer and Amaya Bloch Laine, "L'Europe occidentale," in *L'Année Stratégique* (Paris: Dunod, 1993), p. 25.

12. Frédéric Bozo, *La France et l'Otan* (Paris: Masson, 1991), p. 88.

13. Jonathan Dean, "Losing Russia or Keeping NATO: Must We Choose?" *Arms Control Today* (June 1995): 7.

14. According to the minister of defence, the "granting of associate status in the WEU is part of a European perspective that we wish to open, including in the realm of security, to the countries associated with the [European] Union." See Ministry of Defence/SIRPA, *Propos sur la défense*, no. 39 (December 1993), p. 16.

15. See Bernard de Montferrand, "Le pacte de stabilité en Europe," *Relations Internationales et Stratégiques*, no. 18 (Summer 1995), pp. 23-28.

16. "The French government was not enthusiastic, apparently preferring that the relationship between the new democracies and the EU and Western European Union take policy precedence over NATO enlargement." Stanley Sloan and Steve Woehrel, "NATO Enlargement and Russia: From Cold War to Cold Peace?" *CRS Report for Congress*, 1995, p. 33.

17. Speech of minister of foreign affairs, Alain Juppé, before the Council on Foreign Relations, New York, 28 September 1993.

18. *Journal Officiel*, Assemblée nationale, session of 28 October 1993.

19. The papers were *El País*, *The Independent*, *La Repùbblica*, and the *Süddeutsche Zeitung*.

20. Quoted in *Propos sur la défense*.

21. Quoted in *Les Échos*, 7 January 1994.

22. Bruno Tertrais, "L'Europe Occidentale," in *L'Année Stratégique* (Paris: Dunod, 1995), p. 21.

23. *Nouvelles Atlantiques*, no. 2586, 11 January 1994.

24. Asked about the enlargement of NATO, he replied that the former WTO members did have legitimate security worries, but he thought that other organizations and mechanisms might be better placed than NATO to address them. He mentioned in particular the CSCE, the Charter of Paris for a new Europe, association with the WEU, and the Balladur plan.

25. *Süddeutsche Zeitung*, 9 January 1995.

26. Quoted in *Politique étrangère*, no. 1 (1995), pp.245-59.

27. The foreign minister made these remarks on 30 May 1995, following a NATO ministerial meeting. Quoted in *Propos sur la défense*, no. 51 (May/June 1995), pp. 36-39.

28. *Time*, 4 December 1995.

29. Pascal Boniface, "Europe centrale et orientale: une sécurité encore indéfinie," *Relations Internationales et Stratégiques*, no. 15 (Autumn 1994), pp. 31-37.

30. The cost estimate stems from analysts with the Rand Corporation.

31. Paul Kennedy, *The Rise and Fall of the Great Powers: Economic Change and Military Conflict from 1500 to 2000* (New York: Random House, 1987).

CHAPTER NINE

The Doubtful Mover:
Germany and NATO Expansion

Reinhard Wolf

Introduction

NATO enlargement confronts Germany with a crucial choice. The issue forces the country not just to define its vision for the future of the western alliance but also to decide upon the kind of political landscape it wants to see evolve in Europe. Ultimately, the Germans may have to choose between expanding Western Europe's institutions to their eastern neighbourhood or staying on good terms with Russia. When the issue becomes more pressing again, it thus could put an end to a situation in which political élites have had the luxury of avoiding the setting of clear priorities. NATO's expansion project might create a fork in the road that even Bonn can no longer ignore.[1]

Contrasted with the issue's saliency has been the intensity with which it has been debated among politicians, experts, and the public at large; that is to say, there has hardly been any debate. In stark contrast to the early 1980s, when West Germans fiercely argued about the pros and cons of NATO's missile deployments on German soil, today's path-breaking need for decision arouses little interest, let alone argument, in the Federal Republic. Within the political élite only the Green party unequivocally opposes broadening the alliance. The party spectrum reflects the prevailing attitude among the public, which favours an inclusion of the reformed states of Central and Eastern Europe (CEE), although it dislikes the idea of ever having to send the Bundeswehr to the defence of Germany's eastern neighbours. Only the strategic community appears almost evenly split between proponents and critics of expansion. Yet even the experts have yet to engage in an intense and thorough debate.

Despite this broad support for enlargement, Germany's backing of NATO's current course has never been as solid as it often may have appeared. Unlike the defence minister, Volker Rühe, who was the first and remains the staunch-est advocate of expansion, Chancellor Helmut Kohl and his foreign minister, Klaus Kinkel, have yet to stake out a clear position on the issue. Instead, their support for enlargement is contingent upon continued US pressure as well as on good prospects for widening and deepening the European Union (EU). As Washington's interest in absorbing new members has cooled and prospects for further European integration have become bleaker, Kohl and Kinkel have ac-cordingly advocated stretching out the alliance's expansion process in order to accomodate Russian wishes. The need to concede to the demands of an oth-erwise worried Germany is hence not a persuasive argument in favour of early enlargement.

Germany's Special Stakes in NATO Enlargement

Among other things, the possible enlargement of NATO primarily affects four issue areas that are of particular importance to Germany's interests. There is broad consensus in the country that whatever the alliance finally does is going to have important implications for the following:

- the stability of Germany's eastern neighbours;
- the future of European integration;
- German-Russian relations; and
- the future of NATO and the transatlantic link.

Most obviously, NATO expansion would impinge upon Germany's efforts to stabilize the new democracies located to its east. The collapse of the Berlin Wall and the quick demise of the Soviet empire have confronted Germany's political élite with a host of issues for which it was totally unprepared. While it is true that during the Cold War governments in Bonn had relentlessly called for an overcoming of the unnatural division of Europe, the sudden prospect of liv-ing next door to a potentially volatile region caused German élites nearly to recoil. With Soviet tanks and fortified borders gone, there seemed to be little to arrest the spread of dangerous movements and destabilizing developments whose source lay across the river Oder. Such concerns were quickly given substance by the large influx of eastern migrants (asylum seekers), and were further magnified by the hundreds of thousands of refugees fleeing the wars in former Yugoslavia.

As such, it has become axiomatic that Germany cannot maintain its way of life through keeping out its disadvantaged neighbours, but only by "exporting" its wealth and political values to Central Europe. Once democracy and the market economy have taken firm hold there, it is expected that few will have incentive to leave, or to subvert or attack the region's states. Consequently, Germany would no longer have to fear mass migration and dangerous conflicts close to its borders. The stabilization of its eastern neighbourhood has thus become one of the chief objectives of Germany's foreign policy — as evinced by the large sums of money that have to date been transferred in a bid to ease the CEE countries' economic transformations.[2]

Not surprisingly, then, most Germans appreciate the positive contribution NATO's expansion could make to the political and economic development of the Visegrad countries (i.e., the Czech Republic, Hungary, Poland, and Slovakia), and possibly beyond. An alliance decision to take in a new member might benefit that country's stability in a number of ways. First, the mere prospect of joining NATO is likely to increase a society's resiliency against antidemocratic ideas and movements, for democratic governments and parties would be more vigilant in the face of such threats given that any authoritarian turn would jeopardize the country's accession prospects. Second, eventual membership would further discourage antidemocratic moves that would lead to the country's isolation within the alliance. Third, extending NATO's security guarantee to an eastern state would deter potential adversaries from attacking it. This enhanced feeling of security would make it harder to propagate nationalist and militarist myths that otherwise might be useful were an attempt made to establish a garrison state.

Forestalling such a development would nourish both the country's own democratic system and those of its democratic neighbours, which otherwise would have to face a more aggressively inclined autocracy. Moreover, increased security could be expected to result in a larger influx of foreign investment, further stimulating economic modernization and thereby stabilizing democratic rule. Needless to say, such reassurance effects would also enhance the opportunities for German industry, already the largest investor and exporter to most Central and East European countries.[3] Given both its exposed geographic position and its economic potential, Germany would thus be the principal beneficiary of all these stabilizing effects.

NATO expansion to the Visegrad countries would furthermore facilitate Germany's project of both deepening and widening the European Union between now and the end of the century. One obvious reason why Bonn's political élite remains strongly committed to this ambitious endeavour is, of course, that it desires that Germany's EU partners contribute their "fair share" to the stabilization of the new democracies. However, there is yet another reason, which is even more important in this context: politicians in Bonn fear that any distinctly German effort to stabilize the region might antagonize both their western and eastern neighbours. A return to a national *Ostpolitik* outside of multilateral institutions, it is reasoned, might easily instigate renewed fears of hegemonic designs. Such concerns could not only stifle cooperation between Germany and its eastern neighbours but also promote balancing against Germany, possibly resulting in its international isolation if not outright encirclement.

The combination of deepening and widening is seen as the obvious solution to this problem, for once this project has succeeded, Germany's eastern neighbours would no longer face a loosely constrained behemoth; instead they would be safely anchored within a community in which individual states increasingly played a diminished role.[4] NATO enlargement would indirectly enhance the prospects for widening the European Union inasmuch as it would promote democracy and economic development in Central Europe. Perhaps more importantly, broadening NATO would also facilitate the Union's deepening, particularly the pursuit of a common foreign and security policy (CFSP) within an expanded EU. If access to NATO were denied to new EU members, their security status would clearly differ from that of most of the older members, especially with regard to the US nuclear guarantee. Obviously, these different levels of security would seriously complicate efforts to arrive at common policies vis-à-vis future threats.

The biggest potential drawback NATO enlargement could have for Germany is a souring of its relations with the dominant postcommunist state, Russia. Compared to the other states in the region, Russia is of paramount importance both to Germany's economy and its security. Even today, the Russian Republic is among the most important trading partners Germany has in Central and Eastern Europe.[5] If it manages the transition to a well-ordered market economy, Russia's large population and rich endowment of natural resources will make it an even greater recipient of German exports and investments. Even more obvious is the crucial impact Russia has on German security. It is the only European country ouside of NATO that commands enough conventional and nuclear might to pose a potential threat to Germany, albeit only in the long run. Hence the latter has a fundamental interest in seeing democratic reforms succeed in Russia, as well as in maintaining good relations with it. Otherwise, Germany could find itself again in a dangerous security competition fraught with all the costs and deadly risks that past east-west confrontation entailed for it, a state so centrally located on the continent. To the extent that taking in new members would mean antagonizing or destabilizing a marginalized Russia, Germany could therefore pay a high price for NATO enlargement.

The expansion of the alliance will, finally, affect Germany's vital interest in preserving NATO and the transatlantic link it embodies. Since the end of the Cold War, Germany's élites and public alike have increasingly realized that the Atlantic alliance is endangered, and yet also indispensable to European security.[6] In the eyes of many, the poor performance of both the EU and OSCE in the Yugoslav conflict has underscored the continued need for an active NATO led by a determined United States. At the same time, that conflict has apparently revealed the hazards of an inward-looking America and the potential for a renationalization of security policies of Western European states left to their own devices. Germany has, in the circumstances, increasingly displayed a keen interest in securing a prominent role for NATO and in preserving the American commitment to Europe.[7]

Due to the crucial importance that Washington's leadership and its nuclear guarantee have for NATO's continued viability, keeping America engaged in European security affairs has become one of the top priorities of German foreign policy. Accordingly, one of the big issues from Germany's point of view is how an enlargement of NATO would impinge on alliance cohesion as well as on US interests in the alliance. If accepting new members seems necessary to revitalize NATO and America's European commitments, enlargement would look essential to most Germans. If, on the other hand, such a move came to be seen as a possible threat to the transatlantic link, this would be regarded as an almost forbidding price tag.

In sum, Germany's specific stakes in NATO enlargement neither point unequivocally toward expansion nor do they point away from it. Instead, as soon as this issue becomes more pressing again, those stakes will confront the country with the troublesome need to sort out its priorities in respect of Europe's future security order. Should the Federal Republic concentrate on stabilizing its eastern vicinity, or opt instead for a more encompassing order that avoids new dividing lines in Europe? Should it favour new security commitments for itself and its current allies? Or should it argue against them, out of concern that new obligations entail the risk of entrapping member states in a peripheral war that might ultimately jeopardize NATO's very cohesion?

These and other questions cannot be answered without a thorough and comprehensive analysis of Germany's national interests. Unfortunately, as far as NATO enlargement is concerned, such an analysis has yet to be undertaken. As I will argue later in this chapter, there is so far little indication that the country's political élites and its strategic community have confronted the relevant issues with anything like the seriousness they deserve.

Bonn's Position on Enlargement Takes Shape

Since the collapse of the Berlin Wall the Bonn government has been at the forefront of NATO's efforts to make the alliance more accessible to its former enemies and their security problems. Initially this reformist zeal was linked clearly to Germany's interest in paving the way for East Germany's simultaneous admission to the Federal Republic itself as well as to the alliance to which it belonged. In order to gain the Soviet Union's consent to East Germany's switching sides, Bonn had to prove that the alliance was about to shed its Cold War role and show itself ready to focus on new missions. As NATO's 1990 summit in London approached, therefore, Bonn strongly supported the liaison concept proposed by the Bush administration, calling for regular meetings between the North Atlantic Council (NAC) and Warsaw Treaty Organization (WTO) ambassadors.[8]

One year later, in the fall of 1991, Bonn's foreign minister, Hans-Dietrich Genscher, joined the US secretrary of state, James Baker, in pushing an iniative to upgrade these meetings into what would become the North Atlantic Co-operation Council (NACC). This new institution within NATO was set up to give the postcommunist states a means of regular input into alliance consultations on pan-European security issues. With active support from Germany, the NACC soon established a host of committees and work programs aimed primarily at advancing democratic reforms in the defence establishments of former WTO countries. Through all this, Germany hoped to achieve a further easing of any remaining east-west suspicions, as well as the stabilization and gradual integration of postcommunist countries into western institutions.[9]

For quite some time, Germany's eagerness to draw the reforming eastern states closer to NATO had a natural limit, that being the question of outright membership. When Polish President Lech Walesa and his Czechoslovak counterpart Vaclav Havel expressed their countries' interest in joining the alliance, Bonn's initial reaction was no warmer than that of any other member state. Foreign Minister Genscher cautioned against NATO enlargement, stressing the West's reluctance to take advantage of the Warsaw Pact's dissolution. Instead, he called for further reforms of NATO and the Conference on Security and Cooperation in Europe (CSCE) in order to fill the evolving security vacuum. Other political figures in Germany's ruling coalition displayed similar skepticism. In the few public statements on enlargement made before 1993, they voiced concerns that such a move could isolate Russia and overburden the alliance with conflicts between new members. The solution to the security problems of the CEE states was to be found instead in their eventual admission to the European Community (EC) or to the Western European Union (WEU).[10]

Gradually Bonn came to realize that the growing pressure exerted by the Visegrad countries presented NATO with a dilemma. The new foreign minister, Klaus Kinkel, worried that if the alliance remained utterly opposed to taking in the CEE aspirants to membership, it would undermine its credibility as a community of democratic states. At the same time, he expressed concern that enlargement could weaken the alliance's cohesion while, in the bargain, isolating Russia and Ukraine. To navigate between these conflicting imperatives Kinkel called upon NATO to reconsider its reticence towards the new democracies. Denying any immediate need for decision on enlargement, he proposed to use the NACC to increase efforts to integrate the Visegrad states.[11]

The first German cabinet member to demand outright expansion was the defence minister, Volker Rühe, who subsequently became the country's, if not the alliance's, most ardent supporter of enlargement. Delivering the Alastair Buchan Memorial Lecture at the International Institute for Strategic Studies

(IISS) in March 1993, Rühe called for western efforts to bring political and economic stability to the new democracies in Central and Eastern Europe. To prevent new waves of migrants from threatening the internal stability of Western Europe, the defence minister proposed a "European solidarity pact" and the opening of Euro-Atlantic security structures to the new democracies. "The Atlantic Alliance," he declared, "must not become a 'closed shop.' I cannot see one good reason for denying future members of the European Union membership in NATO."[12]

However, Rühe's clear position did not enjoy unequivocal support within the German government. Far from it. Both the chancellor's office and the foreign ministry repeatedly warned against a rapid expansion that might antagonize Russia. Confronted with an appeal for membership from Poland's prime minister, Hanna Suchocka, Chancellor Kohl made it known that while he favoured some kind of western security guarantee for the CEE states, he could not say whether it should take the form of regular membership in, as opposed to increased levels of cooperation with, the alliance.[13]

Kohl's and Kinkel's concerns apparently received a boost when, in late September 1993, Russia's president, Boris Yeltsin, sent a letter to western governments announcing his strong opposition to an enlargement of NATO. Within days the chancellor and his foreign minister expressed their view that taking in new members was not on the agenda. Kinkel warned strongly against creating new divisions in Europe and, in effect, conceded a veto to Russia, declaring that "nothing can or may happen against (the will of) Russia." Although Bonn's chief diplomat continued to plead for giving some kind of security "signal" to the reform states as well as for opening new avenues for security cooperation to them, he went on to stress that, for the time being, the importance of the relations between NATO and the Central European states was eclipsed by the value of the latter's relations with the European Community. In a similar vein, Kohl recommended EC enlargement as the best option for the Visegrad states while rejecting any need to accept new NATO members in the near future.[14]

Though Rühe publicly criticized what he deemed too cautious an approach concerning enlargement, the German delegation that Chancellor Kohl led to the 1994 NATO summit in Brussels had no intention of advocating any specific measures to procede with expansion.[15] Hence, it had no quarrels with a final communiqué that, instead of giving the leading aspirants an unambiguous membership perspective, only launched the "Partnership for Peace" program designed to enhance security cooperation with all postcommunist states.[16] Thus, for the moment, Rühe's ambitious course seemed to have foundered on his isolation within both the alliance and his own government.

That the German government was still divided on the enlargement issue became obvious when the differences between Rühe and Kinkel escalated into open dispute in the fall of 1994. After Rühe had continued to press for an early decision in favour of NATO expansion, Kinkel publicly criticized the defence minister's policy line in a speech before a gathering of high-ranking German military officers. The foreign minister most obviously challenged his colleague's approach when he voiced strong concerns about a speedy admittance of the Visegrad states.

In Kinkel's view, such a move was apt to create a new division in Europe, thereby antagonizing Russia and isolating both Ukraine and the Baltic states. While not opposing enlargement at a later stage, the foreign minister insisted that such a step had to be combined with a strengthening of the CSCE and linked to the new members' accession to the EU and WEU.[17] With the apparent support of the chancellor, Kinkel succeeded in getting these caveats set forth in the coalition agreement the governing parties had to negotiate in the wake of their razor-thin victory in the October 1994 federal election.[18]

Yet, the impact of Kinkel's caution within the federal government was quickly undone by heavy pressure from the Clinton administration. Within days after the publication of the new coalition agreement, Bonn began to adjust to Washington's changed position. Starting in the summer of 1994, more and more administration officials had called for the early admittance of the Visegrad states. Increasingly it became obvious that Washington's advocates of enlargement were prevailing over the adherents to the "Russia-first" policy.[19]

As the fall meeting of alliance foreign ministers neared, Kohl and Kinkel decided to bow to administration demands to offer the CEE aspirants a clearer membership perspective. In exchange, Bonn demanded Washington's acceptance of an explicit coupling between NATO and EU expansion. It was hoped that embedding NATO enlargement in the wider context of EU evolution would dampen Russia's growing suspicion of western designs. Bonn thus sought a way to straddle the growing gap between American zeal and Russian anger.[20]

Once the North Atlantic Council had principally settled the enlargement issue with its decision to launch an extensive study on NATO expansion, the German government's position gained in coherence. Both Kohl and Kinkel began to stress that enlargement was well on track and not conditioned on Russian consent. While both politicians went on to express their interest in pan-European security structures coupled with a strategic partnership between NATO and Russia, they also fell in line with Rühe's position that the Kremlin could not be given a veto on the alliance's expansion.[21] With NATO firmly set on course, the focus of Germany's intramural debate shifted to the details of enlargement and its implications for western relations with Russia.

Unlike Rühe, the chancellor and his foreign minister continued to pay great attention to Russian anger exemplified by the Kremlin's sudden refusal to sign its individual partnership document with the alliance. Although they did not go as far as to suggest full membership for Russia, Kohl and Kinkel repeatedly implored that Moscow's concerns be taken into account. To this end, the foreign minister proposed a special charter between the alliance and Russia.

According to Kinkel, such a document should institutionalize a broad dialogue based on a code of conduct and obligations to consult on a regular basis.[22]

Kohl, for his part, repeatedly tried to apply the brakes to an early admittance of Poland. At a meeting with Clinton, he emphasized the Kremlin's special sensitivity regarding this particular country and asked Washington not to press for an early expansion decision but rather to wait for the results of the EU's second Maastricht conference, to be concluded in 1997. Once more, the chancellor stressed that admittance to NATO had to be linked to EU integration.[23] In an apparent concession to Russian worries, he again warned against separating these two matters during an interview conducted with Polish television just before his visit to Warsaw. It was only after receiving a telephone call from a worried Polish foreign minister that Kohl declared NATO membership would not necessarily have to wait until EU admittance.[24]

In light of these concerns, foreign policy makers in Bonn were quite happy with the results of NATO's enlargement study and the ensuing alliance consensus to defer decisions on the "who" and "when" of admittance. They particularly welcomed the emphasis the document put on the congruity of NATO and EU enlargement and fully concurred with the stated need to embed the alliance's broadening in a comprehensive development of all-European security structures, including a strong partnership between Russia and NATO. For the rest of the decade, officials in Bonn envision the alliance carefully maneuvering between Russia and the applicants. To these officials, the issue is not an urgent one, as numerous technical matters need further clarification while the potential new members still have to make sure that they can and will meet the stated requirements for admittance.[25]

Bureaucratic Politics and the Enlargement Issue

It should have become clear by now that Bonn never did speak with a single voice on NATO enlargement. The federal government as a whole was never as enthusiastic about this project as it might appear from Rühe's statements alone. In fact, it seems that on this issue, the defence minister was rather isolated within a cabinet dominated by Kohl and Kinkel, both of whom favoured a much more cautious line. As this section will demonstrate, this split was largely due to the divergence in mission and outlook between, on the one hand, the defence ministry and, on the other, the foreign office and chancellery.

Rühe's early and consistent advocacy for speedy NATO enlargement was primarily motivated by a military threat assessment showing the vulnerability of Germany's eastern region. To be sure, in his public pronouncements the defence minister unremittingly presented a host of other, less controversial rationales. Thus, he kept on stressing that NATO had no choice but to transfer stability to the CEE reform states if it wanted to ensure both the consolidation of the new democracies and its own survival as a meaningful security institution. Without such an effort, Rühe claimed, the pacifying effects of political integration, wealth, and democracy could never be realized, so that the west, and in particular Germany, would end up importing the region's mounting instability.[26]

For those not yet persuaded by these grim scenarios, Rühe liked to add that NATO had no right to rebuff the new democracies. Referring to Article 10 of the NATO treaty, the defence minister argued that any country willing to respect the alliance's interests and values and to contribute to its collective defence was entitled to full membership. Hence, NATO simply could not declare itself a closed club: "That's the policy of Stalin, and it will invite lots of trouble."[27]

Actually Rühe was mainly concerned about the military weakness of Germany's eastern neighbours. In the aftermath of his IISS speach, defence ministry sources pointed out that their boss's advocacy for enlargement was based on "serious analysis" ("studierte Gründe"). According to this assessment, Germany's eastern *Länder* would remain exposed unless NATO extended its protection to the states bordering on them. Even after the Russian withdrawals, the experts argued, these *Länder* would be covered just by a "thin veil" of Bundeswehr forces without any allied augmentation. To the east of this thin veil, in the region between the rivers Elbe, Danube, Bug, and Memel, the planners saw a "strategic vacuum," a weak zone hostile forces could easily penetrate.[28] From this strategic perspective, Germany had a vital interest in getting its NATO partners to guarantee not just the Federal Republic's territorial integrity, but also that of its eastern neighbours.

Indeed, Rühe's position on the size, timing, and ramifications of the envisioned intake is much more consistent with this narrow rationale than with the somewhat lofty reasons cited above. The defence minister has always favoured a quick expansion limited to the Visegrad countries. Whatever progress the Baltics, let alone Russia, made on their way to democracy, Rühe cautioned against offering them membership.[29] In fact, from both Rühe's statements and policies one can infer that his primary goal was the integration of the one Central European state of greatest strategic importance to Germany, Poland. Time and again he singled out Poland, stressing that the country had made the greatest progress with political and military reforms and that it, therefore, should become one of the first new members.[30] In the meantime, Rühe's ministry initiated a host of programs and multinational maneuvers aimed at preparing the way for the integration of Polish forces into western command structures.[31]

Rühe's advocacy, however, was motivated not only by strategic concerns but also by his personal ambitions. Before moving to the defence ministry, he had been the long-time foreign policy spokesman of the CDU parliamentary party. It was always clear that he considered foreign affairs his true vocation and would have preferred heading the foreign office instead of the defence ministry. Upon moving to the "Hardthöhe," Rühe tried to fill the post in a way that best suited his own interests. It soon became obvious that he never wanted to be looked upon as the "Bundeswehrminister" but rather as his party's guiding intellect in the realms of foreign and security policy.[32]

Obviously, NATO enlargement is an issue that perfectly fits such ambitions. For one thing, it is a crucial topic of foreign policy because it is apt to define Germany's relations with Russia and the other CEE states. More importantly, the broadening of the alliance is an issue with direct implications for defence, and is accordingly a foreign policy subject about which the defence minister has a legitimate voice. Thus, setting NATO expansion firmly on the agenda must have appeared almost the ideal way to carve out a leading foreign policy role for the defence minister.

That Rühe paid more attention to his personal ambitions and Germany's strategic requirements than he did to the country's broader foreign policy interests might also be deduced from his reactions to Moscow's objections. Early on he insisted that the alliance should expand before the turn of the century, irrespective of any Russian opposition. In his view, these protests were not justified anyway because western efforts to export stability to Central Europe were also in Russia's authentic security interests. While he thought NATO should offer the Kremlin a "strategic partnership," Rühe did not want wrangling over the alliance's expansion to be part of the "partners'" agenda.

Rühe emphasized that NATO should not concede to any outside criticism of its enlargement project. Accommodating Russia, he claimed, would only whet the appetite of those in Moscow who advocated the Kremlin's return to expansionism. Hence, he recommended an uncompromising NATO line, one presenting Boris Yeltsin with a clear choice between confrontation and cooperation. In effect, the defence minister was contending that the alliance could simply afford to ignore the Kremlin's views on enlargement; should the latter react harshly, then that would only underscore the wisdom of taking in the new democracies as soon as possible.[33]

In stark contrast to Rühe, the chancellor and his foreign minister gave precedence to foreign policy rather than military considerations. Early in the debate, Kinkel explicitly highlighted this difference with Rühe when he publicly warned against putting too much emphasis on the military aspects of enlargement.[34] While Kinkel and Kohl welcomed NATO expansion as a necessary complement to an eventual widening of the European Union, they were much more solicitous of Russia. Thus, in the face of the Kremlin's opposition, they needed to be prodded by an increasingly eager Clinton administration and were much more willing to shape the enlargement process in ways that might help to minimize Moscow's estrangement. Consequently, the policy line of both chancellery and foreign office experienced much stronger shifts whenever priorities seemed to be changing in Moscow or Washington.

Kohl's and Kinkel's intrinsic interest in NATO enlargement is largely a function of their desire to deepen and at the same time widen the European Union. Kohl has made further EU integration, particularly in foreign and security policy, one of the top priorities of his remaining years in power.[35] At the same time, his government is deeply supportive of expanding the EU into Central Europe. Integration of the new democracies there is held to be the best means of furthering Germany's economic interests in the region as well as stabilizing its reformist regimes. Moreover, it is seen as the only way to prevent the resurgence of a German-Russian competiton for influence over the lands in the middle.

Of course, these two strategic aims of Germany's EU policy will remain compatible only to the degree new members can and will join in a common foreign and security policy. Therefore, Kohl and Kinkel want to ensure that a wider EU will not be divided into zones with different degrees of security. Their ambitious EU projects imply, therefore, that new EU members must also be allowed to join the alliance. Chancellor and foreign minister alike insist on "congruity," that is, on the principle that EU enlargement must go hand in hand with NATO expansion.[36]

Linking the enlargement of the EU to that of NATO is also a logical consequence of another top priority of the chancellor and his foreign minister, namely to keep good relations with Moscow. Kohl, in particular, has repeatedly referred to Russia as "by far the most important and most powerful country among our partners in Europe's east," and has stressed Germany's "fundamental interest" in seeing its democratic reforms succeed. Consequently, he has strongly warned against any attempts to isolate this country, arguing that they would play into the hands of extremists and reactionaries.[37] Unlike Rühe, the chancellor and his foreign minister have thus kept stressing the necessity to avoid new divisions on the European continent. As a consequence, they have shown great sensitivity to Russian complaints about NATO's expansion plans.[38]

Germany's top foreign policy makers eagerly sought to manage this project in ways apt to minimize Moscow's objections. Apart from offering it a "strategic partnership" with NATO, they have repeatedly tried to massage the enlargement process itself. Accordingly, Kohl himself has asked both the Clinton administration and his own cabinet not to emphasize Poland's favourable prospects for early admission to NATO, because such statements can only annoy the Kremlin.[39] Moreover, both policymakers have often cautioned against a speedy expansion for fear of increasing Moscow's opposition.[40] Above all, Kohl and Kinkel have tried to accommodate Russia by coupling the alliance's enlargement to the widening of the EU, but not primarily so as to delay NATO expansion until the EU is ready to welcome new members.[41] Instead, coupling is held to be a means of depicting the alliance's expansion as part of a larger socio-political process leading to Central Europe's reintegration with the west. Such a broader perspective, it is hoped, should make NATO's enlargement much more palatable to Moscow.[42]

In contrast to Rühe, Kohl and even more so, Kinkel, appear to have given weight to other potential drawbacks of the alliance's expansion. Early in the enlargement debate, the foreign minister publicly raised the "serious issue" that admittance of new members might dilute "NATO's cohesion, purpose, resolve and core functions," instead of strengthening them.[43] More often, however, he expressed his worries about the impact expansion could have on the Baltics and other aspirants unlikely to be among the early joiners. Unlike Rühe, Kinkel's foreign office appears to be deeply concerned that partial expansion of NATO would seem to delineate the alliance's region of interest, possibly thereby diminishing the security of those states left outside. Such an outcome would be regarded as a grave threat to Germany's interest in preventing new dividing lines forming in Europe.

As a consequence, Kinkel and his officials have repeatedly tried to blur the difference between the Visegrad states and the other aspirant countries. By stressing the other states' prospects for admission, the foreign office hopes to mitigate the divisive effect limited expansion could well have in Eastern Europe; yet it seems to be aware that no policy can entirely resolve that dilemma.[44] As long as Russia remains opposed to NATO enlargement, such negative consequences anticipated for western relations with the excluded states will be viewed as a serious detriment to Germany's foreign policy interests.

Notwithstanding, or perhaps because of, their mixed assessment of NATO expansion, the overall position of the chancellery and foreign office is strongly influenced by the policies of the United States government. Even at a moment when Bonn was somewhat more optimistic than it is today about the prospects of NATO's "European Pillar," Kinkel had already reasoned that the US attitude would be essential in any efforts to export stability to Central and Eastern Europe.[45] With the growing disillusionment about the Western Europeans' ability to act on their own, Bonn's interest in preserving American presence and political leadership has only increased.[46]

For fear of a unilateralist or even neo-isolationist turn in the United States, Germany has grown more disposed to help sustain America's interest in NATO, even if this means ceding to Washington's preferences regarding the alliance's future mission and character. It was due only to the massive pressure of the Clinton administration and to the Republicans' triumph in the 1994 Congressional elections that Kohl and Kinkel finally abandoned their firm opposition to the speedy expansion of NATO.[47] Consequently, Washington's latest efforts to reapply the brakes to enlargement have been eagerly echoed by Bonn's foreign policy makers.[48] With regard to the alliance's enlargement policy, analysis reveals that, up to now at least, the dog has been wagging the tail — rather than the other way around.

The Opposition Parties

Compared to the myriad of international aspects associated with NATO enlargement, domestic factors have so far played a rather diminished role in the government's calculations. Although Bonn's ruling coalition scraped by with a mere 10-vote majority in the last federal elections (in October 1994), it seems very unlikely that the opposition parties will greatly influence Germany's position on NATO expansion over the near term. The only party that might theoretically exert such influence on the federal government is the Social Democratic Party (SPD), which controls roughly a third of the parliamentary votes. Yet, following the federal elections the SPD had been strained by intense bickering between its former chairman, Rudolf Scharping, and his charismatic rival, Gerhard Schröder. During the summer of 1995 the struggle between the two over leadership led to a severe crisis within the party.[49]

Accordingly, at the time of this writing, the SPD appears not to be in a position to challenge the government or influence its foreign policy. It remains to be seen if the new chairman, Oskar Lafontaine, will be able to give his party a more distinct foreign policy profile. Concerning NATO expansion, this task will be far from easy since, over the past two years, the SPD's views on enlargement have adapted more to the government's position than the other way around. For the moment, the small Green party and the marginalized ex-communists (PDS) are the only parties in the Bundestag that oppose outright the alliance's expansion project. In the following few pages, I explore in a bit of detail the various opposition party perspectives on enlargement, starting with the largest of them.

The SPD's attitude concerning enlargement underwent significant shifts, ranging from downright skepticism to nearly unconditional support, before settling back into renewed doubts. Just before NATO's Brussels summit in January 1994, the party's foreign policy experts were still opposing any intake of new members. Both its long-time security expert, Egon Bahr, and the shadow foreign minister, Günter Verheugen, termed expansion a risky, even disastrous, move that was bound to revive the bloc confrontation between east and west. While Bahr recommended the concepts of "security partnership" and a "common European house" as alternative policy foundations, Verheugen called for an all-European security system built around the CSCE.[50]

Within a single year, the SPD's incoming party chairman, Rudolf Scharping, and the parliamentary party's foreign policy spokesman, Karsten Voigt, managed to change the Social Democrats' line almost completely. Whereas at the 1994 Munich Wehrkunde conference Scharping had only ventured to express principled support for "an evolutionary enlargement of NATO," by the following year he was touting the integration of the new democracies into NATO and the EU as the most reliable antidote against a renationalization of defence and security policies. At that time, however, he still put considerable emphasis on parallel measures NATO needed to take in order to ensure that its expansion did not create new security problems. Specifically, he mentioned a partnership treaty with Russia as well as intensified relations with those countries that could not expect to be among the first to join.[51]

Over the following months, leading Social Democrats became almost enthusiastic supporters of the enlargement project. Karsten Voigt, in particular, turned into and remains a forceful advocate of expansion and has tried to use his position as president of the North Atlantic Assembly to speed up that process.[52] In effect, Voigt, Scharping, and also Verheugen moved very close to defence minister Rühe's position, at least with regard to the *timing* of expansion. They favoured an early intake of the Visegrad countries and warned against creating new obstacles. Notably, they all stressed the need to decouple EU and alliance enlargement, so as to spare the most advanced NATO aspirants a longer delay.[53] In striking contrast to the emotional opposition the SPD had, until recently at least, been mounting against government proposals to use German forces in future out-of-area conflicts, the party's position in the NATO-expansion debate was clearly congenial with that of the mainstream of the ruling coalition.

It remains to be seen whether, following the sudden ousting of Scharping from his position as party chairman, the Social Democrats will try to challenge the coalition's policy on enlargement. Both Lafontaine's speech before his election and the foreign policy resolution passed at the Mannheim party congress suggest that the SPD may move away from the consensus with the ruling parties and try again to capitalize on its image as the party of peace and détente. The congress approved a draft resolution backed by Lafontaine that rules out German participation in combat missions out of area. Moreover, the resolution called for a deferral of NATO's expansion until a decision on the future shape of a comprehensive security order for Europe had been reached. Otherwise, it is claimed, Russia would feel cornered and the prospects for its reforms, doomed.[54] Conceivably, the SPD's renewed skepticism concerning enlargement might, over time, induce the party to use this issue for an open challenge of the government's foreign policy. As long as early expansion enjoys considerable support among the party's foreign policy experts, however, such a prospect seems not very likely.

Up until recently, democratic opposition to NATO enlargement has fallen to the Green party. Although in recent years the Greens have modified their traditional opposition to the alliance, they still view it primarily as an "instrument of the Cold War." They strongly doubt its ability to tackle what they see as the new security challenges, namely nationalism, militarism, and "economic selfishness." These problems, they claim, would be better dealt with by strengthening the OSCE. In their view, expanding NATO will not enhance European security but rather revive the confrontation with Russia. Interestingly, the Greens are the only German party that openly mentions the negative effects enlargement could have on NATO's functioning as a security institution. In particular, and not unlike many American expansion critics, Green representatives raise doubts that NATO's cohesion could withstand expansion, nor do they believe it would be possible to implement security guarantees for the new members were the latter to be victims of aggression.[55]

Not surprisingly, NATO expansion is also rejected by the Party of Democratic Socialism (PDS), the successor to East Germany's communist party. The PDS sees the alliance as an irritating remnant of the Cold War that needs to be replaced by more encompassing security institutions, such as an enhanced UN and OSCE.[56] Consequently, a broadening of the alliance is criticized as a step in the wrong direction. In the party's view, this project is bound to put the Kremlin's back up against the wall, thereby dooming all prospects for reforms in Russia.[57]

German Society and NATO Enlargement

There is no indication that, in coming years, either the public or the strategic experts will exert a major influence on official policy. In striking contrast to the early 1980s, when the alliance's planned deployment of Pershing and cruise missiles aroused substantial public opposition, enough eventually to reverse the initially supportive position of the Social Democrats, today neither the public nor the informed observers seem to care a lot about NATO's need to make a crucial choice on membership. Within Germany's small security-studies community, enlargement is hardly a topic of heated discussion. Nor has there been much in-depth analysis of the pros and cons of expansion.[58] Instead, participants in the debate confine themselves to the mere confession of their faith in certain arguments. Not surprisingly, the opinions held by the less-informed citizens are even less substantiated, as demonstrated by the staggering inconsistency of the public's overall view. One might argue that, as of now, German society has not even witnessed a real debate on the enlargement project. As a result of this low degree of politicization, political élites are unlikely to heed many arguments and views emanating from society.

The discourse among German specialists on foreign policy and strategic issues has offered little intellectual guidance and not much critical inspiration to political practitioners. By and large, the public debate among academics and analysts seems to have had — at best — marginal influence on official policy. It has rather followed practical political steps instead of fostering them. Moreover, the debate so far has mainly focused on the question of whether the alliance should be expanded at all, with scant attention being devoted to the modalities of an eventual enlargement.[59] In assessing the "pros" and "cons" of NATO's taking in new members, the experts have rarely presented any ideas of which practitioners had been unaware. Nor have they added much candour or analytical rigour to familiar arguments. In both respects, the Federal Republic's security-studies community presumably can still learn quite a bit from its western counterparts.

Germany's debate on the merits of expansion is largely focussed on the phenomenon's likely impact on Russia and the emerging Central European democracies. Proponents of enlargement have all taken up Rühe's claim that Germany cannot forever live at the edge of the western world, thus it has a vital interest in getting the alliance to export its stability to the Federal Republic's eastern neighbours. By doing so, it is contended, the west as a whole and Germany in particular will achieve two goals simultaneously. First, the admission of new members will solidify their political and economic reforms and thereby ensure that these countries become reliable partners for decades to come. Second, expansion, it is said, will firmly anchor the CEE reform states in the west and thereby eliminate a strategic "no-man's-land" that has, so repeatedly, been an object of outside interventions and a fomenter of German-Russian rivalry.[60]

The opponents' counterclaim centres on the negative impact NATO enlargement might have on Russia's reforms and foreign policies. Critics of expansion argue that taking in former WTO members will marginalize Russia. The Russian population, it is feared, could perceive such a development as a major failure of those reformers who staked so much both on the country's westernization and on developing cooperative relations with current NATO countries. With their domestic position seriously undermined, the reformers would have either to radicalize their policies vis-à-vis the west and the CEE reform states or risk being replaced by a reactionary government. In the worst case, critics argue, NATO would end up with a Kremlin returning to autocracy at home and expansion abroad. As a consequence, German enlargement critics anticipate a second Cold War that would put paid to all hopes for effective pan-European security cooperation.[61]

Neither "Russia appeasers" nor "NATO enlargers" take great pains to refute each others' arguments, and neither group makes a serious and comprehensive effort to assess the net effect NATO enlargement might have on stability in Central and Eastern Europe. Expansion critics rarely, if ever, address the possible consequences a "closed shop" policy might entail for the applicants and NATO itself. Usually, they merely assert that, due to their socio-political nature, any instabilities in Central and Eastern Europe are better dealt with by a combination of EU enlargement, an enhanced OSCE, and active democratization policies by the west.

In like manner, many advocates of enlargement avoid the issue of Russia's likely antagonization simply by claiming that NATO's expansion will actually benefit it, because it will serve to stabilize Russia's western neighbours.[62] By implication, NATO can easily cope with the Russian problem through teaching the Russians their true foreign policy interests.[63] Other enlargement proponents seem to hope that NATO can dampen Moscow's ire through offering the Kremlin political and economic compensations, such as membership in the G-7. At any rate, they claim, the current alliance members must give Russia neither a "droit de regard" nor a "veto" when the legitimate security aspirations of the new democracies are at issue.[64]

The enlargement advocates display similar nonchalance towards counterarguments about another contested issue — the impact expansion could have on the vitality of NATO. Of course, both sides contend that their policy preference is the only one that can ensure the alliance's future. However, most proponents of expansion effectively sidestep the issue by ignoring the interests of individual member states, concentrating instead upon NATO as if it were a unitary actor. In their view, the simple fact that expansion will give it a new mission will suffice to prevent the alliance's atrophy. What risks and costs this would entail for today's individual member states, and why they should be willing to bear them, proponents do not address in this context.[65]

Enlargement skeptics at least take this crucial consideration into account and express their concerns that NATO would overburden itself with a proliferation of security commitments, internal conflicts, and diverging perspectives. Consequently, they challenge the proponents' implicit assumption that in the case of aggression against a new member, it could count upon receiving effective protection from the older member states.[66]

Yet even the expansion skeptics do not raise the one issue, let alone discuss it, that arguably should be the litmus test of any national debate on the broadening of security obligations: they fail to ask whether Germany actually has an interest in defending various prospective member states. Particularly, they refrain from querying whether it is conceivable that Germany might declare war on an aggressive Russia, unless the Federal Republic itself were to come under attack.[67] Formulating and answering this kind of question ought to be a primordial task for any country's security-studies community, for it can discuss such an issue with much more candour than can government and political élites. That Germany's experts evade this issue almost completely cries out for an explanation.

Two factors appear to be especially relevant in this context. The first concerns the great confidence German élites and experts have in international institutions. Over the past decades, they have almost become "instinctive multilateralists," because through their enormous successes in NATO and EU Germans have learned to pursue national interests almost exclusively through international institutions.[68] Due to this idiosyncratic experience, German élites tend to overrate the prestige and binding power that institutions possess, vis-à-vis their member states.

The second factor, which is strongly related to the first, is that a great many Germans, east and west, have grown accustomed to discussing international problems primarily from an ethical point of view, rather than in terms of national interest or power politics.[69] This emphasis on the moral perspective becomes even more pronounced as soon as the discussion turns to those countries that, in the past, were victimized by German forces. Compared to their other western counterparts, many German experts are still very reluctant to ask whether, to paraphrase Bismarck, the defence of a Central European state could ever warrant the bones of the nation's soldiers.[70]

That this question needs to be discussed becomes apparent if one studies recent opinion polls. A survey conducted in late 1994 shows a large majority of Germans agreeing with NATO's expansion plans. When asked if the alliance should give security guarantees to prospective EU members in Eastern and Southeastern Europe, almost 72 percent responded positively. Fifty-eight percent favoured admitting to NATO Poland, the Czech Republic, and Hungary even in advance of EU expansion.[71] Yet many of the enlargement supporters also evidenced a strong distaste for its potential implications. Queried about their willingness to send German forces into combat, a mere 25 percent approved using the Bundeswehr for the defence of Poland against a hypothetical Russian attack — less than half the number of those favouring German participation in a military raid against Libya, should that country try to build nuclear weapons.[72]

This stark inconsistency between support for enlargement on the one hand, and an unwillingness to come to the aid of an envisioned ally on the other, was also confirmed by a more recent poll published in June 1995. It shows that general support for enlargement turns into clear opposition once the military implications of NATO expansion are spelled out. When the obligation to help defend new members was mentioned, support for enlargement dropped from 33 to 27 percent, while opposition rose from 25 to 41 percent.[73] Both polls thus demonstrate that, up to now, the greater part of the German population has not paid much attention to the enlargement project. Apparently, most Germans have yet to form an educated and thus more rational opinion on the subject. Presumably, greater awareness of the problem's complexities will weaken the public's overall support for the broadening of the alliance.

Conclusions

Germany's support for NATO's expansion plan is not as rock-solid as it may often appear. While Defence Minister Rühe is likely to remain a staunch advocate of rapid enlargement, the future positions of Foreign Minister Kinkel and, far more important, the chancellor are much less clear. As I have argued,

Chancellor Kohl's position is chiefly influenced by three evolving factors: the process of European integration; America's NATO policy; and the fate of the Russian reformers. Up to the autumn of 1995, Kohl's loyalty to the Clinton administration's enlargement course and his interest in widening and deepening the European Union had the upper hand over his desires to placate Yeltsin and help the reformers in Russia.

However, Kohl's cautious support for enlargement weakened the moment Washington again began to advocate moving at slower speed. His support might flag even further should American eagerness for enlargement continue to wane or should Germany's ambitous EU projects begin to look like failing. Presumably, Kohl's plea that Washington defer a final NATO decision until sometime after the Maastricht review conference has to be seen in this context. Hence, the chancellor's current backing of a steady, albeit slow, expansion course should not yet be taken to represent his final word. In the future, he may well favour an even longer deferral of the enlargement decisions that are currently envisioned for 1997.[74]

Given Kohl's unchallenged position within his government and the recent shifts within the main opposition party, an eventual change of the chancellor's mind would almost certainly translate into a modification of German policy. Neither Rühe nor Kinkel, let alone the endangered Liberal Party (FDP), would be in a position to prevent such a change of course. The SPD and the smaller opposition parties would almost certainly support one. Nor would public opinion exert any major influence in the matter. It is far from obvious that a majority of the public will continue to favour the alliance's broadening. It seems more than likely that, when NATO's decision on the who and when of expansion draws nearer, the gap between the public's backing of enlargement and its unwillingness to show military solidarity will be closed at the former's expense. In that case, neither the SPD nor the coalition parties would reap much benefit from promoting the expansion project. Accordingly, they would be free to adjust their course to changed circumstances.

That the public's majority support should not be taken for granted is also partly due to the disappointing quality of the German debate over expansion. So far, both the political élites and the security-studies community have largely failed in their efforts to educate the rest of the population on the country's stakes in NATO's broadening. Instead of openly discussing the trade-offs and dilemmas associated with taking in new members, many politicians and experts have chosen to dispute even the very need for choice. The most obvious instance of this unfortunate tendency has been the widespread downplaying of Russia's negative reaction to an eventual enlargement.[75] Much the same might be said regarding some of the other possible drawbacks of expansion — for instance, in respect of the negative impact a partial or piecemeal enlargement might have on those CEE states left out in the cold.

This analytical deficiency is often compounded by a rhetoric that much too easily commingles (if not, replaces) strategic reasoning with moral principles. NATO enlargement is at one and the same time depicted as a moral imperative and a strategic necessity. Thus, leading politicians have defended their plea for alliance expansion by casually condemning the concepts of the national interest and the balance of power, calling the latter in particular outmoded and ethically indefensible.[76] Such sweeping claims are hardly conducive to an intellectual climate in which sound analysis of geopolitical issues can flourish.

In the case of NATO broadening, these sentiments discourage not only the appreciation of Russian security concerns, but also impede the assessment of the allies' stakes in enlargement and, by implication, the latter's impact on alliance cohesion. Above all, a premature intermingling of strategic analysis with moral sentiments often obscures the distinct relevance that national costs and benefits have for foreign policymaking. Little wonder then, that the German public still favours the pose of international solidarity while, at the same time, shrinks from carrying out an envisioned pledge, when doing so seems costly.

In a way, then, the deficient quality of the German enlargement debate is indicative of the country's difficulties in coming to grips with its changed position in a new Europe. With its long and successful tradition of multilateral decisionmaking, its strong distaste for geopolitical reasoning, and its conspicuous reluctance to discuss openly its national interests, Germany is still ill-equipped for selecting its own priorities. Naturally, these general inhibitions are especially strong when the decision in question concerns that part of Europe that has had to suffer most under German aggression and occupation. In such a context, Bonn will maintain a strong propensity for seeing Germany's interests to be extensively defined by the preferences of its chief partners. To some degree, this is inevitable, given the Federal Republic's exposed geographic location.

Yet, where far-reaching issues are concerned, decisionmaking in multilateral settings must presuppose, first of all, an extensive discussion and clear understanding of one's own interests. Otherwise, intergovernmental harmony may soon be followed by a national dissatisfaction with multilateral decisions and, consequently, lead to their inability to be implemented. Ultimately, this could seriously undermine the effectiveness as well as the prestige of hitherto successful institutions. Seen from this perspective, both Germany and the alliance could only benefit from the German debate on NATO's future roles gaining in depth, frankness, and intensity.

Notes

I would like to thank Robert Dorff, David Haglund, Gunther Hellmann, Karl-Heinz Kamp, Franz-Josef Meiers, Peter Rudolf, and Oliver Thränert for their most helpful comments and criticism.

1. On the propensity of German leaders to avoid tough foreign policy choices, see Timothy Garton Ash, "Germany's Choice," *Foreign Affairs* 73 (July/August 1994): 65-81.

2. According to the federal ministry of finance, by January 1995 Germany had provided DM 45.5 billion in financial aid to the Central and Eastern European reforming states, and a further DM 100 billion to the successor states of the former Soviet Union. These sums amount to two-thirds of *all* western aid to these countries. See "Deutsche Außenpolitik in einer neuen Weltlage. Rede vom Bundesminister des Auswärtigen, Kinkel, vor der Deutschen Gesellschaft für Auswärtige Politik am 24. August 1994 in Bonn," in Auswärtiges Amt, ed., *Außenpolitik der Bundesrepublik Deutschland: Dokumente von 1949 bis 1994* (Köln: Verlag Wissenschaft und Politik, 1995), p. 1083. I would like to thank Michael Sturm for sharing the ministry of finance figures with me.

3. See "Ansprache von Bundesaußenminister Klaus Kinkel anläßlich der Feier des 125 jährigen Jubiläums des Auswärtigen Amtes am 16. Januar 1995 in Bonn," *Internationale Politik* 50 (April 1995): 81; "Rede von Bundesaußenminister Klaus Kinkel auf der Münchner Konferenz über Sicherheitspolitik am 5. Februar 1995," ibid. 50 (August 1995): 94. In 1993, Germany's trade with Central and Eastern Europe amounted to almost 33 percent of total OECD trade with the region (author's calculation based on figures from OECD and the German ministry of economics). During the following year, the Federal Republic was the biggest foreign investor in the Czech Republic, the Slovak Republic, and Bulgaria, and ranked second in Hungary and Poland. See FAZ Informationsdienste, ed., *Osteuropa-Perspektiven Jahrbuch 1995/96* (Frankfurt, 1995). Again, the author gratefully acknowledges the help of Michael Sturm in providing him with these data.

4. This rationale is most succinctly articulated in the so-called Schäuble paper, but it can also be found in other prominent statements. See CDU/CSU-Fraktion des Deutschen Bundestages, *Überlegungen zur europäischen Politik* (Bonn, 1 September 1994), pp. 2-4. Also see "Europa ist Kern unserer Außenpolitik," speech by Chancellor Kohl before the Bundestag, 8 November 1995, *Das Parlament*, 24 November 1995; "Rede des Vorsitzenden der SPD, Rudolf Scharping, über die gemeinsame transatlantische Sicherheit auf der Münchner Konferenz für Sicherheitspolitik am 5. Februar 1995," *Internationale Politik* 50 (April 1005): 90-103; "Vortrag des Bundesministers der Verteidigung, Volker Rühe, über Deutschlands Verantwortung in und für Europa, gehalten am 19. Mai 1994 an der Universität Oxford," *Europa-Archiv*, no. 15 (1994), pp. D443-48.

5. In the first half of 1995, the total volume of trade between Germany and Russia amounted to DM 11.6 billion. It was only marginally surpassed by German trade with Poland (DM 11.8 billion). However, German exports to Russia dropped by 12 percent, to DM 4.7 billion, and thus were less than exports both to Poland and the Czech Republic. See "Polen wichtigster Handelspartner in Osteuropa," *Frankfurter Allgemeine Zeitung*, 24 October 1995.

6. Even an influential faction within the Greens has recently come to appreciate NATO and the US presence in Europe. Polls show that public support for NATO, which in the immediate wake of unification had briefly plummeted, is today as strong as ever. In 1994, 75 percent of the West Germans and 60 percent of the East Germans deemed the alliance "essential" to German security. See Ronald D. Asmus, *Germany's Geopolitical Maturation: Public Opinion and Security Policy in 1994* (Santa Monica: RAND, 1995), p. 18, fig. 3:6.

7. Witness the various German proposals for new transatlantic charters, treaties, and free-trade zones. Klaus Kinkel, "NATO Requires a Bold but Balanced Response to the East," *International Herald Tribune*, 21 October 1993; Idem, "Germany Sees an Evolving Agenda for a Still Much Needed Alliance," ibid., 30 March 1995; "Vortrag des Bundesministers der Verteidigung, Volker Rühe, an der Universität Oxford"; Rudolf Scharping, "Deutsche Außenpolitik muß berechenbar sein," *Internationale Politik* 50 (August 1995): 43.

8. Michael R. Beschloss and Strobe Talbott, *At the Highest Levels: The Inside Story of the End of the Cold War* (New York: Little, Brown, 1993), chap. 11; Stephen F. Szabo, *The Diplomacy of German Unification* (New York: St. Martin's, 1992), pp. 88-93.

9. Raymond L. Garthoff, *The Great Transition: American-Soviet Relations and the End of the Cold War* (Washington: Brookings Institution, 1994), pp. 621-22.

10. *Archiv der Gegenwart*, 25 February 1990, p. 34267; "NATO rät Staaten Osteuropas vom Beitritt ab," *Frankfurter Allgemeine Zeitung*, 3 April 1991; radio interview with CDU MP Karl Lamers, *Mittagsmagazin des Westdeutschen Rundfunks*, 15 January 1992, 12:15 p.m.; radio interview with CDU MP Karl-Heinz Hornhues, *Funkjournal der Deutschen Welle*, 18 February 1992, 11:15 a.m.

11. "Auf der Suche nach einem Mittelweg," *Frankfurter Allgemeine Zeitung*, 6 March 1993.

12. Volker Rühe, "Shaping Euro-Atlantic Policies: A Grand Strategy for a New Era," *Survival* 35 (Summer 1993): 135.

13. "Enlargement of NATO: This Will Be an Important Topic at the Summit — But Will also Be a Long Process, as Experience Shows," *Atlantic News*, 8 September 1993; "Rühe: Die Nato nach Osteuropa hin öffnen," *Frankfurter Allgemeine Zeitung*, 8 September 1993; Herbert Kremp, "Die Nato blickt nach Osten," *Die Welt*, 11 September 1993; Claus Gennrich, "In New York rückt Kinkel die deutschen Leistungen ins Licht," *Frankfurter Allgemeine Zeitung*, 28 September 1993.

14. "Bedenken Jelzins gegen eine Ausweitung der Nato nach Osten," *Frankfurter Allgemeine Zeitung*, 2 October 1993; TV interview with foreign minister Kinkel, *ZDF-Spezial*, 4 October 1993, 7:25 p.m.; "Wörner: Ausdehnung der NATO nicht aktuell," *Süddeutsche Zeitung*, 7 October 1993; TV interview with Chancellor Kohl, *SAT 1*, 11 October 1993.

15. "Rühe warnt die Nato vor 'Vetorecht' für Rußland," *Frankfurter Allgemeine Zeitung*, 9 December 1993; "Kinkel: NATO-Erweiterung ein langfristiger Prozeß," *Süddeutsche Zeitung*, 8 January 1994.

16. See paras 12 and 13 of the "Declaration of the Heads of State and Government Participating in the Meeting of the North Atlantic Council Held at NATO Headquarters, Brussels, on 10-11 January 1994," reproduced as Appendix XII, *NATO Handbook* (Brussels: NATO Office of Information and Press, 1995), pp. 269-75; TV interview with Foreign Minister Kinkel, *ARD-Mittagsmagazin*, 10 January 1994, 1:10 p.m. See also a speech given by Kohl shortly after the Brussels summit at the Wehrkunde conference in Munich ("European Security and Germany's Role," p. 7).

17. "Rühe: Osterweiterung der NATO bald möglich," *Süddeutsche Zeitung*, 19 July 1994; "Rühe will Klarheit über Nato-Erweiterung," *Frankfurter Allgemeine Zeitung*, 28 September 1994; "Erneuter Ausblick der Nato nach Osten," *Neue Zürcher Zeitung*, 3 October 1994; "Ewiger Frieden," *Der Spiegel*, 3 October 1994, p. 36; "Differenzen zwischen Kinkel und Rühe in der Ostpolitik," *Frankfurter Allgemeine Zeitung*, 7 October 1994; "Außenminister Kinkel geht auf Distanz zu Rühe: Gegen rasche Erweiterung der NATO nach Osten," *Süddeutsche Zeitung*,

7 October 1994; Martin Winter, "Ministerzwist verärgert Kohl," *Frankfurter Rundschau*, 8 October 1994.

18. "Die Nato soll erweitert werden. Die außen- und sicherheitspolitischen Vorhaben der Koalition," *Frankfurter Allgemeine Zeitung*, 15 November 1994.

19. See Douglas Stuart's contribution to this volume, as well as Peter Rudolf, "The Future of the United States as a European Power: The Case of NATO Enlargement," *European Security* (forthcoming).

20. "Annäherung im Streit um NATO-Erweiterung," *Süddeutsche Zeitung*, 23 November 1994; "Bonn besorgt über Drängen der USA," *Süddeutsche Zeitung*, 25 November 1994. The communiqué adopted by the North Atlantic Council largely reflected this German concern, for its fifth paragraph stated that "enlargement of NATO will complement the enlargement of the European Union, a parallel process which also, for its part, contributes significantly to extending security and stability to the new democracies in the East." Final Communiqué of the Ministerial Meeting of the North Atlantic Council Held at NATO Headquarters, Brussels, on 1 December 1994.

21. "NATO Enlargement/Kohl: Developing a Concept in Close Contact with Russia," *Atlantic News*, 22 December 1994; Paul F. Horvitz, "With Clinton, Kohl Expresses Support for NATO Growth," *International Herald Tribune*, 10 February 1995; Klaus Kinkel, "Die NATO-Erweiterung: Ein Beitrag zur gesamteuropäischen Sicherheit," *Internationale Politik* 50 (April 1995): 22-25; "Leider hat Moskau immer noch Angst," *Der Spiegel*, 10 April 1995, pp. 20-22; George Brock, "Kohl Cautions Nato against Rush to Expand Eastwards," *Times* (London), 4 July 1995.

22. Kinkel, "Die NATO-Erweiterung"; "Bei NATO-Erweiterung russische Ängste beachten," *Süddeutsche Zeitung*, 26 May 1995; "NATO um Rücksicht gegenüber Moskau bemüht," ibid., 27/28 May 1995. The idea of a "strategic partnership" between Russia and NATO had also been floated by the German defence minister. Both its lack of substance and Rühe's apparent indifference to Russian concerns indicate that this idea was primarily intended as a palliative for the Kremlin. "Rede des deutschen Verteidigungsministers an der Karls-Universität."

23. Martin S. Lambeck, "Kohl bei Clinton: Abstand zu Polen," *Die Welt*, 10 February 1995; "Vier Minister sollen erreichen, was die Nato als Ganzes nicht kann," *Frankfurter Allgemeine Zeitung*, 27 February 1995.

24. Brock, "Kohl Cautions Nato"; "Junktim mit EU-Mitgliedschaft?," *Frankfurter Allgemeine Zeitung*, 5 July 1995; "Kohl ändert Redemanuskript," ibid., 7 July 1995.

25. "Die deutsche Handschrift ist deutlich zu erkennen," *Frankfurter Allgemeine Zeitung*, 29 September 1995; communication to the author, Bonn, November 1995.

26. Volker Rühe, "Redefining Europe's Security Interests," *Wall Street Journal Europe*, 9 September 1993; "Rede des deutschen Verteidigungsministers, Volker Rühe, am 8. Oktober 1993 an der Karls-Universität in Prag," *Europa-Archiv*, no. 3 (1994), pp. D101-4; "Vortrag des Bundesministers der Verteidigung, Volker Rühe, an der Universität Oxford."

27. Rick Atkinson and John Pomfret, "EU and NATO Compete for Control," *International Herald Tribune*, 7 July 1995; "Rede des deutschen Verteidigungsministers, Volker Rühe, am 11. Mai 1995 in Bonn über die Nordatlantische Allianz als Fundament einer neuen Friedensordnung in Europa," *Internationale Politik* 50 (August 1995): 93.

28. Herbert Kremp, "Strategischer Hohlraum und die neue Bündnis-Diskussion," *Die Welt*, 16 April 1993. Interestingly, this concern did not originate in the military sections of the defence

ministry, i.e., the "Führungsstab der Streitkräfte" (FüS), but in its planning staff. Background information, Bonn, 3 November 1995.

29. Rick Atkinson, "Allies Seek New Ties to Bind NATO," *Washington Post*, 10 September 1994; "Differenzen zwischen Kinkel und Rühe in der Ostpolitik," *Frankfurter Allgemeine Zeitung*, 7 October 1994; "Öffnung nach Osteuropa ein längerer Prozeß," *Süddeutsche Zeitung*, 23 August 1995; "Es gibt da schon Unterschiede," *Frankfurter Allgemeine Zeitung*, 23 August 1995.

30. "Rühe: Osterweiterung der NATO bald möglich," *Süddeutsche Zeitung*, 19 July 1994; "Wie weiter zwischen dem Westen und Rußland?" *Frankfurter Allgemeine Zeitung*, 12 May 1995; Karl Feldmeyer, "Die Nato spielt auf Zeit," ibid., 29 August 1995.

31. "Rühe: Die Nato nach Osteuropa hin öffnen," *Frankfurter Allgemeine Zeitung*, 8 September 1993; Volker Rühe, "Deutsche Sicherheitspolitik: Die Rolle der Bundeswehr," *Internationale Politik* 50 (April 1995): 29.

32. Karl Feldmeyer, "Im allgemeinen einig," *Frankfurter Allgemeine Zeitung*, 6 March 1995.

33. Charima Reinhardt, "Rühe warnt Jelzin vor Isolierung," *Frankfurter Rundschau*, 21 April 1995; "Scharfe Antwort Rühes auf Moskaus drohende Töne," *Süddeutsche Zeitung*, 2 May 1995; "Keine Expansions-Strategie," ibid., 30 May 1995; Karl Feldmeyer, "Nicht vor dem Jahr 2000," *Frankfurter Allgemeine Zeitung*, 10 October 1995.

34. Herbert Kremp, "Die Nato blickt nach Osten," *Die Welt*, 11 September 1993; TV interview with Kinkel, *ZDF-Spezial*, 4 October 1993, 7:25 p.m.

35. "Europa ist Kern unserer Außenpolitik."

36. "Erklärung des Bundeskanzlers, Helmut Kohl, am 13. Januar 1994 vor dem Deutschen Bundestag zu den Ergebnissen des NATO-Gipfeltreffens," *Europa-Archiv*, no. 3 (1994), pp. D135-36; "Differenzen zwischen Kinkel und Rühe in der Ostpolitik," *Frankfurter Allgemeine Zeitung*, 7 October 1994; "Annäherung im Streit um die NATO-Erweiterung," *Süddeutsche Zeitung*, 23 November 1994; "Ansprache von Bundesaußenminister Klaus Kinkel," pp. 80-84; Klaus Kinkel, "Identität und Handlungsfähigkeit der EU. Erklärung der Bundesregierung zu aktuellen Fragen der Europapolitik," *Das Parlament*, 30 June 1995, p. 4. See also the memorandum of the CDU/CSU group in the Bundestag (the so-called Schäuble paper), which seems to be very close to Kohl's own views: "Überlegungen zur europäischen Politik," pp. 3-4.

37. "Rede von Bundeskanzler Helmut Kohl zur Lage in Tschetschenien vor dem Deutschen Bundestag in Bonn am 19. Januar 1995," *Internationale Politik* 50 (April 1995): 84-88; "Erklärung von Bundeskanzler Helmut Kohl vor der Presse anläßlich seines Besuchs in Washington am 9. Februar 1995," ibid., pp. 104-5; "Jelzin lehnt Erweiterung der NATO erneut ab," *Süddeutsche Zeitung*, 4 September 1995. To some extent, Kohl's willingness to take into account Moscow's objections may also be due to his personal sentiments. Reportedly, he still feels that the Federal Republic ought to show its gratitude for the Kremlin's having consented to German unification. Background information, Sankt Augustin, 2 November 1995.

38. "Erklärung von Bundeskanzler Helmut Kohl"; Klaus Kinkel, "NATO Requires a Bold but Balanced Response"; "Erklärung des Bundeskanzlers, Helmut Kohl, am 13. Januar 1994"; Kohl, "European Security and Germany's Role," p. 7; "Differenzen zwischen Kinkel und Rühe"; "Rühe über Rußland besorgt," *Süddeutsche Zeitung*, 15-17 April 1995; "Junktim mit EU-Mitgliedschaft?"; "Rußland warnt scharf vor Ost-Erweiterung der NATO," *Süddeutsche Zeitung*, 5 February 1996; "Kohl in Moskau — Wutausbruch Jelzins gegen die Ost-Erweiterung der Nato," *Frankfurter Allgemeine Zeitung*, 20 February 1996.

39. Lambeck, "Kohl bei Clinton"; "Kohl ändert Redemanuskript," *Frankfurter Allgemeine Zeitung*, 7 July 1995.

40. "Rühe: Die Nato nach Osteuropa"; "Annäherung im Streit"; "Bonn besorgt über Drängen der USA"; "Vier Minister sollen erreichen."

41. It seems likely that Kohl first sought to couple the timing of both processes, only to realize that such a stance would unduly antagonize Poland and other Central European aspirants to membership.

42. "Bonn besorgt über Drängen der USA."

43. Kinkel, "NATO Requires a Bold but Balanced Response."

44. "Ewiger Frieden," *Der Spiegel*, 3 October 1994, pp. 36-37; "Differenzen zwischen Kinkel und Rühe"; "Kinkel lobt die baltischen Staaten," *Frankfurter Allgemeine Zeitung*, 21 August 1995; "Rühe irritiert Auswärtiges Amt mit Äußerungen im Baltikum," *Süddeutsche Zeitung*, 24 August 1995; "Das darf Herr Rühe nicht tun," *Frankfurter Allgemeine Zeitung*, 24 August 1995.

45. "Auf der Suche nach einem Mittelweg." See also "Wörner: Ausdehnung der NATO nicht aktuell."

46. Thus, in a speech before the parliamentary assembly of the WEU, Kinkel called NATO the "central guarantor of European security and stability" due to its ability to "anchor the US presence in Europe." See "Rede des deutschen Außenministers, Klaus Kinkel, am 19. Juni 1995 in Paris vor der Parlamentarischen Versammlung der Westeuropäischen Union," *Internationale Politik* 50 (August 1995): 128; and "Rede von Bundesaußenminister Klaus Kinkel auf der Münchner Konferenz über Sicherheitspolitik am 5. Februar 1995," ibid., 50 (April 1995): 93-96.

47. "Annäherung im Streit um NATO-Erweiterung."

48. "Die deutsche Handschrift ist deutlich zu erkennen."

49. Ultimately, the crisis loomed as a menace to the SPD's role as chief opposition party. Hence, at one point, its CDU rival even decided to refrain from public criticism that might otherwise fuel the erosive processes. See Ulrich Deupmann, "Frustrierte Blicke in den Abgrund," *Süddeutsche Zeitung*, 21 September 1995.

50. Radio interview with Verheugen, SFB 3, "Das Interview," 8 January 1004, 0:05 p.m.; TV Interview with Bahr, N-I V, "Villa Bonn," 9 January 1994, 9 p.m.

51. Rudolf Scharping, "For a New Strategy of the Alliance," Munich Security Policy Conference, 5 February 1994; "Rede des Vorsitzenden der SPD, Rudolf Scharping." See also "Voigt kämpft für erweiterte NATO," *Frankfurter Rundschau*, 19 November 1994.

52. "Arbeitsgruppe stellt Plan zur Nato-Erweiterung vor," *Die Welt*, 17 May 1995; "Reformüberlegungen für das transatlantische Bündnis," *Das Parlament*, 19/26 May 1995.

53. Rudolf Scharping, "Deutsche Außenpolitik muß berechenbar sein," p. 43; Günter Verheugen, "Basic Issues of German Foreign Policy," *Internationale Politik und Gesellschaft*, no. 3 (1995), p. 264.

54. "Beschluß des Bundesparteitages Mannheim 1995. Antrag A 1, Landesverband Baden-Württemberg. Außen- und Sicherheitspolitik der SPD: Die Beschlüsse von Wiesbaden weiterentwickeln."

55. Speech by Green parliamentary leader Joschka Fischer before the Bundestag on 15 December 1994, *Das Parlament*, 23 December 1994; statement by Green foreign policy spokesman Ludger Volmer before the Bundestag, 6 September 1995, ibid., 22 September 1995; TV discussion with Volmer, "Zur Sache," WDR, 26 September 1995, 7:30 p.m.

56. *Programm der Partei des Demokratischen Sozialismus*, 31 January 1993, pp. 31-32.

57. Speech by Heinrich Graf von Einsiedel before the Bundestag, 27 October 1995, *Das Parlament*, 10 November 1995.

58. I have yet to come across a single major article in a German journal that is specifically devoted to the value of broadening NATO. To date, the most opinionated contributions to the debate have been published in two small "pro and con" forums in the weekly *Die Zeit* and in a Social Democratic journal. See the articles by, respectively, Christoph Bertram and Theo Sommer, in "Soll das westliche Bündnis die Staaten Osteuropas aufnehmen?" *Die Zeit*, 7 January 1994. As well, see Oliver Thränert, "NATO-Erweiterung? Vorerst nicht!", and Peter Schmidt, "NATO-Erweiterung: möglichst bald"; both in *Internationale Politik und Gesellschaft*, no. 2 (1995), pp. 191-96.

59. For a notable exception, see Karl-Heinz Kamp, "Zwischen Friedenspartnerschaft und Vollmitgliedschaft — Die NATO und die Erweiterungsfrage," *Interne Studien*, no. 102/1995 (Sankt Augustin: Konrad-Adenauer-Stiftung, June 1995), pp. 38-49.

60. Bertram, "Soll das westliche Bündnis?"; Schmidt, "NATO-Erweiterung"; Arnulf Baring, "Wie neu ist unsere Lage? Deutschland als Regionalmacht," *Internationale Politik* 50 (April 1995): 12-21; Lothar Rühl, "Bedürfnis nach Sicherheit," *Die Welt*, 9 December 1993; Idem, "Jenseits der 'Partnerschaft für den Frieden'," *Europa-Archiv*, no. 4 (1994), pp. 101-8; Ludger Kühnhardt, "Der Osten des Westens und die 'russische Frage'," ibid., no. 9 (1994), pp. 239-47.

61. Sommer, "Soll das westliche Bündnis?"; Thränert, "NATO-Erweiterung?"; Ernst-Otto Czempiel, "Bausteine einer europäischen Friedensordnung," *Europa-Archiv*, no. 4 (1994), p. 93; Walter Schütze, "Sackgasse oder Königsweg? Die Ost-Erweiterung der NATO," *Blätter für deutsche und internationale Politik*, no. 8 (1995), pp. 924-35; Berthold Meyer, "Die Ost-Erweiterung der NATO — Weg zur Einheit oder zur neuen Spaltung Europas?" *HSFK-Report 5/1995* (Frankfurt, April 1995), pp.45-47. For the same criticism voiced by three German peace research institutes, see "Unzuständig, unzulänglich, überfordert," *Frankfurter Allgemeine Zeitung*, 22 June 1995.

62. This argument is also often used by enlargement proponents within Germany's political élite, such as Rühe, Scharping, Voigt, and the prominent CDU MP Rudolf Seiters. See "Keine Expansions-Strategie," *Süddeutsche Zeitung*, 30 May 1995; and Rudolf Seiters, "Eine Partnerschaft mit der Nato liegt im Interesse Rußlands," *Die Welt*, 21 April 1995.

63. Pleas for western efforts to persuade Russia of NATO's benign intentions are made by Bertram, "Soll das westliche Bündnis?", and Schmidt, "NATO-Erweiterung."

64. Kühnhardt, "Der Osten des Westens"; Rühl, "Jenseits der 'Partnerschaft für den Frieden'," p. 105; Baring, "Wie neu ist unsere Lage?" p. 18.

65. Ludger Kühnhardt, "Europa ist nichts ohne die USA," *Die Welt*, 16 June 1995.

66. Josef Joffe, "NATO vor! Oder?" *Süddeutsche Zeitung*, 2 December 1993; Idem, "Die NATO — kein Fühlwohl-Verein," ibid., 21 September 1995; Gunther Hellmann and Reinhard Wolf, "Wider die schleichende Erosion der NATO: Der Fortbestand des westlichen Bündnisses ist nicht selbstverständlich," *Jahrbuch für Politik* 3 (Fall 1993): 285-314; Uwe Nerlich, "Neue

Sicherheitsfunktionen der NATO," *Europa-Archiv*, no. 23 (1993), pp. 663-72; Michael Stürmer, "Deutsche Interessen," in *Deutschlands neue Außenpolitik.* vol. 1: *Grundlagen*, ed. Karl Kaiser and Hanns W. Maull (München: R. Oldenbourg, 1994), pp. 39-61.

67. Karl Feldmeyer, "Fragen zur Nato-Erweiterung," *Frankfurter Allgemeine Zeitung*, 28 April 1995.

68. On this point see Baring, "Wie neu ist unsere Lage?" p. 13; John S. Duffield, "German Security Policy after Unification: Sources of Continuity and Restraint," *Contemporary Security Policy* 15 (December 1994): 170-98; and Garton Ash, "Germany's Choice," p. 71.

69. See the somewhat startling remarks of Foreign Minister Kinkel on the occasion of the 125th anniversary of Germany's foreign office: "Die letzten 50 Jahre sind ein grundsätzlicher Neuanfang gegenüber den 75 Jahren davor! Machtbalance und Vormachtdenken sind überholt. Sie taugen nicht als Konzepte für die Zukunft! Seit 1949 ist auch die Außenpolitik voll eingebunden in den Wertekanon unseres Grundgesetzes." ("The last 50 years amount to a fundamental renunciation of the preceding 75 years. Balance of power and hegemonial thinking are obsolete. Since 1949 foreign policy is also fully integrated into the canon of values set forth in our basic law.") "Ansprache von Bundesaußenminister Klaus Kinkel anläßlich der Feier des 125jährigen Jubiläums des Auswärtigen Amtes," p. 81. Naturally, one is left to one's own speculations as to how and why Germany's basic law should render obsolete the balance of power.

70. For the observation that when debating NATO broadening, Germans tend to stress a moral perspective more than their allies, see Karl Feldmeyer, "Unterstützung und Sympathie," *Frankfurter Allgemeine Zeitung*, 7 January 1994; and Klaus-Dieter Frankenberger, "Zwischen Moral und Staatsinteresse," ibid., 1 June 1995. See also Verheugen, "Basic Issues of German Foreign Policy," p. 264, for the argument that due to its responsibility for World War II, which led to the division of Europe, Germany must not exclude CEE states from western institutions.

71. Asmus, *Germany's Geopolitical Maturation*, pp. 19-20 (fig. 3:8).

72. Ibid., p. 44

73. Renate Köcher, "Unerwartete Wende," *Frankfurter Allgemeine Zeitung*, 14 June 1995.

74. Statements Kohl made in Moscow in early 1996 attest to the chancellor's flexibility as regards the speed of the enlargement process. According to Yeltsin, Kohl opined that "this problem can be deferred a little bit to another date," and went on to say that "one must not talk about it today." Claus Gennrich, "Die Europäer sollen in einem Block leben und nicht in zweien," *Frankfurter Allgemeine Zeitung*, 21 February 1996. See also "Kohl in Moskau."

75. For a critique of this shortcoming, see Kamp, "Zwischen Friedenspartnerschaft und Vollmitgliedschaft," pp. 30-31; and Schütze, "Sackgasse oder Königsweg?" p. 934.

76. In addition to sources cited elsewhere in this chapter, see "Rede von Bundesverteidigungsminister Volker Rühe über die pazifische und atlantische Dimension gemeinsamer Sicherheit, gehalten an der Stanford University in San Francisco am 27. Februar 1995," *Internationale Politik* 50 (April 1995): 105-11. German difficulties in coming to grips with the concept of national interest are perhaps best exemplified by Rudolf Scharping's statements. While calling for an "open naming of German interests" at one point, at another he can reassure his auditors that Germany has learned the lessons of its national disaster and thus will not "return to the classic pattern of a country which defines its interest in national terms" [das seine Interessen national bestimmt]. See "Deutsche Außenpolitik muß berechenbar sein," p. 39; and Scharping's speech at the 1995 Wehrkunde conference.

Notes on Contributors

John Barrett received his Ph.D. in International Relations from the London School of Economics, and is currently the Head of the Policy Planning Section on the International Staff at NATO Headquarters. Previous research postings have been in Germany, at the Universität Tübingen, and in Canada, at the University of British Columbia, and the Canadian Centre for Arms Control and Disarmament. From 1989 to 1991 he served in the Bureau of International Security and Arms Control Affairs of the Canadian Department of External Affairs. His publications span an array of security concerns, with particular emphasis on arms control.

Pascal Boniface, who received his Ph.D. in 1985 in International Law from the Université Paris-Nord, is Director of the University's Institut de Relations Internationales et Stratégiques (IRIS). He has published widely in the areas of strategic studies and French defence policy, and is currently editor of the quarterly, *Relations Internationales et Stratégiques*. He has also directed the publication of some two dozen works on international relations, nuclear strategy, and defence problems. In addition to his scholarly activities, Dr. Boniface worked for two years at the French National Assembly, and has been an advisor to two Defence Ministers.

Paul Buteux is Director of the Centre for Defence and Security Studies at the University of Manitoba. Educated at the London School of Economics, he has published extensively on NATO and on Canadian defence and foreign policy. He has recently completed a project on the future of nuclear deterrence. Currently, he is working on the application of the theory of security communities to European security issues.

Robert H. Dorff is Visiting Professor of Foreign Policy at the US Army War College, where he teaches and conducts research in the Department of National Security and Strategy. He received his Ph.D. from the University of North Carolina at Chapel Hill. Since 1980 he has served on the faculty at North Carolina

State University, where he is currently an Associate Professor of Political Science. Dr. Dorff is a native German speaker, currently conducting research on German peace support operations, and on the future of NATO and the implications for German security policy.

Michel Fortmann, who holds the Chair of Military and Strategic Studies at the Department of Political Science, Université de Montréal, was educated in France and Canada, earning his Ph.D. in Political Science from the Université de Montréal in 1984. Since that time, he has published widely in the areas of arms control, regional security, and Canadian defence and security policy. His current research focusses on multilateral institutions and international relations theory.

David G. Haglund, from 1985 to 1995 the Director of the Centre for International Relations at Queen's University, is Head of its Department of Political Studies. He received his doctorate from the Johns Hopkins School of Advanced International Studies in Washington in 1978, then taught at the University of British Columbia until coming to Queen's in 1983. Besides publishing several books and numerous articles on European and transatlantic security issues, he has written extensively on the international political economy of minerals. His current research focusses on NATO's evolution. Dr. Haglund is a former NATO Fellow.

Josef Joffe is a columnist and editorial page editor at the *Süddeutsche Zeitung* in Munich, as well as a contributing editor of *U.S. News and World Report*. His articles appear frequently in major newspapers and journals in Europe and North America, and he has also published widely in scholarly books and journals dealing with international security. Dr. Joffe, who holds a Ph.D. from Harvard, is an affiliate of that university's Center for International Affairs, and has had fellowships at the Carnegie Endowment and the Woodrow Wilson Center in Washington, where he has also taught at the Johns Hopkins School of Advanced International Studies. He currently is teaching international relations at the University of Munich.

Andrei Kortunov has recently been heading the Department of Foreign Policy at the Institute of USA and Canada Studies, Russian Academy of Sciences, where he was Deputy Director, and is currently President of the Moscow branch of the Russian Science Foundation. He has held fellowships at the Heritage Foundation and at the University of California (Berkeley). Dr. Kortunov has authored numerous works analyzing US-Soviet relations, international security issues, and Soviet and Russian domestic and foreign policy. He is currently studying Russia's relations with the west and Russian policy in the CIS.

David M. Law, currently Associate Director of the Centre for International Relations at Queen's University and a Skelton-Clark Fellow in the Department of Political Studies, has also been active in private- and public-sector consulting in the areas of transformation analysis, strategy development, and project management. Prior to 1984, he served for ten years with the Political Directorate of NATO where his last position was Head of the Policy Planning Unit. In addition to transatlantic and European security issues, his research interests focus upon the impact of technological change on state profiles and governmental systems in post-Soviet and western communities.

S. Neil MacFarlane is Professor of Political Studies and Director of the Centre for International Relations at Queen's University. His recent research has focussed on ethnic conflict, international organizations and regional security, and the foreign and security policies of the former Soviet republics. He received his doctorate from Oxford, and has had previous positions at the University of Virginia, the University of British Columbia, Harvard University, and the International Institute for Strategic Studies. In the late summer of 1996 he will return to Oxford, where he will hold the Lester B. Pearson Chair in International Relations.

Pierre Martin is Assistant Professor in the Department of Political Science at the Université de Montréal, where he has taught international relations and quantitative methods since 1990. He holds a Ph.D. from Northwestern University. His research focuses upon the politics of international economic relations and pubic opinion analysis. His writings have appeared in numerous journals relating to Canadian politics and international relations, as well as in several edited volumes.

Jeffrey D. McCausland, a Colonel in the US Army, is currently Director of European Studies at the US Army War College. He holds a Ph.D. in International Relations from the Fletcher School of Law and Diplomacy, Tufts University. During his military career he has served in a variety of command and staff positions in the United States and Europe, including an assignment to the office of the Deputy Chief of Staff for Operations working on the Conventional Armed Forces in Europe Treaty (CFE) from 1988 to 1989. He commanded the 3rd Battalion 17th Field Artillery, VII Corps during Operations Desert Shield and Storm. He was previously a member of the Department of Social Sciences, West Point; a visiting fellow at the Center for International Affairs, Harvard University; and a research fellow at the International Institute for Strategic Studies, London. He has published broadly on European and defence issues. In the late summer of 1996 he will take up an assignment with the Marshall Center, in Germany.

Douglas T. Stuart holds the Robert Blaine Weaver Chair in Political Science and is Director of International Studies at Dickinson College. He received his Ph.D. in International Relations from the University of Southern California in 1979, and has since published many books and articles in the areas of US-European security relations, Asian security, and arms control. Dr. Stuart is a former NATO Fellow and a regular lecturer at the US Army War College. His current areas of research are European security and American military policy in post-Cold War Asia.

Reinhard Wolf is Assistant Professor in the Department of Political Science, Martin Luther University, Halle-Wittenberg. He received his Ph.D. in 1991 in Political Science from the Free University of Berlin. Between that year and 1993 he was a Research Fellow at the Stiftung Wissenschaft und Politik, in Ebenhausen. He has been a Research Associate at the Massachusetts Institute of Technology, the University of Maryland, and the Royal Institute of International Affairs. He has published widely in the areas of European security and the future of NATO.

Index